YAHWEH REVEALED

— BOOK TWO —

Understanding the Almighty

SERIES

John A. Naphor

Yahweh Revealed
Book Two of *Understanding the Almighty* Series

© 2015 John A. Naphor

Published in Succasunna, New Jersey, by CORNERSTONE PUBLISHING.

www.godculture.net

CORNERSTONE PUBLISHING can bring a live speaker to your event. For more information please visit www.godculture.net

Book cover design and interior formatting by BookStylings.com

Dedication

This book is dedicated to Yahweh, our Father in heaven through our Lord and Savior Jesus Christ, without whom I would have no life, to my wife Devi and my three beautiful children, your love, support and sacrifice mean everything to me, to my parents for your continuous prayer and support, and to all those who have influenced my life in Christ.

TABLE OF CONTENTS

Introduction

The essence of God has always been a mystery to humanity. People from every nation, tribe and tongue, and from every worldwide culture from the beginning of time have continually asked the age old question, "Is there a God?" If so, "Who is He?" It would be my guess that at some point you have found yourself wondering the same thing as well. Is God Yahweh? Is He Allah, Buddha, or even Jesus Christ?

If you are like so many, you may even feel they are all the same and each culture merely uses a different name to address Him. How many times have you heard it said, "There are many pathways to God?" I have also found that a rapidly expanding number of modern men "enlightened" by contemporary science deny that God even exists. They view the Bible the same way Napoléon Bonaparte did when he proclaimed, "Religion is excellent stuff for keeping common people quiet. Religion is what keeps the poor from murdering the rich." In other words, he felt the Bible is merely a book of fables that is nothing more than a means of controlling the ignorant masses.

Then there is the question of know-ability. Is God knowable? Does He actually care about humanity or has He abandoned His "grand experiment," apathetically leaving mankind to wallow in the chaos of our own devices? Watching the evening news certainly makes it seem so. What sort of God would allow ISIS and many of their counterparts to brutalize humanity the way they do? How could a loving Creator permit the starvation and murder of innocent young children? The answers to such seemingly inexplicable questions in conjunction with the essence of Almighty God are the topics we will address within the pages of the following discourse.

In my previous book *God Culture*, we discovered how God interacts with mankind. We discovered how every situation of life has been designed to bring man to the point of salvation. Because Yahweh operates from the standpoint of foresight, His ways seem to be mysterious to us. However, once we learn His culture, brought to life through covenant, we begin to gain an understanding of the trials and tribulations experienced throughout our lives. Within God's covenant of grace we begin to view our trials for what they truly are; opportunities to enter His presence.

For God, life is all about eternity. The trials and tribulations we experience along the way are merely designed to drive us to our knees with the end goal of knowing that He is our only path to deliverance. Salvation is the entire purpose of the covenant, and ultimately, salvation is the meaning of life.

In the following pages we will delve deeper into the identity of God. You will discover how scripture reveals both His nature and His will, and how and where Jesus Christ fits into the picture. I will begin to unveil for you the nature of God's ultimate plan for all of creation.

Comprehending the essence of Yahweh, in as much as human frailty allows, will guide you into discerning His will for your life. As the cloak is lifted you will discover how to approach our Maker. You will begin to nurture a personal relationship with Him and become aware of the majestic, and sometimes even, painstaking processes the Lord has undertaken to redeem His most beloved act of creation—humanity. Once armed with this incredible knowledge the Lord will unleash His power into your life. From that point, life will never be the same. Everyone around you will be affected.

If you read *God Culture* you are about to continue the journey you began. If not, welcome to the *Understanding the Almighty* series. The information contained within these resources will unlock the mysteries of God for you. As the veil is rent and your eyes opened you will never see God the same way again.

In the following pages you will begin to uncover the essence of our Father, Yahweh. If you act upon the information you are about to receive, Yahweh will hand you the keys to the kingdom of God. You have heard that knowledge is power. It most certainly is and *"the fear of the Lord is the **beginning** of knowledge."* (Proverbs 1:7) Comprehending the will of God, and thus, Understanding the Almighty is where our journey begins. Therefore, let's jump into the winnowing flames of Almighty God and allow Yahweh, *"the all consuming fire,"* (Hebrews 12:29) to refine our lives. You are about to experience divinity. Welcome to *Yahweh Revealed*.

CHAPTER 1

God is Love

You may not realize it but you *can* know God. In fact, He has been reaching out to you your entire life, even since the day you were born. You can know His nature, His ways and His personality. You were *born* to know Him in this manner. His sole desire is to reveal to you His essence that you may intimately know Him. God's sole desire is to be joined to you for eternity. Therefore, let us begin by discussing the quality that is the very essence of Almighty God.

All too often we see the Lord as punishing and angry when in reality this is the exact opposite of God Almighty's true nature. Keep in mind that God does not just possess the quality we are about to discuss. He *is* this quality. Without it, not only would mankind be unfit for salvation, but mankind would not exist at all. Man was created for it, and in it, mankind, namely you, fulfill the desire of God's heart. Consider that thought as you watch the evening news tonight and process the day's current events. Think about how far man has fallen from grace.

If you have not yet realized it, the quality I am referring to is the love of God. If you are like most people you have lived your entire life up to this point and are just now recognizing that you have been created as the object of God's affection.

> *"For the Lord's portion is His people . . . He circled him, He instructed him, He kept him as the apple of His eye."*
> **—Deuteronomy 32:9-10**

When you think about the Lord, is His love for you the foremost quality in your mind? Quite frankly, it should be. Love is exactly how God regards you. He proved it in the life, death and resurrection of Jesus Christ, who just happens to be Yahweh Himself, manifested in flesh and blood.

It appears to me that the majority of mankind, regardless of race or religion, has misplaced the true nature of Almighty God. He is so much more than just the swear words you have learned from your friends and relatives. He is miles above both vengeance and pride. He is infinitely more than whatever religion you portend to practice. It seems that we have changed His nature into a statue, a prayer, and as recently revealed to those in the West, a jihad—but we have forgotten that He is a living, perhaps even breathing, being, who as incredible as it may sound, gave His life for the ones He loves.

Mystify Me

I recently had a conversation with a gentleman who in his pursuit of God has turned to Sufism, which is a type of Islamic mysticism. Sadly, this gentleman grew up Roman Catholic and it was not long before I realized that he had given up on Christianity due to a gross misunderstanding of God's nature. Truthfully, I don't blame him. It is sad to admit, but it was obvious that no one has ever presented the truth of God's Word to him. All he has ever received is a misguided set of rules, regulations and rituals. In all honesty, nothing more than a religion deprived of true understanding and devoid of any and all power.

His objection, although quite common, is not so easily answered without diligently peering into God's Word with wisdom and understanding. That is the purpose of this series. His grievance is that, "God was angry in the Old Testament and continually proved that He is merciless by ordering the slaughter of innocent men, woman and children. Why would anyone want to believe in a merciless God? I just don't think God would act that way."

As a result, and like so many others, this misunderstanding has caused him to look for a god that does not actually exist. He has no concept of covenant and without that it is not possible to understand God and His ways. In his mind, he has created a god that thinks like he does and acts according to what *he* deems to be righteous. I do not need to tell you how dangerous this doctrine can be. In addition, it has caused him to look for something less concrete and more mystical—where things can be interpreted according to one's personal beliefs and feelings. That is not a revelation of God. It is a revelation of self.

True Love

What I find interesting, and what is becoming increasingly more common as the world and its religions evolve with globalization, is the overlooking of the violence within the pages of other religious books, namely the Q'ran, which ironically, he has turned to for peaceful guidance. Many people today are swift to condemn Jehovah while completely ignoring, *"Slay them where you find them,"* (Al-Baqarah 2:191, the Q'ran) and *"Allah loveth not the transgressors."* (verse 190) Why does Allah get a pass, particularly by the progressive left wing of society? How does burning people alive and lopping off the heads of the innocent make Islam a "Religion of Peace?" **George W. Bush**

Even more troubling than the physical acts of terror is the Muslim concept of God. Are you able to discern Allah's true nature from the Surah's (Q'ran versus) identified above? This is the real problem. Unlike the New Covenant in Jesus Christ, there is not only a basis for violence in the Q'ran, it is encouraged. Taking the words of the Q'ran literally will always lead to bloodshed. *"Allah loveth not the transgressors,"* and, therefore, neither do his followers.

This is not the case for the disciple Jesus Christ. The God of the Bible loves every human being regardless of race or religion, and irrespective of sin. The shedding of blood by the disciple of Christ is a gross transgression of the law of Christ. It is a blatant act of disobedience that is in direct opposition to *"loving your enemies"* and *"blessing those who curse you."* (Matthew 5:44) As you are about to see, it is the opposite of everything Jesus both lived and died for.

When realizing that Yahweh is the creator of mankind it makes perfect sense for Him to love us. Yahweh desperately loves the sinner. In fact, *"God so loved the world,"* transgressors included, *"that He gave His only begotten Son"* (John 3:16) to expunge our sin and welcome us back into His presence.

That is perfectly logical if you ask me. I still love my kids even when they rebel. In fact, there is nothing any of my children can do to cause me to stop loving them and I am merely flesh and blood. Any act of "tough love" is simply an attempt to keep them on the right and righteous path. How much greater is the love of God whose entire essence is love, than even the most compassionate of men.

This, however, is not the case with Allah. Allah loveth *not* the transgressors. He precisely stated so in the Q'ran. There is no denying its meaning regardless of the linguistic interpretation. It says the same thing in Arabic that is does in English, Spanish, French, or any language, for that matter. This is not an attempt to bash Muslims. I have many Muslim friends and family members and I love them dearly. They, by the way, also love me. Therefore, do not believe all the stereotypes, and for the sake of world peace, I agree with those who proclaim that all Westerners should get to know their Muslim brethren. How else can we share the gospel with them?

With that said, however, I am compelled by Yahweh to *"speak the truth in love,"* (Ephesians 4:15) and to *"shed light upon the darkness."* (2 Corinthians 4:6, et al.) This book is about *"coming to the knowledge of the truth."* (2 Timothy 3:7) Therefore, we must be able to make the necessary distinctions between truth and deception when searching for the true nature of God.

Which sounds more like true love? In other words, which deity sounds more like a loving God; Yahweh, who stepped out of the glory of heaven and into the realm of death—who died for your sin, and did so even while you were still a transgressor of His law; (Romans 5:8) or Allah, who clearly states that he does not love you in your present condition, (Al-Baqara 2:190) and who requires *your* blood—whom *you* must die for to reach? Do not be fooled, Allah cannot love any of us, Muslims included. We are all transgressors of God's law. According to the Q'ran, *"Allah loveth not the transgressor."* If this is the case, can Allah and Jehovah really be the same God?

The reality of the human condition is that *"all have sinned and fall short of the glory of God."* (Romans 3:23) We are all sinners—from the best of us to the worst of us, and everyone in between. There is not a human alive who has not transgressed the law of God. Therefore, every human being has been disqualified in the eyes of Allah due to this one completely overlooked precept; He does not love the transgressor of his law. As a result, he simply cannot love humanity.

Therefore, even the prophet Mohammed was skeptical of his salvation. Can you imagine? The founder and prophet of Islam—the one who speaks for Allah and is the highest authority in Allah's kingdom on earth died unsure of his eternal plight. This is the complete opposite of Jesus Christ. Do you remember His words to the thief on the cross? *"Today you will be with me in paradise."* (Luke 23:43) Jesus knew exactly where He was going and who He was bringing with Him. He still knows. If you make Him your Lord and Savior you too will be with Him in paradise.

This is untrue of "the prophet." Thus, every Muslim continues to this day to include a petition for Mohammed's soul in their daily prayers. In fact, even speaking his name is always followed by the plea, "Peace be upon him." If that is true, and it is, where does it leave you, my Muslim brother or sister? I refer to you as a sibling because we have the same forefather in Abraham. If Mohammed's fate is unsure, you are undoubtedly condemned. If that sounds harsh, it is. I must, however, as stated above, speak the truth to you in love. Allah is harsh. There is no mercy for the transgressor. You cannot escape the scale.

With this in mind, let's spend a minute or two examining the law. If you are reading this and are having a little trouble believing that you are a transgressor of God's law, simply peer into your own thoughts. Consider your own actions and how many times you have both thought and acted negatively toward another human being. Is this *"loving thy neighbor as thyself?"* (Mark 12:31) I am not discussing self-abatement here; I am simply revealing our true nature and how easily we discard those of whom we are animus toward.

How many times have you acted upon such thoughts and lashed out at someone? Aren't you thankful that God does not act upon the same thoughts and lash out against us? That is the misperception of my friend whom I alluded to earlier, as well as, the countless number of atheists pervading our world today. Their perception is that God is evil. They believe He is lashing out at humanity.

Therefore, rather than submit to an "evil" God, it is better just not to believe. This is nothing more than sticking your head in the sand. As you will see, the true evidence points directly to God. How about we believers? Is this your perception of God as well? Perhaps this is why we run from God and refuse to submit our lives to Him. We feel the moment we do, He will take something from us.

Contrary to popular belief, such thoughts never cross Yahweh's mind. *"For I know the thoughts that I think toward you, says the Lord, thoughts of peace and not evil, to give you a future and a hope."* (Jeremiah 29:11) Notice that God states it is He who knows His thoughts. Mankind does not. It seems that modern humanity has it all wrong. The Western world believes God is an ogre. The Middle East believes He is a murderer and the Far Eastern religions believe He is merely an energy source floating about the universe.

God is not any of these. He is love. He does not think negatively of, or about you. The exact opposite is true. Every thought He has regarding you is positive. He proved it by redeeming you in Christ even while you were still a transgressor of His law.

> *"But God demonstrates His own love toward us, in that **while we were still sinners**, Christ died for us."*
> **—Romans 5:8**

When contrasted side by side it becomes abundantly clear that God and Allah are diametrically opposed to one another. In Christ, all are one and everyone who calls upon the name of the Lord can and will be saved. (John 14:20) Allah loveth not the transgressor. Who is love? Who do you think will save you?

Without Love personified in the person of Jesus Christ you must futilely try to win Allah's favor through a jihad that can never satisfy his thirst for blood. Not even Mohammed could do it and believe me, history proves that he tried. In Allah, you have no hope because he *is* not, and *does* not, possess the essence of love. Neither does any other so called deity. It is not their nature. Most are not even real, let alone alive! (We'll get to the living Allah's identity shortly) Therefore, both God and salvation are not just distant, they are non-existent without a redeemer. Jesus is *"the way, the truth and the life. No one comes to the Father except through Him."* (John 14:6) Sin simply will not allow it. Without Christ, sin has permanently separated you from the presence of God.

For the sake of full disclosure, however, and to be completely fair, the Muslim will claim and rightly so, that "slaying them where you find them" is taken out of context. As a stand-alone phrase it may be. An "obedient Muslim," particularly one who does not treat the Q'ran as the literal word of Allah, will only apply this command when aggressed upon. Of course the working definition of aggression is something of a moving target, but that is another discussion for another time.

Let's give them the benefit of the doubt, however, and assume that our interpretations of being attacked equate. It still does not alleviate the problem. The concept of loving the sinner, which is a club that all of humanity are members of, is still non-existent. Conversely, the love of Yahweh manifest in the person of Jesus Christ encompasses all of humanity, the sinner and the non-Christian included.

*"For God so loved **the world** that He gave His only begotten Son."*
—John 3:16

When those around Him saw what was going to happen, they said to Him, 'Lord, shall we strike with the sword?' And one of them struck the servant of the high priest and cut off his right ear. But Jesus answered and said, 'Permit even this.' And He touched his ear and healed him."
—Luke 22:49-51

Once again we see Jesus as love personified. *Even when attacked* Yahweh still loves, as is demonstrated by Jesus healing the ear of the man sent to kill Him. Have we ever seen such a demonstration of compassion from either Allah, the "prophet" or any of his followers. History cries out against them! Jesus, on the other hand, died for all. He loves all—even His enemies. To this day Jesus loves the enemies of the cross. HaShem shows no personal favoritism. (Romans 2:11) All are one in Christ.

In Mohammed, we experience the exact opposite of love, mercy and forgiveness. History clearly demonstrates that Islam is rooted in unprovoked imperialistic violence. Contrary to the acts of the Messiah, Jesus Christ, the prophet Mohammed ordered, and may have even participated in the slaughter of Banu Quarayza, where somewhere between 400 and 900 Israelites were beheaded in the year 627 AD. That is merely one act of violence to be both ordered and inspired by the Islamic prophet throughout history. The Hadith (the life and times of Mohammed) is full of them.

God, who is Love, proclaimed the following, "***You have heard it said***, *you shall love your neighbor and hate your enemy.*" Isn't that what Allah really said in, "Allah loveth not the transgressors, slay them where you find them, et. al?" "***But I say to you***, *love your enemies, bless those who curse you, and pray for those who spitefully use you and persecute you that you may be sons of your Father in heaven.*" (Matthew 5:43-45) Need I go on?

Jesus Christ comes from the perspective of love. Love fulfills the law. (Galatians 5:14) With the law having been completed, and, therefore, taken out of the way, (Colossians 2:14) the sin that it brings to life ceases to exist. Therefore, we can enter the presence of Yahweh through the Lord Jesus Christ, who is God personified. "*God is love.*" (1 John 4:8) Therefore, He is the reference point of forgiveness. All must come to and through Him for salvation. One doctrine comes from the perspective of Love, all others from the heart, mind and sin-stained opinion of sinful man.

Whose word do you trust, a perfect and holy God or a sin-crazed man? It is completely up to you. Who do you think cares for you more? Before you answer that question I must warn you; not only is man's love conditional, according to the Word of God, man's heart is inherently evil.

> *"As it is written: 'There is none righteous, no, not one; there is none who understands; there is none who seeks after God.* ***They have all turned aside;*** *they have together become unprofitable;* ***there is none who does good,*** *no, not one.'"*
> —**Romans 3:10-12, Psalm 53:2-3**

Psalm 53, which is the scripture Paul cross referenced in Romans chapter three says, "*God looks down from heaven upon the children of men.*" What does He find? Nothing but unrighteousness, misunderstanding and disobedience toward Him—the same thing He is still finding today. Regardless of your religion, would you agree that it is time for a change in perspective? Perhaps God is not who you thought He was. Furthermore, perhaps you are not who you thought you were either.

In truth, the law cannot save your eternal soul no matter what form of religion it takes. Did God order the slaying of men, woman and children in the Old Testament? Undoubtedly. Was there a reason? As Sarah Palin so aptly proclaims, "You betcha!" After reading what follows, however, I will let you be the judge. Is God really unmerciful? Is any sin innocent? To find out, let's have a look at the dwelling place of sin. Sin, resulting in judgment finds its origin in the bottom of the abyss. Therefore, let's take a gander at hell and judgment from the point of view of perfect Love. You are about to enter the heart and mind of Yahweh.

Repent and Relent

If you take an honest look at the Bible, you will find that in every instance judgment only comes upon the willfully disobedient. God never has and never will slay the righteous (Those in right standing with Him) along with the wicked. (Genesis 18:25) His love, lack of partiality and sense of justice simply will not allow for it. Contrary to what most have been taught, Yahweh is so merciful that time and again we find Him *relenting* from judgment in the pages of the Bible—even in the Old Testament! I have no doubt whatsoever that He is still relenting today.

> *"Then the men turned away from there and went toward Sodom, but Abraham still stood before the Lord. And Abraham came near and said, 'Would You also destroy the righteous with the wicked? Suppose there were fifty righteous within the city; would You also destroy the place and not spare it for the fifty righteous that were in it? Far be it from You to do such a thing as this, to slay the righteous with the wicked, so that the righteous should be as the wicked; far be it from You!* **Shall not the Judge of all the earth do right?**'"

What a great question that is. Have you ever asked it yourself? I sure have.

> *"So the Lord said, 'If I find in Sodom fifty righteous within the city,* **then I will spare all the place** *for their sakes.'"* (Now you know why America and the better part of Europe is yet to be reduced to rubble.)
>
> *"Then Abraham answered and said, 'Indeed now, I who am but dust and ashes have taken it upon myself to speak to the Lord: Suppose there were five less than the fifty righteous; would You destroy all of the city for lack of five?'"*

"So He said, 'If I find there forty-five, I will not destroy it.'"

"And he spoke to Him yet again and said, 'Suppose there should be forty found there?'"

"So He said, 'I will not do it for the sake of forty.'"

"Then he said, 'Let not the Lord be angry, and I will speak: Suppose thirty should be found there?'"

"So He said, 'I will not do it if I find thirty there.'"

"And he said, 'Indeed now, I have taken it upon myself to speak to the Lord: Suppose twenty should be found there?'"

"So He said, 'I will not destroy it for the sake of twenty.'"

"Then he said, 'Let not the Lord be angry, and I will speak but once more: Suppose ten should be found there?'"

"And He said, 'I will not destroy it for the sake of ten.'

So the Lord went His way as soon as He had finished speaking with Abraham; and Abraham returned to his place."

—Genesis 18:16-32

In truth, God only found four righteous and He did save them. The rest, however, refused; even though they had been repeatedly warned to submit to the living God. Therefore, as the movie, *A Knight's Tale* so poetically opined as the evil Adhemar suffered his first and final defeat, the rest had been "weighed, measured and found wanting," (Daniel 5:27) as fire and brimstone rained out of heaven to obliterate the two cities.

This is not a solitary event folks—neither the judgment nor the relenting. All over the Bible we find God both judging, and in the case of repentance, relenting. *"Then God saw their works, that they turned from their evil way; and God relented from the disaster that He had said He would bring upon them, **and He did not do it.**"* (Jonah 3:10)

Keep in mind that in the immediately proceeding example, the disaster was about to come upon the city of Nineveh, which was part of the ancient Assyrian Empire and a gentile (non Jewish) city. God has always loved and shown mercy to *all* of His children, Jews and gentiles alike. His affinity toward Israel is, and always has been, about the Messiah. The coming of the Messiah, in both His first and second comings, also is, and always has been about the salvation of the *entire* human race—Jews, gentiles, infidels, or however you would like to categorize us, included.

Therefore, God would do anything to protect His lineage knowing it must remain intact for the benefit of *your* salvation. Is God showing favoritism to Israel? If your salvation were not at stake I might consider that claim, but since it is, I would argue that the favoritism being shown is toward you, the one born outside of the covenant of promise.

Furthermore, and just to make sure you understand that God truly has no favorites, there was a time when He was going to destroy Israel, as well. Israel is not exempt from the consequences of disobedience and sin, just as you and I will be held accountable when our ultimate day arrives.

"And the Lord said to Moses, 'Go, get down! For your people whom you brought out of the land of Egypt have corrupted themselves. They have turned aside quickly out of the way which I commanded them. They have made themselves a molded calf, and worshiped it and sacrificed to it, and said, This is your god, O Israel, that brought you out of the land of Egypt!'" And the Lord said to Moses, 'I have seen this people, and indeed it is a stiff-necked people! **Now therefore, let Me alone, that My wrath may burn hot against them and I may consume them. And I will make of you a great nation.'"**

"Then Moses pleaded with the Lord his God, *and said: 'Lord, why does Your wrath burn hot against Your people whom You have brought out of the land of Egypt with great power and with a mighty hand? Why should the Egyptians speak, and say, He brought them out to harm them, to kill them in the mountains,*

and to consume them from the face of the earth? Turn from Your fierce wrath, and relent from this harm to Your people. Remember Abraham, Isaac, and Israel, Your servants, to whom You swore by Your own self, and said to them, I will multiply your descendants as the stars of heaven; and all this land that I have spoken of I give to your descendants, and they shall inherit it forever.' **So the Lord relented** *from the harm which He said He would do* **to His people.** *"*
—Exodus 32:9-14

Both the judgment and the relenting recorded in the pages of the Bible is merely a shadow of things to come. *"That which has been is what will be, that which is done is what will be done, and there is nothing new under the sun."* (Ecclesiastes 1:9) The righteous will be saved and the disobedient will be judged. Ecclesiastes 1:9, which in the estimation of most appears to be completely insignificant, is the key to understanding the future of not just the entire human race, but as you will shortly see in the book of Revelation, the entire universe. To those of us willing to follow God, God is not hiding His ultimate plans from humanity.

"And the Lord said, 'Shall I hide from Abraham what I am doing,
since Abraham shall surely become a great and mighty nation, and
all the nations of the earth shall be blessed in him? For I have
known him.'"
—Genesis 18:17-19

The Coming of Our God

Just as God did not hide His plans from Abraham, He is not hiding what He is about to do from us either. Here is a look at the future of mankind. I would encourage you to pay attention to this. As always, it will not turn out well for the willfully disobedient. Let's have a look at the return of Jesus Christ.

"Then I saw a new heaven and a new earth . . ."
—Revelation 21:1

*"Now I saw heaven opened, and behold, a white horse. And He who sat on him was called Faithful and True, and **in righteousness He judges** and makes war. His eyes were like a flame of fire, and on His head were many crowns. He had a name written that no one knew except Himself. He was clothed with a robe dipped in blood, and His name is called The Word of God. And the armies in heaven, clothed in fine linen, white and clean, followed Him on white horses."*

"Now out of His mouth goes a sharp sword, that with it He should strike the nations. And He Himself will rule them with a rod of iron. He Himself treads the winepress of the fierceness and wrath of Almighty God. And He has on His robe and on His thigh a name written:"

"KING OF KINGS AND LORD OF LORDS."
—Revelation 19:11-16

I will never forget the day my four year old daughter came home from food shopping with my wife and disclosed to me that she saw Jesus in *Shop Rite*, our local food store. Like anyone else most likely would have, I incredulously asked her, "Of course you saw Jesus. What did He look like?"

While expecting to hear a description of the handsome, crystal blued eyed, Caucasian, Jesus Christ depicted by nearly every European artist that has ever put brush to canvas—with His majestic locks of flowing brown hair; her answer still astounds me to this day. That is not the Jesus she saw. She said, "He had white hair and His eyes and His shoes were really shiny. He was wearing a long robe and had a gold ring around his whole body."

As you might imagine, I nearly fell out of my chair. I said, "Wait a minute, tell me that again. What did you see?" She repeated the encounter—white hair, shiny eyes and all! In that instant I realized my four year old daughter had just come face-to-face with her Messiah. She was not imagining, lying or however you might explain a child's embellishments. She had seen Jesus in a manner that most adults never knew existed. How many people do you know who teach their children that Jesus has white hair, a fire in His eyes and a sword in His mouth? I know—me neither! Although I agree that my radical, Jesus freak-like nature makes me the most likely candidate to do so, I never read Revelation to her. Most adults cannot comprehend it. Yet my daughter did not see the European version of Christ, she saw the Jesus of Revelation.

The only explanation is that my four year old had a face-to-face with Jesus. In hindsight, I suppose it should not have surprised me. *"But Jesus said, 'Let the little children come to Me, and do not forbid them; for of such is the kingdom of heaven.'"* (Matthew 19:14) *"And he said: 'Truly I tell you, unless you change and become like little children, you will never enter the kingdom of heaven.'"* (Matthew 18:3) Although I now believe Jesus was revealing Himself both to me and my daughter, (She no longer remembers the incident) I must admit, I was both amazed and a little jealous. Why didn't He appear to me? Have you ever had that reaction? Someone tells you something glorious and your first reaction is jealously.

I guess I will just have to wait and ask Jesus myself when my eventuality materializes. In the meantime, however, you may be wondering why the image she described is so astounding. Check out the following description of the resurrected and restored to the right hand of glory, Jesus Christ of Nazareth.

*"Then I turned to see the voice that spoke with me. And having turned I saw seven golden lamp stands, and in the midst of the seven lamp stands **One like the Son of Man**, clothed **with a garment down to the feet and girded about the chest with a golden band. His head and hair were white like wool, as white as snow, and His eyes like a flame of fire; His feet were like fine brass, as if refined in a furnace**, and His voice as the sound of many waters; He had in His right hand seven stars, out of His mouth went a sharp two-edged sword, and His countenance was like the sun shining in its strength."*
—Revelation 1:12-16

It was at that moment, *"when out of the mouth of babes"* I heard *"perfect praise,"* (Matthew 21:16) that I realized two things. **1)** My daughter possessed knowledge that could only have been revealed to her by God, and **2)** We have gotten it all wrong. We are two thousand years removed from Jesus being *the Lamb of God,* (John 1:29) and are on the verge of meeting Jesus as *the Lion of the tribe of Judah,* (Revelation 5:5) who will come to both judge the world for sin and obliterate it in the process!

The resurrected Jesus will not return as the meek Lamb of God, *"who was made a little lower than the angels."* (Hebrews 2:9) The return of Christ will be the polar opposite of His initial appearance. *"The Lord is a Man of war."* (Exodus 15:3) The risen Christ will return in the full manifestation of His glory. He will possess all the power of His almighty Father, Yahweh. The next Jesus the world meets will not have flowing light brown hair and blue eyes (As if He ever did), but will have the snow-white hair of the glory of God and a flaming fire in His eyes! With the sword of Almighty God His return will smite evil from the planet. All those opposed to His will, His ways, and His timing, will be eliminated from existence. Resistance is futile.

Most people do not realize that the Yahweh of the Old Testament is exactly the same Yahweh revealed throughout the New Covenant in Jesus Christ. God has not changed, humanity has. Unlike the Old Testament, in Christ, humanity can sinlessly approach God. However, Yahweh always has and always will judge sin. Prior to the manifestation of Jesus Christ, humanity remained under the law, and thus, under judgment. In Christ, the law has been fulfilled and thus, the curse of the law has been eliminated from all those who believe. To enjoy this privilege one *must* be in Christ. All those outside will be judged. As you can see from Revelation 19 above, it will not end well for those rejecting the New Covenant of grace.

As extreme as this may be, Yahweh is not satisfied to lose His precious children. Love will not allow for it. *"The Lord is not slack concerning His promise, as some count slackness, but is longsuffering toward us,* **not willing that any should perish**, *but that all should come to repentance."* (2 Peter 3:9)

The ultimate act of relenting is Love manifested in the person of Jesus Christ. In Christ, God has relented to all of humanity. Anyone and everyone can receive mercy from God. All you need to do is ask. *"And it will be that everyone who calls upon the name of the Lord shall be saved."* (Acts 2:21) Love has put the ball in your court. You get to decide your eternal future. Judgment or acceptance is in your control. God has done all the work necessary to provide for your salvation. Your only work is to receive Jesus Christ by faith and the process is not complicated. Simply make the decision to accept God's way and not your own. The destruction of sin is the purpose of the law. The fulfillment is in Jesus Christ, *"the Lamb slain before the foundation of the world."* (Revelation 13:8)

Evil Continually

If you are God, however, why not just force *everyone* to comply? Wouldn't that be more merciful than death? I suppose that all depends upon your outlook on life. In truth, it is all about freedom. God created humanity to be free. Liberty is a core value in God culture. It is the devil who oppresses. As always, however, the choice to be eternally free is your own.

Do you want to be free? Countless masses of humanity have died in the struggle for freedom. Yet as soon as we realize the mess we have created we ask God to rescind our liberty. We blame God for our iniquity and demand that He take back our free will and decide for us. Make a note of what I am about to say. God will not decide for you! You are free to do as you please. It is the greatest gift and perhaps the gravest curse in all of creation. In it, *you* decide your eternal destiny.

Therefore, when sin comes to unmitigated fruition death is the only option. If left unchecked, the wicked will pollute the hearts and minds of all humanity. Have you ever considered why God judged the people of Noah's day. God was not being cruel. He was being merciful.

> *"Then the Lord saw that the wickedness of man was great in the earth, and that every **intent** of the thoughts of his heart **was only evil continually.**"*
> **—Genesis 6:5**

Consider what was in store for a world where the only thought someone could conceive was an act of unbridled evil. And you thought Hitler's Germany was cruel? That was merely one man leading one nation and look at all the suffering caused by evil personified corrupting the hearts of his followers. I cannot even imagine what the Great Tribulation will be like, once *"the man of sin,*" (2 Thessalonians 2:3) otherwise known as the anti-Christ, is revealed.

I had an opportunity several years back to visit the concentration camp known as *Dachau*, located just outside of Munich (Munchen for all you non-Americans), Germany. Interestingly enough, I had a client who experienced the horrors of Dachau for three long years. He was imprisoned there. Dachau was his home. Therefore, I was particularly interested in visiting this house of horrors turned museum for myself. I could not fathom what I encountered upon arrival.

Imagine a place where the goal of your torturers is to keep you alive as long as possible for the sole purpose of testing how much pain you could endure and how your body would react to such torture. In many cases, the victims would be brought right to the brink of death. Then, in an excruciating act of "mercy" they would be brought back to life, just to experience the horror of a torturous death once more.

Some of the human experiments included hypothermia, altitude, procedures performed upon your internal organs without anesthesia, and the most horrifying and inhumane experiment of all, the removal of ones cranium while keeping the brain intact and attached to the body. The purpose of Hitler's demonically possessed monsters in human flesh was to test whether or not God's precious child could remain alive without a head. Thank God for death in the case of those poor souls.

Now consider the world in which Noah resided. Not one human soul could conceive of anything except evil. Even in Hitler's Germany there were numerous righteous souls. Do you recall the movie, *Schindler's List*, and the selflessness by which Oscar Schindler defied the Nazi regime and saved countless Jewish souls and lineages? Apart from Noah and his family, such a man did not exist in Noah's day.

Under these conditions Dachau would have been a paradise. Do you still fault God for judgment? Can you now see the perspective of mercy that God always operates from? Eradicating the people of

Noah's day was an act of mercy not cruelty. Judgment always leads to the salvation of the righteous. Think about it, Jesus was judged on the cross so you could live in eternity.

Hell and Judgment

Have you ever considered why hell is such a horrific place? In the midst of all the evil that has been cast into the abyss, the love of God is not present. There is nothing to restrain the masses of demonic cruelty. Therefore, it is a place that exceeds mere torment. It is a realm of gruesome barbary. Is this what humanity really wants for mankind? Without the gift of death and the mercy of judgment, that would be the perpetual existence of an immortal humanity residing on an everlasting planet.

Therefore, think about your perception next time you blame God for judgment. Judgment is an act of mercy. Just as what God Himself was willing to perform in Christ, judgment is the sacrifice of one for the good of all.

"You do not realize that it is better for you that one man die for the people than that the whole nation perish."
—John 11:50

Were the people of Sodom and Gomorrah, for example, really innocent? They were undoubtedly worshipping other gods and living in outright rebellion toward their Creator. In light of modern day world culture's, does that sound familiar? They were living hedonistic lives which sometimes even included the sacrifice of their own precious children. Is that any different than the holocaust of abortions committed over the last fifty years by a modern day enlightened humanity? The men of Sodom were ready and willing to gang rape the visitors who graced their "majestic" city and they had the unanimous support of the masses. The entire city gathered to watch. Doesn't that also sound familiar?

Think about what is gracing our airwaves and computer screens as we speak. Consider the fact that same sex marriage has the unanimous support of the democratic party to the point of lighting up the White House in the colors of the rainbow. While you are at it, consider how far from the promise of God the symbolization of the rainbow has fallen.

Was God justified in putting and end to such debauchery? Peer into modern culture before you answer that question. With sin still present in the world, perhaps it is merely the embodiment of the sacrifice that has changed.

In our post-modern culture we are seeing similar circumstances unfold before our very eyes. Society continues to be influenced by the Godless modern world leaders, as well as, today's pop cultural icons. As a result, we watch our children degrade and move further from their Creator day after day—even to the point of murder. What did you expect to happen when nearly anything goes in society and God has been removed from both the hearts and minds of the people, as well as, the public square?

Incredibly, this licentious behavior is concealed by the names of freedom, equality and tolerance. Unless, of course, the freedom requested is the tolerance for the public worship of Yahweh, and in particular Jesus Christ. Very few public figures have tolerance for that. As a result, the world's moral lines are continuously being blurred and pushed forward to the point of being vanquished. World news has been confirming this fact for decades. The same leaders that have been elected to serve the public good are leading the people down the path of eternal destruction.

Without a Savior, God cannot tolerate the presence of sin. It does not, and cannot exist in the full manifestation of His presence. Sin brings with it a death penalty that will eventually be carried out. That is the whole point of judgment. It is also the beauty of salvation.

When you accept God's love in the form of Jesus Christ as the Savior of your soul, your judgment is passed over. You receive eternal life and you become spiritually immortal, and thus, "Hell hath no fury!" **William Congreve**

The Second Death

Immortality is the exact opposite of the destiny that awaits those who rebel against the King of all kings. I believe we have misinterpreted the fate of the unbeliever. For centuries, the church has taught that the unbeliever will spend an eternity roasting within the blackened flames of hell. This, however, is inconsistent with both the nature of God, "*who is love,*" (1 John 4:8) and His Word. Let's turn to John the "Revelator" for more.

> *"Then I saw a great white throne and Him who sat on it, from whose face the earth and the heaven fled away. And there was found no place for them. And I saw the dead, small and great, standing before God, and books were opened. And another book was opened, which is the Book of Life.* **And the dead were judged** *according to their works, by the things which were written in the books."*
>
> *"The sea gave up the dead who were in it,* **and Death and Hades delivered up the dead** *who were in them. And they were judged, each one according to his works. Then* **Death and Hades** *were cast into the lake of fire.* **This is the second death.** *And* **anyone not found** *written in the Book of Life was* **cast into the lake of fire.***"*
>
> **—Revelation 20:11-15**

You have just witnessed God Almighty's final act of mercy—the "Second Death!" The Second Death is not an eternity spent burning in the outer darkness or languishing in the flames of hell. The Second

Death is the eternal destruction of both death and hell, as well as, the rebellious souls of all those who oppose God, both human and angelic. In other words, the first death is the destruction of your physical body. The second death is the obliteration of your soul and spirit.

The idea of eternal punishment comes from several scriptures that use the phrase, *"forever and ever,"* when referring to God's ultimate plan for the unbeliever. Let's have a look at Revelation 20:10, for example. *"The devil, who deceived them, was cast into the lake of fire and brimstone where the beast and the false prophet are. **And they will be tormented day and night forever and ever.**"* Revelation 14:11 is another. *"And the smoke of their torment **ascends forever and ever**; and they have no rest day or night, who worship the beast and his image, and whoever receives the mark of his name."*

This certainly sounds like eternal punishment. Does it not? The problem, however, is that we are reading this verse of scripture in English and not in Greek. In general, the Greek word "aion" is translated: "Forever." However, its real meaning is an "age." There are actually two meanings for the word "age."

1. "Age" can mean a human lifetime, or life itself. So it can be a limited time, as long as someone (Or some*thing* in the case of Lucifer, the fallen angels and even hell and death) is going to live.

2. "Age" can also mean an unbroken age (Such as the time period prior to the implementation of a new and sinless heaven and earth, or the millennial reign of Christ.), a perpetuity of time, *or an eternity*. So it *can* mean forever and ever, but it does not have to, and in most cases it does not.

The one exception is the time span of eternity. The "aion" of eternity is never ending.

The meaning of the word is interdependent upon the context in which it is used. According to the Word of God, and evidenced by its being cast into the Lake of Fire, even hell is subject to an "aion." The second death puts a time limitation on hell and an end to its reign. Therefore, it is my opinion that casting hell and death into the Lake of Fire puts an end to hell's fury.

In case you are wondering, we see the same thing in the Old Testament, as well. If we look at Daniel 12:2, for example, we find the following: "*And many of those who sleep in the dust of the earth shall awake, some to **everlasting** life, some to shame and everlasting contempt.*" The Hebrew word translated as everlasting is the word "olam." It has a very similar meaning to the Greek word "aion." Just like the word "aion," "olam" can mean everlasting or it can be a span of time that has no foreseeable end. There is an end to it, but the end is so far in the distance that humanity cannot foresee, nor perhaps even, comprehend the distance.

In most cases "olam" does not mean everlasting. The word "olam," for example, is used when describing Jonah's time spent in the belly of the great fish. Scripture goes on to clarify that although the span of time may have seemed like an eternity to Jonah, it was actually three days and three nights. Therefore, "everlasting" cannot apply to "olam" in the case of Jonah. We can point to where the time span ended.

Therefore, when we reconcile the time span, or "aion," being applied to hell, we can clearly point to where it is expunged from existence. Revelation 20:14 puts an end to hell in the Lake of Fire. That is the difference and the reason we apply the literal "everlasting" or "eternal" to the fate of the believer. Nowhere in scripture can we see where the faithful disciple of Jesus Christ meets their demise. The New Heaven, the New Earth and the New Jerusalem, according to scripture, have no end, and therefore, we can apply "everlasting" to the meaning of "aion" to the inhabitants of the New Jerusalem.

Keep in mind that I am not preaching or teaching Universalism, nor am I claiming hell is not real. I am not arguing that all men will be saved. Scripture is abundantly clear that this is not the case. The point I am making is that the onset of a New Heaven and a New Earth ushers in a new age, or aion, if we use the Greek terminology. At this time both hell and death, as well as, Lucifer, the fallen angels and every human soul who set themselves in opposition to the Lord will be cast into the Lake of Fire and obliterated. That is what fire does. It either purifies, as is the case of gold being refined in the fire, or it destroys everything cast into it. Since the scripture does not state that the wicked are going to be purified at the end of the age, the only other option is the purification of eternity *from* the wicked, which is the destruction of every form of evil.

The onset of this new age, which manifests the New Heaven and the New Earth, is the beginning of eternity. The redemption of creation is what causes the New Jerusalem to descend out of heaven from God. This is both where and when the throne of God and the Lamb makes its permanent abode in oneness with a redeemed humanity—thus, the eternal aion begins. Even the one thousand year reign of Christ, which is an aion of itself, is temporary. In eternity, death is non-existent. Pain, sorrow and torment is non-existent.

> *"And God will wipe away every tear from their eyes; there shall be no more death, nor sorrow, nor crying. There shall be no more pain, for the **former things have passed away.**"*
> **—Revelation 21:4**

How is this possible if the torment of hell continues on perpetually? Does that sound like the nature of our loving Father? Where does the context of this concept come from? It is contrary to everything else we find in scripture regarding the nature of our heavenly Father.

Nowhere in scripture do we find evidence of our memories being purged of our loved ones. Furthermore, the scripture states that "*the sea gave up the dead, and death and Hades* (the place of the dead) *gave up the dead*," (Revelation 20:13) as they get in line to experience the Great White Throne judgment which finalizes their destiny as a date with the Lake of Fire. This is a radically different fate than those who die in Christ, "*who are always confident, knowing that while we are at home in the body we are absent from the Lord.* (2 Corinthians 5:6)

Wouldn't knowing that your precious child is burning in everlasting flames while you are basking in the heavenly bliss be a torment in its own right. Eternity is not an act of mind control on the part of our Father. It is an act of mercy and all of the redeemed will be conscious of God's incredibly merciful act.

Scripture clearly illustrates that consciousness still exists in heaven as all those slain for the Word of God come out from under the heavenly altar and cry out in a loud voice, "*How long, O Lord, holy and true, until You judge and avenge our blood on those who dwell on the earth?*" (Revelation 6:10) It is undeniable that their memories have not been purged. They have been martyred for the Word of God. Yet they still recall the events leading up to their deaths. Therefore, the end of hopeless torment is to be celebrated. The saints of God will forever rejoice in God's goodness when He puts an eternal end to all suffering.

Would you who are sinful punish your kids for a lifetime? Do you not have mercy on them at some point? In mercy, we even "put down" our pets. Yet we deprive our heavenly Father of His most majestic characteristic; mercy, when we fail to separate the glory of the sinless and eternal new age from the temporal suffering of hell and death.

It appears to me, based upon scripture, that suffering meets its ultimate demise in the Lake of Fire where the smoke of its love charred ashes rise for eternity. All rebellion, along with all life, whether spiritual or physical in its nature, (i.e. Angelic or human) that has been cast into the Lake of Fire will cease to exist. Everything cast into the Lake of Fire meets utter destruction. If this were not so, what is the point of the Lake of Fire? Why not just leave hell and death where they are and leave the rebellious to languish in eternal hopelessness? If not to destroy them; why move them? The answer is that Yahweh is ever merciful and at the end of the age He utterly obliterates hell in the Lake of Fire along with all of its inhabitants.

In my opinion, and based upon both scripture and the ever merciful nature of God, this is the true meaning of both the words, "aion" and "olam" in relation to eternal damnation. Is it possible that the translators and commentators have gotten it wrong? Were they too limited by the English language or too influenced by the status quo to convey its proper meaning? Is eternal damnation and everlasting torment the ultimate in fear mongering? Is it as **James Hogg**, the Scottish Poet and author of *The Private Memoirs and Confessions of a Justified Sinner*, stated, "Nothing in the world delights a truly religious people so much as consigning them to eternal damnation?"

To be honest, if you have ever read the Q'ran the concept of eternal torture sounds much more like the nature of Allah than our loving Father, Yahweh. Ultimately, however, that is for you to decide. The purpose of this book is to search for and reveal truth.

To solidify this idea, let's visit the Words of Love personified. Check out what our Lord and Savior, Jesus Christ, has to say about the topic. *"And do not fear those who kill the body but cannot kill the soul. But rather fear Him who is able to **destroy** both soul and body in hell."* (Matthew 10:28)

God is not referring to Satan in this scripture. It is Yahweh who will obliterate the wicked. Notice the word, "destroy." It comes from the Greek word, "apollumi," and it means, "to fully destroy;" "to cut off entirely." It means to "cancel out," and to "utterly perish," "by experiencing a miserable end," which would certainly be the case if one were to experience the horrors of hell for an undeterminable span of time just prior to being vanquished by the Lake of Fire. Apollumi implies absolute and permanent destruction.

Therefore, it appears that in the end Yahweh will utterly destroy the body, soul and spirit of the wicked. According to Jesus, the rebellious will be wiped away—literally expunged from existence. When will this occur? As far as I can tell, the Book of Revelation discloses that the destruction of the wicked occurs when they are cast into the Lake that burns with fire and brimstone. In eternity, all forms of evil shall cease to exist.

If that is not enough to convince you, here are several other scriptures that describe the ultimate end of the wicked. What follows is the fate of all who rebel against the one and only true and living God. Check out the following passages taken from Psalm 37:

> *"For yet a little while and **the wicked shall be no more**; indeed,*
> ***you will look carefully for his place**, but it shall be no more."*
> **—Psalm 37:10**
> This undoubtedly illustrates the obliteration of both the
> unbeliever and hell (their place) from existence.

> *"But the wicked shall perish; and the enemies of the LORD, like*
> *the splendor of the meadows, **shall vanish**. Into smoke **they shall***
> ***vanish away."***
> **—Psalm 37:20**

What smoke is the Psalmist referring to? *"And the smoke of their torment will rise for ever and ever."* (Revelation 14:11)

In other words, the torment has been reduced to nothing but mist by the Lake of Fire. Consider what happens to smoke as it rises. The deconstructed matter is changed into vapor as it perpetually ascends into untraceable nothingness. That is all that will be left of the wicked's existence in Yahweh's eternity—nothingness! Just like any fire, even though the flames have been extinguished, the smoke continues to rise.

*"But the transgressors **shall be destroyed** together; the future of the wicked shall be cut off."*
—Psalm 37:38

One of the things I have learned from studying the Word of God is that just like your earthly parents, when God wants to make something clear He has a tendency to repeat Himself. Call it nagging if you will. When it comes to the ultimate fate of the wicked, God continuously nags and lectures His children to both educate and lead them away from the Lake of Fire. Most do not realize that even Jesus taught more about hell than He did about heaven. As always, Yahweh is not trying to hide His plans. He is not speaking in mysteries or using speech that is difficult to discern. The exact opposite is true. He is disclosing His plans in plain language that even a child can understand. God lets us know exactly where He stands. In the process, He lets us know where we stand as well.

*"As smoke is driven away, so drive them away; as wax melts before the fire, **so let the wicked perish at the presence of God.**"*
—Psalm 68:2

*"For behold, the day is coming, **burning like an oven**, and all the proud, yes, all who do wickedly **will be stubble**. And the day which is coming **shall burn them up**, Says the LORD of hosts, That will leave them neither root nor branch."*
—Malachi 4:1

*"He who has the Son has life; he who does not have the Son of God **does not have life.**"*
—John 5:12

God could not be any clearer then He is John 5:12. Even the most famous scripture in all the Bible makes the end of the wicked abundantly clear. *"For God so loved the world that He gave His only begotten Son, that whoever believes in Him **shall not perish**, but have everlasting life."* (John 3:16)

Either one has everlasting life, or one dies. You cannot have both and God is certainly not a masochist. He does not derive pleasure from the pain of another. In truth, I could go on and on for quite some time displaying scriptural evidence of the destruction of the wicked. For brevity's sake, however, I'll spare you all the gory details. For the wicked, all semblance of life ceases at the time of your final judgment. We will not remain alive simply to experience everlasting torture. It is scripturally inaccurate and somewhat insulting to a God who *"desires mercy and not sacrifice, and the knowledge of God more than burnt offerings."* (Hosea 6:6)

With that said, neither hell, nor destruction was created to be the final destination of humanity. That is what God created heaven for. Hell was created to be the holding place of the angels of heaven who rebelled against God.

> *"And the angels **who did not keep their proper domain**, but left their own abode, He has reserved in **everlasting** chains under darkness **for the judgment of the great day.**"*
> **—Jude 1:6**

Once again we see the misinterpretation of the word, "aion." Hell was reserved, complete with some sort of shackles, by the way, to hold the rebellious angels and keep them from tormenting humanity until the end of the age (aion) that culminates in their eternal destruction within the Lake of Fire.

Think again about why hell is such a torturous place. In hell, evil is left unchecked. God, *"who is love,* does not abide there. He does not inhabit hell. He has a presence there. (Psalm 139:8) It is part of

His permissive will, but He does not abide in hell. Hell is the place where Satan and his insidious followers have complete and total reign. It has become their new domain due to their dissidence. Do you still want to play with fire, no pun intended?

Hell did not become man's reality until *after* the rebellion of Adam and Eve in the Garden of Eden. Rebellion brought sin and death into the present. Listen to what God says about "the place of the dead" in regard to the object of His affection's rebellion against Him:

> *"Therefore my people have gone into captivity, because they have no knowledge; their honorable men are famished, and their multitude dried up with thirst.* **Therefore Sheol has enlarged itself and opened its mouth beyond measure***; their glory and their multitude and their pomp, and he who is jubilant,* **shall descend into it.***"*
> **—Isaiah 5:13-14**

Because man made the decision to ignore God and follow his own ways, which is the same decision Lucifer made, man reaped the same final destination. Hell was actually enlarged to make room for those who were never intended to inhabit its horror. Both hell and death were created from the beginning of time, and perhaps even before, with the ultimate goal of being eliminated from eternity, along with Satan and all those who followed his insidious plan. Unfortunately, humanity got caught in the cross fire.

Therefore, in one final act of mercy, the Lord has eliminated man's eternal suffering by casting those who refuse to enter glory into the Lake of Fire. From there, all who oppose God will be utterly eliminated from existence. This is *"the second death,"* (Revelation 20:14 and 21:8) and this in itself is an absolute horror. When contrasted to the glory of eternal life, there can be no greater horror than the utter destruction of your eternal spirit, soul and body. Think about that for a second. Even your consciousness will cease to exist.

Since the idea of destroying His most precious act of creation is as horrific to God as it is to mankind, He made a way for all of humanity to spend eternity in His presence. He introduced physical death to mankind, and incredibly, in the ultimate act of everlasting love He stepped into it Himself.

The Taste of Death

As you read what follows, keep in mind that death was not created to be the ultimate fate of mankind. Mankind was created for eternal life. It was only when sin entered humanity that death became necessary for sin's destruction. The Word becoming flesh, (John 1:14) Jesus Christ, who is God personified, is the fruition of Yahweh's triumph over death.

> *"But we see Jesus, who was made a little lower than the angels, **for the suffering of death** crowned with glory and honor, **that He, by the grace of God, might taste death for everyone.**"*
> **—Hebrews 2:9**

Because Jesus "tasted" death for all of us, we are no longer required to die, spiritually speaking. As we just learned, according to Revelation 20:14, death is cast into the Lake of Fire and is completely annihilated from existence, along with hell and all of the torment that is associated with its inhabitants.

Think about what fire does to anything it touches. It utterly consumes it. It reduces it to ash, in essence, transforming it to nothing. Do you realize that fire, due to the heat it produces, is one of the only elements in existence that can change the form of matter? Remember, matter can neither be created nor destroyed in the natural realm in which we currently exist. It can only be changed. Therefore, when death and hell are introduced to the Lake of Fire, a fundamental change occurs in eternity. They are utterly consumed and reduced to ash. In essence, evil is eradicated from existence. Just like fire burns the dross off of gold, the Lake of Fire purifies eternity as immortality triumphs over death.

Unfortunately, this leaves no room for the unbeliever. There is no longer a place for them in God's eternity where sin and death are completely eradicated. Therefore, since perfect justice precludes them from salvation, in God's final act of mercy He does not leave the damned to suffer. He casts them into the Lake of Fire and eliminates them from existence. *"This is the second death."* (Revelation 20:14) The war is over. Love has triumphed!

Sin Filter

I have found that most people do not understand that in Jesus Christ, God is no longer at enmity with sinful man. The second death is not a forgone conclusion. You are not preordained to being dismantled by the Lake of Fire. It is a choice that you, and only you, can make. God has made a way to deal with sin both before and after our physical deaths. Incredibly, God became a filter to sin and relented. Just as a filter removes impurities from air or water, Jesus removes the impurity of sin from His most precious act of creation—you. This is why Jesus exclaimed, *"No one comes to the Father except **through** Me."* (John 14:6) Jesus is a sin filter! *"In Him is Life, and the life is the light of men."* (John 1:4)

No wonder the angels proclaimed the war with mankind was over on the eve of Jesus' birth. For those who believe, sin has been filtered from mankind and the sting of death has been nullified. (1 Corinthians 15:55) Love had come in His full manifestation. To build upon this truth, let's have a look at the miracle of the very first

Christmas, which is the the birth of Christ and the fulfillment of God's love for humanity.

— CHAPTER 2 —

Peace Treaty

You may not expect this, but I have been known to be a bit of grinch during the Christmas season. Although I love Jesus with all my heart, when it comes to Christmas... bah humbug! I have come to detest the malls, traffic, and unnecessary spending. (Yes, for the most part the gifts we buy our loved ones will make no difference in the lives of a culture with an average of 4 televisions, 3 computers, 3 cell phones, and 2 cars per household—who also possess closets full of so many articles of clothing that we have to periodically discard them into our local Salvation Army box to keep our closets from overflowing onto the floors of our homes) The entire commercialization of the season never ceases to put me in a bit of a grouchy mood. I am not kidding. I am the modern day grinch.

Perhaps you are wondering why I feel this way. It never ceases to amaze me, that as the world is lining their homes with Christmas lights and drinking rum-laced egg nog at the corporate Christmas party, the thought of Jesus Christ crucified rarely crosses the minds of those "celebrating" the birth of our Lord. I am "grinchy," for lack of a better term, because Christmas is no longer about Christ. It has become mostly an excuse to get drunk with your friends and to take on a fifteen percent interest rate for an item that will be thrown out in less than a year. It is about rallying the corporate sales numbers to ensure that the stockholder remains invested. Christmas has morphed into the Messiah of Wall Street, not the salvation of mankind!

Jesus Christ of Nazareth did not give up the glory of heaven and suffer a torturous death so the world could pretend to be happy for a month while they get deeper into debt for the benefit of the corporate investor. Therefore, let's have a look at the wonder of Christmas and reconsider what we are truly celebrating. What did Yahweh reveal in the birth of Christ? To find out, check out the message of the heavenly host.

The Heavenly Host

*"Now there were in the same country shepherds living out in the fields, keeping watch over their flock by night. And behold, an angel of the Lord stood before them, and the glory of the Lord shone around them, and they were greatly afraid. Then the angel said to them, 'Do not be afraid, for behold, I bring you **good tidings** of **great joy** which will be to **all people**. For there is born to you this day in the city of David, **a Savior**, who is Christ the Lord. And this will be a sign to you: You will find a Babe wrapped in swaddling clothes, lying in a manger.'"*

*"And suddenly there was with the angel a multitude of the heavenly host praising God and saying: 'Glory to God in the highest, **and on earth peace, goodwill toward men!**'"*
—**Luke 2:8-14**

Before we proceed in analyzing this message, think back on the statement made by the prophet Jeremiah in chapter 29:11, *"For I know the thoughts that I think toward you, says the Lord, thoughts of peace and not evil, to give you a future and a hope."* Doesn't that sound like *"goodwill toward men?"*

When viewed from this perspective, does my Sufis friend's objection, that God is lashing out at humanity, have any validity at all? Is God's nature evil? To the contrary, it is man's nature that is evil. Man's sinful nature has been the cause of judgment all along. Sin is the reason for the season. Christmas is about transforming man's nature, and thus, his eternal destination from the throes of hell to the glory of heaven. The reason for the season is actually the alleviation of judgment. That is a gift worth opening, don't you think?

God's love is unquestionable. His every action is with humanity's best interest at heart. His thoughts and deeds regarding mankind have never changed. *He* never changes. (Malachi 3:6) His ways and His ultimate plan for humanity and the universe have been immovable from the Old to the New Testament. He *is* love. When the fulfillment of time came He offered Himself for all in fulfillment of His own Word. If you truly think about it, God becoming our atoning Lamb is simply mind boggling. Why would the creator of heaven and earth and every form of life, lower Himself to become that which He created? Would you do that?

Angels Among Us

To truly comprehend the announcement proclaimed to the shepherd's we must have an understanding of the ministry and function of angels. What is their God intended purpose for interacting with mankind? Do you realize that God loves you so much that He created supernatural beings to guard and watch over you? Yes, you are that important to Him.

First, however, I must clear up a tremendous and quite frankly, theologically dangerous misconception that I persistently hear repeated over and over again. Human beings will never become angels. When you die you will not all of a sudden sprout wings and sail about the clouds. You will be as human in heaven as you are on earth. You were created in the image of Love. For all of eternity that is how you will remain. In addition, angels are not some chubby little "Buddha like" creatures that flutter around the ether shooting arrows at potential lovers. Cupid is not love, God is.

> *"But to which of the angels has He ever said: 'Sit at My right hand till I make Your enemies Your footstool.' Are they not all **ministering spirits** sent forth to minister for those who will inherit salvation?"*
> **—Hebrews 1: 13-14**

Although there are many classes of angels, this is an example of those appointed to assist mankind. Angels are "ministering spirits" created *by* God and sent *to* men for the purpose of serving those who will inherit salvation. The Word of God defines the "heirs of salvation" as all who are believers in Yahweh.

Faith in Jesus Christ is believing that the ultimate plan of Yahweh leads to salvation. This requires a certain level of trust on the part of the believer. In order to insure His plans are met, Love sent supernatural ministers to assist His beloved. Once the truth is recognized there is no doubting how deeply Yahweh cares about our well-being.

The word "ministry" or "minister" means "to serve." That is their function. That is where we get the idea of guardian angels from.

The terminology never appears within the pages of scripture, however, the primary function and role of the angels is clearly defined. They are obedient and powerful supernatural ministers sent to assist those who will inherit the kingdom of God.

That, by the way, is also *your* function, minus the supernatural part, when you enter ministry in whatever capacity God places you. We have been created in the image of Love. Therefore, we are expected to act and serve in love toward both God and man. In Christ, we are all ministers of the Almighty.

Of the various functions of angels we see them sent to carry out judgment, to heal, to administer worship and praise, to make war, protect etc . . . Have I said anything thus far that man has not been created to administer as well. Love (God) is amazingly consistent in His expectation of those He created.

There are also those who are sent to bring a man, or mankind as a whole, a particular message. We see this illustrated with the angels, as well as, the heavenly host in the Christmas account above. The word "host," by the way, refers to an army. It comes from the Greek word "stratia" and it means, "an encampment," or an "army." However, this army did not come to make war with mankind as will occur at the end of time. The Lord of hosts sent this army to announce peace. Love had come to reconcile with His most prized possession—you.

Peace on Earth

Hence the angel's message was "*on earth peace* and *goodwill* (not ill-will) *toward man.*" God's message was that as far as He is concerned the problem of sin is over and done with. The Messiah, the Savior of the world, Jesus Christ of Nazareth has come. The battle for your soul is over and God has won the war. Judgment no longer needs to be your destiny. In Christ, you can be redeemed.

Interestingly enough, the Greek word "peace" used here is "eirene," pronounced, *i-ray'-nay*. It means, "quietness, rest, prosperity and/or peace." The words "good will" mean that God's will for us is His goodness, not His anger or any means of harm. Do you remember Jeremiah 29:11? God is incredibly consistent in His message to mankind. The word "toward" comes from the Greek word "En." It means, "a fixed position."

Here is the good news. That is what the word gospel means. It comes from the Greek word, "euaggélion," and it means, "good news." The euaggélion, or gospel, is that God has taken a fixed, or *immovable position*, of *His will* being *peace* and *goodness* toward mankind. Those are *His* words, delivered by *His* angels, for the benefit of you and me. He expressed it and brought it to pass in the person of Jesus Christ of Nazareth, the Savior of all those who believe. Jesus *is* the gospel! He *is* the good news. In the blood of Christ, Yahweh has signed an everlasting peace treaty with humanity. In Jesus Christ, even the most dreadful transgressor is complete, and yes, I even dare say, holy! Love died for all.

However, the question, why go through the trouble of sending an entire army of angels to make an announcement? still remains. In fact, why send Jesus at all? Hey, God didn't mess up, man did. Why not just flood the earth or blow it up and start over? That certainly would have been easier since for God creating is as simple as you and I speaking. In fact, for Him it is a whole lot simpler. He is not bound by language nor any lack of understanding.

As we discussed earlier, the answer to judgment is love. He simply loves us. Love is God's motivation for creating not just mankind, but everything in the entire universe. The totality of creation is for the benefit of humanity.

*"He chose us in Christ **before** the foundation of the world, that we should be holy and blameless before Him **in love**, having **predestined us to adoption as sons** by Jesus Christ to Himself,*

according to the good pleasure of His will, to the praise of the glory of His grace, by which He made us accepted in the Beloved."
—Ephesians 1:4-7

The war with humanity is over and as far as God is concerned there is peace and goodwill toward man on the earth. Ephesians 1:4 is actually an amazing piece of scripture. It states that God knew you before you were ever created. Not only that, it declares that God knew you before the earth, or even the world, and possibly before the entire universe ever existed! It declares that you are holy, which means set apart to Him. You are blameless, meaning your sin is forgiven. In *His* eyes you are without fault. It says He adopted you and made you a son or daughter—a child of God, before you ever existed on this planet or in this natural realm. It says that it brought him pleasure and that it was His will to create and adopt you. You have been accepted in Love. All *you* have to do is trust that Christ is who He says He is.

When Christ is your Savior all of eternity belongs to you. God has always known you. He has known you in the Spirit from before "*let there be light*" set time and space in motion. In the Person of Jesus Christ, He has made peace with you. He yearns to be reconnected to you. He has longed for you since the day your conception separated you from His Spirit. If you do not respond to His call, He will reach out continually until you breathe your last breath. The only question is whether or not you are willing to love Him back. Will *you* make peace with *Him*? I encourage you not to wait as we do not know the date of our ultimate demise. Then, and only then, has time run out.

Counter Punch

In order to gain a better understanding of what happened over two thousand years ago in the birth of Christ, and why it was even necessary, we must go all the way back to, and even before the beginning of mankind. The birth and ministry of Christ was a response to what was lost in the Garden of Eden over six thousand years ago. It appears to be a counter to the "move" Satan made upon mankind in the Garden of Eden. The object of God's affection was stolen from right under His nose—or so it appeared.

In truth, God delivered a knock-out blow from the inception of time. Don't ever forget that God had the foresight to anticipate not just every move, but every single thought that Satan ever has or ever will have in the future. Yahweh is the pinnacle of wonder.

Let There Be Light

So let's rewind the videotape and look back into God's perfect will for mankind. You will find that God had a forever plan of peace from the beginning of time. Satan never had a chance. He still doesn't. No matter what is happening in your life do not ever forget that God is the supreme being in the universe. His wisdom and power is unmatched and His will for you is good, not evil.

Everything you see around you is a result of His love for you. Every aspect of creation is for the benefit of humanity. Therefore, let's peer into antiquity and discover the miraculous wonders of the Ancient of Days. The universe and everything in it was constructed just for you.

> *"In the beginning God created the heavens and the earth. The earth was without form and void; and darkness was on the face of the deep. And the Spirit of God was hovering over the waters. Then God said, "Let there be light"; and there was light."*
> **—Genesis 1:1-3**

You may think I am weird when I say this, but I can spend hours meditating on the first three chapters of the Book of Genesis. It actually fascinates me. The more I learn, particularly about the science of the cosmos, the more fascinated I become with the Genesis account. Allow me to share a small bit of the riches contained within just these three verses of scripture.

As you read this you will soon realize that the matchless wonder of creation was all revealed out of love for mankind. Science is not just something to be processed in the mind. The universe, and everything in it, is not merely some random act of chance as modern scientists and the media may have you believe. It is a direct result of the love of God. There is a spiritual purpose to everything you see in the universe.

Don't forget that God is omnipresent. Omnipresence means God is present in all things. In other words, God has saturated the natural realm with Himself. *"Do you not know that your bodies are the temple of the Holy Spirit?"* (1 Corinthians 6:19) This includes the believer in Jesus Christ. It is also how God *"**upholds** all things by the Word of His power,"* (Hebrews 1:3) and why *"He is before all things, and **in Him** all things consist."* (Colossians 1:17) This makes perfect sense when you consider that *"all things were made **through Him**, and without Him nothing was made that was made."* (John 1:3)

When looked at spiritually and physically, the entire cosmos points directly to God and His immense love for humanity. Thus, when God said, *"Let their be light . . ."* the creation of the universe was not just an empty location containing physical properties. It is a manifestation of God Himself, and thus, contains both the essence and presence of Almighty God. God did not just create the universe, He became an active part of it.

Thus, the Word of God is perfectly clear about how the universe as we know it came to exist. Although the Lord does not disclose the process He used, apart from speaking creation into existence; He makes it known beyond any shadow of doubt that *He created* the universe and God's love for humanity is the reason He created all things. Creation was an act of love. It is a gift from above.

Therefore, do you think God's ultimate creation, which is human life, would be easy to replicate? Could it have been possible for the image of God be so simplistic that mere humanity could comprehend its wonder? Of course not. The wonder of life is designed to reveal the greatness of God. We do not even understand the human brain, but once redeemed *we have the mind of Christ.* (1 Corinthians 2:16) We have only explored five percent of the ocean floor. We know more about the surface of the moon than the depths of the sea and we believe we can fathom the majesty of Yahweh?

Our minds have been created in the similitude of God Almighty. No wonder we can only tap into a minute aspect of the potential God has bestowed upon us. Sin has stolen our power. Once redeemed, however, we are reconnected to Greatness. That is just one aspect of humanity. It is one minute example of Yahweh's vastness. Infinite wisdom created unmatched complexity in both humanity and the universe. Love would allow nothing else.

When science peers into the human body, and even the cosmos, they witness the wonder of the Almighty. Creation was designed for you to recognize God's unmatched power in comparison to the frailty of mortal men. It is evidence of His existence. God left His fingerprints everywhere in the universe and not just for the purpose of man to *discover* Him. It is for the purpose of apprehending Him. Isn't it funny how science has attempted to reverse the truth and place both man and nature above the Creator? In the process, we have set ourselves in opposition to Almighty God.

Scientists continually look to the heavens for the catalytic event that set the universe in motion. Although they are yet to figure out exactly what happened, more and more scientists are coming to the conclusion that it had to be created by an infinitely intelligent and powerful Creator. There had to have been a catalyst. In reality, they need to look no further than the first phrase contained in the Torah and the Bible. Love was the catalyst. *"In the beginning God created . . ."* The world was once perfect. My how things have changed.

Lost In Translation

"The earth was without form and void; and darkness was on the face of the deep." (Genesis 1:2) As we all know, whenever one language is translated to another there are certain nuances within the languages meaning that are lost. I also believe that the more languages the text is translated into the more inaccurate it becomes. This makes sense if you consider the fact that the subsequent translations continue to be rendered from an interminably, even if ever so slightly, flawed text.

The children's game "telephone" clearly illustrates this concept. Therefore, we should never conclude that the texts of the Bible are flawed due to translation as both atheists and the religion of Islam, for example, would have you believe. We simply need to know that if we encounter confusion or anything that may be perceived as inaccuracy, we can simply return to the original language of the compositions and recover the intended content.

Although this is rarely an issue instances do arise. Even more importantly, the original languages seem to supply a more detailed intent on the part of the Author. A Concordance of the Bible can easily help you accomplish this seemingly insurmountable task. I believe the sentence, *"The earth was without form and void,"* falls into this particular category.

The translators did not know what to do with one particular word in the sentence so they translated it to the best of their understanding. This does not mean they were correct. God, however, *always* is! As incredible and inconsequential it may seem, the word I am referring to is the word, *"was."*

As we move forward you are about to see the manifestation of how Love created the perfect environment to testify of His glory. In truth, God need not say a word to show His majesty.

"The heavens declare the glory of God; and the firmament shows His handiwork. Day unto day utters speech, and night unto night reveals knowledge. There is no speech nor language where their voice is not heard. Their line has gone out through all the earth, and their words to the end of the world."
—Psalm 19:1-4

What follows is the wonder of God's creation. In the birth of Jesus Christ, Yahweh announced the redemption His crowning achievement, which is none other than you. You are the entire reason that *Yahweh Revealed* His majestic cosmos. The creation of the universe was all about humanity. Therefore, I would encourage you to read on. You are about to discover just how much trouble God went through, not just to manifest you, His most beloved act of creation into His image, but to redeem you from the destruction of the Lake of Fire. Therefore, let's press on and discover *Jehovah Shalom*, the God of peace.

CHAPTER 3

The Glory of God

It seems that there is a conflict between scientists and theologians. I must admit that for reason's other than pride and ego, I do not understand why. Science does not conflict with the Word of God, it simply confirms it. In fact, the Word of God is one of the inspirations for Sir Isaac Newton and many of his contemporaries to begin searching the cosmos in the first place. This makes perfect sense when you realize that God is the creator of the universe and the cosmos was designed by Him with the dual purpose of supporting life and expressing His glory. The heavens have been designed to point you in the direction of a loving Creator who does not just possess love, as stated earlier, He is love.

Young and Old

With that said, the conflict stems from the idea that the Word of God allegedly establishes that the age of the earth to be approximately six to ten thousand years old, while modern science dates the earth at roughly 4.54 billion years. Theology places humanity (Homo sapiens) at approximately six to ten thousand years, while science targets two hundred to two hundred-fifty thousand years of age. Genealogical evidence coupled with techniques such as radio carbon dating contribute to the controversy. I am not here to argue which is correct. I simply do not know, and as you will see, from a theological perspective, it does not matter.

However, how can a theologian explain the fact that archaeological records place the skeleton known as "Lucy," the name given to the remains of a female *Australopithecus Afarensis*, an extinct hominid species thought to be closely related to the genus Homo, as far back as 3.2 million years, particularly, when Genesis places "the beginning" of mankind at the creation of Adam? Furthermore, how can one reconcile a six thousand year old earth when examining the same data?

Theologians have brushed off the problem by claiming that carbon dating is an inaccurate form of measurement. Although no one can argue it to be inerrant, I believe the better and, perhaps, even more accurate answer may be found in the word "was." I know what you are thinking, "Seriously dude? Your answer is was?"

Before you scoff, let's have a look at the original Hebrew/Chaldee text. In it, the word "was" does not appear in Genesis 1:1. What *does* appear is the word "became." What is the significance? Read the text as it originally appears. Instead of saying, "*The earth was without form and void*," it should read, "*The earth **became** without form and void*." That changes the meaning completely. The inference points to some form of a pre-Genesis earth.

In other words, there quite possibly may have been civilizations, perhaps even advanced civilizations, on the earth prior to the event that caused the earth to *become* without form and void. If this is true, it certainly explains how carbon dating can place humanoid creatures as far back as 3.2 million years. It also explains how dinosaurs and other pre-historic creatures can date back to the millions of years when many theologians and young Earth creationists argue a six-thousand year old earth.

You may ask me, "Do you believe in a young or an old earth?" I believe both are possible and I believe the biblical account agrees. I also believe that issues such as this are irrelevant in every way except for scientific knowledge. The age of the heavens and earth, and the amount of time man has resided here are irrelevant to the nature and stature of Jesus Christ. My only interest in the pursuit of scientific data is for the confirmation of the truth of God's Word, in addition to the fact that I simply enjoy the discovery. It causes me to love Him even more as I learn to wonder at His greatness.

I also believe there is one other important factor to consider. The evidence can be argued that man in his *current* form as human beings, that is, Homo sapiens, date back to the Genesis account. However, I also believe the universe is billions of years old, quite possibly 13.7 billion years old, and that it is entirely possible that "manlike" creatures existed prior to the earth *becoming* without form and void. Why is this important? The issue of love is at stake.

Human beings did not evolve as common animals as many atheists might have you believe. When you consider that all of the inorganic matter in the universe only contains 235 bits of exponential information, and a mere protein molecule (The building block of life) contains 1500 bits of exponential information, the mathematical possibility of life evolving from inorganic matter is not just remote, it is impossible. 1 plus 1 does not equal 6.38.

Furthermore, a single human cell contains 20 million bits of exponential information. *20 million* is a long way from 235, especially when you consider that each organism broken down element by element reverts back to 235. Where did these massive leaps in complexity originate? Who organized the matter in such a precise manner and injected the additional data? Random chance?

Mathematically speaking, the primordial stew defies both logic and mathematics, especially when you examine the incredible leaps in genetic information as you climb the ladder of complexity. Mathematics, as well as, the observable evidence of biogenesis (Life from life) confirms the impossibility of both abiogenesis (Life from inorganic matter) and evolution.

We did not just randomly select from frogs, fish, or monkeys, or have a one celled common ancestor. You did not descend from a banana. Humanity is special to God. Man is infinitely more precious to God than any other being ever created. Love *created* someone to love and to be with. No evolutionist will ever understand this incredible nuance. You will never find the "missing link" in the fossil records. There is no singular point in time that any organism ceased being what it was to become something new. It simply does not exist. Love created life. Life could not evolve. It is far too complex. If you do some unbiased research, you too will find that it is mathematically and biologically impossible.

With that said, carefully note the following biblical text as evidence that the earth may have been altered at some point in the distant past:

> "I beheld the earth, and indeed it was without form and void; and the heavens, they had no light. I beheld the mountains, and indeed they trembled, and all the hills moved back and forth. I beheld, and indeed **there was no man**, and all the birds of the heavens had fled. I beheld, and indeed the fruitful land was a wilderness, and **all its cities were broken down** at the presence of the Lord,

by His fierce anger."
—Jeremiah 4: 23-26

There are two possibilities rendered here. Number one, is that the prophet Jeremiah was gazing at the past. Number two, is that he was peering into the future. Since we have prophetic textual evidence of what God is going to do with the earth in the future, and it does not resemble Jeremiah's prophecy, I must conclude that Jeremiah was looking into the ancient past.

This could potentially explain some of the puzzling feats of engineering and construction employed by such cultures as the ancient Egyptians, Mayans, and civilizations that created such wonders as Stonehenge, the Pyramids, Pumapunku, etc . . . that would be difficult to reproduce even today. Scientists have noted that the cuts in the stone at Pumapunku are so precise that they could not have been accomplished without power tools and/or laser technology.

I have seen gold trinkets resembling airplanes, (They actually look like fighter jets) that were found in an area covering Central America and coastal areas of South America. According to *World-Mysteries.com*, they are estimated to belong to a period between 500 and 800 CE. Since they are made from gold, however, accurate dating is impossible and based essentially on stratigraphy which may be deceptive. "However, we can safely say that these gold objects are more than 1000 years old." They certainly are not less than one hundred years old. I always thought it was the Wright brothers who discovered flight.

Is it possible these ancient artifacts survived the catastrophe that caused the earth to become without form and void? Perhaps we will never know, but in truth, we have merely scratched the surface of understanding the world we live in. I suppose you will have to draw your own conclusion, but in my opinion, it certainly is compelling. I know how much we all love television, but *Ancient Aliens* were not from outer space. If they existed, they were most likely created just like you and me and resided on the very same chunk of space rock that we do.

City of Lights

As a result, I am compelled to ask myself the question, what could have been the cause of this catastrophic event that may have either destroyed or severely altered the then present state of the earth? Once again note the following scriptures.

> *"And war broke out in heaven: Michael and his angels fought with the dragon; and the dragon and his angels fought, but they did not prevail, nor was a place found for them in heaven any longer. So the great dragon was cast out, that serpent of old, called the devil and Satan, who deceives the whole world; he was cast to the earth, and his angels were cast out with him."*
> **—Revelation 12:7-9**

What most casual readers do not realize that biblical scholars have learned is that the Book of Revelation is not necessarily in chronological order. Parts of it move parenthetically back in forth in time. The scripture of the war in the heavens is one such example. Also, notice that the war was between two groups of angels. Lucifer lead the rebellious angels, and Michael, who happens to be the only angel in the word of God expressly named to have the position of Arc angel, lead the others.

Many scholars have speculated that Lucifer (Satan) is an Arc angel as well. I personally reject that due to the fact that of all the mentions of Lucifer within the Word of God, the title of Arc angel never appears on his resume'. Furthermore, the word "Arc," denotes the highest position amongst the angels which can only be held by one angel. It is like being the world's fastest man. It is certainly not subjective and it can only, by its very nature, be held by one person.

At the time of this discourse, no one could argue that Usain Bolt is not the fastest man in history. The stop watch doesn't lie.

By the way, there are only three angels that are actually named in the Bible. They are: Michael, Lucifer and Gabriel, the messenger angel. In addition to demonstrating the greatest power of the three, only Michael is *named* as the top dog. Additionally, it is illogical that an all-knowing creator, who is Love, would put the rebellious Lucifer at the top of the pecking order. Those purporting this are ignorant of Lucifer's true purpose. He was created to be powerful, but not that powerful.

Jesus also gave a short but fascinating recount of the above event. *"I saw Satan fall like lightning from heaven."* (Luke 10:18-19) When Satan rebelled against God there was no longer room for him in heaven. Only love can exist in the presence of God. By his dissidence, Satan has disqualified himself. Therefore, he was cast down to the earth to create a proving ground for humanity. Love only exists if the free-will to love and choose is present. This, by the way, was God's plan all along. No one in heaven was surprised by Satan's discord.

Therefore, for the purpose of maintaining order, man must pass the same test that one third of the angelic population failed. Since only love can be present in heaven, man's eventual and everlasting abode, Satan's sole purpose is to prove you belong. Isn't it sort of comical that Satan does not even know how he is being used? He is so full of pride and ego that he fails to even notice. That only makes me revere the all-knowing Yahweh even more. However, this event was not without physical consequence.

What happens when lightning strikes something? A lightning bolt recently struck a telephone poll near the neighborhood in which I live. The power was incredible. It did not just crack the poll. It shattered the poll into thousands of splinters and transformed the cement sidewalk next to it into glass.

Think about that. For the most part, lightning destroys whatever it strikes. That which is not destroyed is often times transformed, as was the case with the sidewalk. An event of such magnitude involving a multitude of supernaturally powered angels being cast to the earth would cause much more than mere disorder on the blue planet. Just like the sidewalk near my home, it would undoubtedly transform it, and thus, may have caused the entire earth to *become* without form and void.

In essence, the entrance of evil may have shattered the planet just as lightning splintered the pole near my home. When the pieces fell back into place, the cracks in the natural were clearly evident. The strength of cement had been commuted into the fragility of broken glass. The perfect had become imperfect. Evil had left its mark.

Also notice in the Jeremiah prophecy, which actually looks like Genesis chapter one in reverse, that the heavens were devoid of any light and *indeed* there was no man. Cities, however, had already been built. This precludes it from being a *post*-Adam event, since the lack of cities only existed *prior* to Adam in the Book of Genesis. Within just a couple generations, Nod, the first city was built.

Since that time, there has not been an instance when there was no sun or stars in the sky. From that time, the light has always shown. The description may refer to the time when *"darkness covered the face of the deep."* Also, since Adam was created there has not been a time when at least one man was roaming the blue planet.

Finally, it would require a multitude of human-like creatures to build cities. In the Jeremiah prophecy there are none. In conclusion, there could have been man-like creatures prior to Adam. The Jeremiah discourse seems to point to this conclusion. Keep in mind, however, and the reason I have touched on this controversial topic, is that they were not the image of God. They were vastly different from you and me in nature. They did not possess the same essence of love that present kind humanity does. They were not created to be one with God. Love was not finished until His image had been replicated. It was all part of the plan. Even within the appearance of chaos God is perfect.

Jeremiah continues on and declares that, "*All the cities were broken down.*" In the future, when we inhabit the New Jerusalem and have no need of the sun for light, the city is certainly not broken down. Our present cities will be wiped out, not left broken down. When God creates a *New* Heaven and a *New* Earth there will not be a trace of evidence that the former civilizations ever existed. There will be no indication that our current earth or even universe ever existed. In the absence of sorrow, suffering, and pain, what once was will have been wiped clean.

In truth, the New Jerusalem will be the greatest and most modern city ever known. It will contain the very essence of Love. The New Jerusalem is not a rebuilt city. It descends out of heaven from God. It is placed upon a New Earth that surpasses its predecessor's glory from its perfect inception. It contains no darkness. It is ablaze with the glory of God and the Lamb is its light. (Revelation 21:23 and 22:5) There will be no hatred and no violence there. Only love will prevail.

The aforementioned cities of Jeremiah's account have no light. They have been eradicated and darkened. It makes perfect sense that the entrance of Satan would bring darkness, destruction and ultimately death. That is consistent with both his nature and his character. "*The thief does not come except to steal, kill and destroy.*" (John 10:10) He is the opposite of Love. He is the beginning of all the evil and hatred present upon the earth today. There is no life or light in him. It appears to me that this must denote the past and that there must have been intelligent human-like creatures on earth in this pre-garden of Eden world.

Take careful note of the following. There is another difference between them and us which precludes the Lord from destroying life as we know it, certainly in a spiritual sense, and possibly even in a physical sense. There is a reason He broke everything down and created man to inhabit the Garden of Eden. The difference and the reason for our existence is that we can be inhabited by God.

Yahweh is so in love with mankind that He has chosen to be conjoined to us. In fact, it is even deeper than that. When you allow Him, He will penetrate your being, thus consummating His love for you and actually become one with you. Having been created in His image makes us so similar to Him that He can unite and dwell *within us*. God made a "forever" choice when He created humanity. As amazing as it may sound, God has chosen *you* to be His temple.

> *"Do you not know that your body is the temple of the Holy Spirit who is in you?"*
> **—1 Corinthians 6:19**

Do you still believe that you are ordinary? No, you are so much more than you could have ever imagined. You are extraordinary in His love! Could you have ever imagined that all that information is contained in the word "was?" Perhaps I am a bit strange. These are the kinds of things I think about in my spare time. I guess someone has to do it.

The Trinity in Isaiah

Let's get back to the Genesis account . . . *"And darkness was on the face of the deep. And the Spirit of God was hovering over the face of the waters."* I will spend a little more time on the darkness shortly, but we see something revealed here that is of utmost importance. Its significance is based upon God's desire to share information with the ones He loves. He wants you to recognize His nature. He wants you to love Him for who He is. Most do not realize that Yahweh announced His plan to reveal the coming Messiah long before the birth of Christ. The initial annunciation occurred centuries before that fateful first day of Christmas. In the above scripture we see God's Spirit.

With the first revelation of God's name, Elohim, (Genesis 1:1) which is a plural name for a singular God, we find that the nature of God is derived in multiplicity. Just one sentence later, with the revelation of the Holy Spirit, (Genesis 1:2) God begins to disclose exactly who He is as He Messianically walks with Adam and Eve in the Garden of Eden (Genesis 3:8).

Later in the Book of Isaiah, which was written seven hundred forty years before the birth of Jesus Christ, we actually see God's triune nature revealed in one singular revelation:

> Come near to Me, hear this: **I have not spoken in secret from the beginning**; *from the time that it was,* **I was there**, *and now the* **Lord God** *(1), and His* **Spirit** *(2) have sent* **Me** *(3)*
> **—Isaiah 48:16**

This is clearly a Messianic annunciation of the Lord Jesus Christ. It clearly denotes the triune nature of the Lord Almighty, as Yahweh the Father, Yahweh the Holy Spirit and Yahweh the Messiah revealed in the pages of the Old Testament. It is confirmation of John 1:3, *"All things were made through Him, and without Him nothing was made that was made."* Love wanted us to recognize Him when He walked among us. *"I will walk among you and be your God, and you shall be My people."* (Leviticus 26:12) How did we miss Him? God may as well have screamed it from the mountain top. Yet so many still reject His voice.

Make note of the fact that God is not trying to hide anything. He is revealing it. He does not speak in secret, but openly to anyone willing to listen. God's sole desire is to reveal His true nature to those whom He loves. He wants you to personally know Him. That includes knowing about Him. He wants you to become intimately familiar with His nature, His ways, His Word, His covenant, His culture and His personality. He does not want you to miss Him when He calls and, therefore, He has made Himself completely recognizable once you know where and how to look for Him. Love is always a reciprocal act. This is what differentiates Him from every other deity man has ever conjured up.

This does not mean that He does not have secrets. He does. "*The secret of the Lord is with those who fear Him, and He will show them His covenant.*" (Psalm 25:14) As you progress in your knowledge of the Lord you will find that He is not keeping secrets *from* you. He is keeping them *for* you. You must, however, be in a place spiritually to receive them. He will not let His secrets fall by the wayside. They are vastly too important and reserved only for those who truly love Him. The Lord is always consistent in His ways when you learn to understand Him, albeit in whatever limited capacity we have the ability to.

I'm in a Fog

Let's now peer into the darkness . . .

> *"And darkness was on the face of the deep. And the Spirit of God was hovering over the face of the waters. **Then God said**, 'let there be light'; and there was light."*
> **—Genesis 1:2-3**

The order of this revelation is no accident and is of utmost importance. First we see darkness, then we see the creation of light. With the implementation of modern technologies such as the Hubble Space Telescope and various mathematical breakthroughs, scientists can now see the radiation signatures of the early universe which allows them to allegedly go back and examine the remnants of the creation event within a millisecond of the actual occurrence. I am not smart enough to understand how that is done, therefore, I use the word "allegedly." You know it as the "Big Bang Theory" (BBT) which connotes a tremendous release of energy and matter that set the universe into its current state of expansion.

Scientists have recently theorized that for the first three hundred seventy-seven thousand years or so of the universe, that is an approximate number, this is not intended to be a science book, it was devoid of all light. The particles for light, such as photons, ions etc . . . existed, it was simply too hot for light to function. Therefore, the universe was murky and in a plasma-like state. There was no clarity. "*Darkness was on the face of the deep.*" (Genesis 1:2) It was not until after this brief period, by cosmological standards, that the newly formed universe had cooled enough for the particles to function properly in the production of light. Then all of a sudden, as if "Someone" flipped a switch, the universe burst into illumination!

As awesome as that is, here is the incredible part. Genesis 1:3 states, "*And God saw the light, that it was good; **and God divided the light from the darkness**.*" Science now believes that after the 377,000 year period, a phenomenon known as "decoupling" occurred. In essence, it means that the particles of light that were bound together during "recombination," the early state of the universe, divided from one another. Recombination is what caused the universe to be foggy in its plasma-like state. It was like looking through translucent glass. Upon decoupling, the universe became transparent and the light became distinguishable from the darkness.

Decoupling, which means "separation," or if we are to use the terminology of Genesis, "division," eliminated the dark and foggy state of the universe. Both light and darkness now became visible. They were indistinguishable prior to this event. Due to the intense heat, the molecules were melded together in the plasma-like state state of matter. Upon decoupling, the production of light occurred exactly as Genesis 1:3 so accurately and amazingly stated, "*God divided the light from the darkness.*"

This scientific breakthrough has rendered the Book of Genesis to be completely accurate in its account of how the production of light was created. *"And darkness was on the face of the deep. **Then** God said, "Let there be light."* He actually said, *"Light be,"* and bam! The particles of light had been created. At this point, however, the universe was in its infancy and as previously stated, due to the immense heat, the light particles could not properly function. Therefore, Yahweh having implemented the second law of thermodynamics, cooled the universe. In so doing, *"God divided the light from the darkness."* The possibility of day and night now became distinguishable. Day one was finished.

Incredibly, Jesus both revealed and used the same process of creation in His healing of the blind man in Bethsaida. Check out the following progression of events. In His incredible wisdom, Jesus uses every opportunity to disclose His true identity to humanity. As technology races toward eternity we are now catching revelations that are intended specifically for our modern-day generation. The fact that He does so in ways that only contemporary science can recognize is a testament to the wonder of His greatness. What follows is an exact replica of the light producing Genesis account adapted by the one and only Jesus Christ to shed light upon the hearts and minds of a modern humanity searching the cosmos for truth.

> *"Then He came to Bethsaida; and they brought a blind man to Him, and begged Him to touch him. So He took the blind man by the hand and led him out of the town. And when He had spit on his eyes and put His hands on him, He asked him if he saw anything."*
>
> *"And he looked up and said, '**I see men like trees, walking.**'* (Note the murkiness of his sight) *Then **He put His hands on his eyes** again and made him look up. And he was restored **and saw everyone clearly**.* (Followed by transparent clarity) *Then He sent him away to his house, saying, 'Neither go into the town, nor tell anyone in the town.'"*
> **—Mark 8:22-26**

Just as in the beginning of creation, the blind man's first experience of luminescence was murky and indistinguishable. Jesus' first touch of the blind man left his eyes nebulous and hazy. It was not until God got personal with His creation, *"that God saw the light, that it was good,"* and divided the light from the darkness, that the light became distinguishable from the darkness.

In like manner, it was not until Jesus got personal with the blind man, spitting is not very personal, and touched his eyes directly, that the blind man saw clearly. The direct touch of Jesus Christ will always divide the light from the darkness.

God, by the way, just like the instruction of Jesus given to the formerly blind man, did not tell anyone how He did it. Faith is a personal discovery that every human being must come to on their own. Therefore, every human being gazing into the eyes of the blind man had to choose whether or not to believe. Similarly, the whole of humanity is faced with the same choice when peering into the eyes of the cosmos. At first glance, God may appear murky, and to some, even, dark. However, as we are touched by His grace through faith in Jesus Christ, His goodness and mercy becomes clear as day, and incredibly, as technology progresses, Yahweh is revealed.

*"But you are a chosen generation, a royal priesthood, a holy nation, His own special people, that you may proclaim the praises of Him who called you **out of darkness into His marvelous light.**"*
—1 Peter 2:9

I would encourage you to take this to heart as this is the message Jesus is conveying through the encounter. Jesus Christ is *"the image of the invisible God, the firstborn over all creation."* (Colossians 1:15) He is *"the brightness of His glory"* and *"the express image of His person . . . who upholds all things by the Word of His power."* (Hebrews 1:3)

Science has theorized that the creation of the universe occurred exactly the way God said it did in the Book of Genesis. Where then is the conflict between science and theology? The heavens have declared the glory of God and modern science blinded by atheism is yet to have their eyes opened. They cannot see through the fog of sin. I praise God, however, that the further science peers into the cosmos, the more clearly their decoupling becomes. Eventually, God will become so transparent that denial becomes merely an act of vanity.

Think about it, how could Moses, or whomever you believe authored the Book of Genesis, have possibly possessed such information? How could the subsequent authors of the New Testament have layered the same mysteries into the life of the Messiah? If you know anything about statistics there is only one possible answer. God told them. Yahweh is *"the author and finisher of our faith."* (Hebrews 12:2) Getting lucky, as many atheists will portend, is a statistical impossibility with something so complex as the creation of the universe. In the Word of God, Yahweh has revealed the knowledge of Himself to mankind.

Water, Water Everywhere

Although I live in the Northeast, I love the Bible Belt. I am always amazed as I drive down the highway and see all of the "Jesus" billboards, crosses erected near the highways, and the outward profession of Jesus Christ by our southern brothers and sisters in America. Not too long ago, I was driving up Route 287 in New Jersey, when I noticed a billboard that proclaimed the love of God for humanity. I was so shocked that I doubled back and drove by it again to make sure I was not imagining things. Outward displays of Christianity are rare in the Northeast. This, however, is not the case with our Southern neighbors. In addition, they also have something that is a bit rare in the Northeast, as well, Christian Radio.

While in Greensboro, North Carolina, I ran across Glenn Beck on the radio. I realize he is not classified as Christian radio, but where

I come from it is close enough! Even the *one* station near my home that had good quality teaching of the Word of God has been replaced with the endless drone of Christian pop. As a musician, all I can say is, "Ugh!" Not that Christian pop is a bad thing, it is simply all the same. It is like the redundancy of a 1980's hair metal band. You had to have a high voice and a ballad on your album. The ballad captured the female audience and we all know why that is so important. Like any other business, Christian pop has discovered a formula that "works," and now every artist sounds exactly like *Hillsong United* and *The Newsboys* . . . but back to the lesson at hand.

Spiritually speaking, New York City and Sodom and Gomorrah are not that far apart! They are in the same spiritual zip code, if you know what I mean. The liberal madness known as the Northeast cannot be all that far from judgment and can only be surpassed in its debauchery by San Francisco, or, perhaps, Bangkok, Thailand.

Keep in mind as you are reading this that my political bent falls on the extreme of both sides of the aisle. I once heard someone say, "If something is worth doing, it is worth overdoing." Obviously, I have made that a practice in my life. Quite honestly, overdoing everything comes naturally to me.

As a financial advisor, I am quite naturally a fiscal conservative. I believe in lower taxes, less government interference, and so forth. At the same time, I have been to court on numerous occasions testifying on behalf of my illegal alien friends in hope of gaining their freedom from their previously oppressive nations. On other social issues, such as abortion, I am on the polar opposite side of the aisle. As a disciple of Jesus Christ, I believe He was of a similar ideology. Jesus Christ was the perfect progressively liberal, staunch conservative, wrapped up in one human package. Jesus overdid everything He came into contact with. It ultimately sent Him to the cross.

Anyway, as they were talking, they began discussing a brand new scientific discovery that caused me to nearly drive off the side of the road. My spirit did a summersault. Apparently, several weeks prior to my trip to Greensboro, on May 12, 2014, scientists publicly released that they had discovered that the earth's mantle contains three times the amount of water as all the oceans combined—and that it has a "float system" that lets water in and out in order to maintain the ocean's level. So much for melting iceberg's flooding New York City! I guess it will have to be fire and brimstone again.

Two scientists, who happen to be University professors, discovered that located deep inside the earth's mantle is a mineral called, Ringwoodite. Despite the intense heat, water, discovered in a previously unknown form, is a part of Ringwoodite's elemental make up. Science has estimated that if all of the water were simultaneously released, there is enough water to deluge the earth to the point that only the highest mountain peaks may be visible. In other words, there is enough water to flood the entire planet.

As cool as that is, and as damaging as it is to the global warming community, (which is most likely why the media buried it) that is not what got me excited. I immediately recognized the Genesis account of the great flood. What, you ask?

Scientists have always wondered where the source of earth's water came from. Oceans are not easy to fill. Various theories have been floated about, such as comets (which are frozen ice-balls flying through space) pelting the earth and depositing the perfectly viscous life giving miracle substance known as water. The oceans, however, are so vast that the violence of that many strikes would most likely preclude life from forming in the first place—assuming life could randomly evolve from an inorganic primordial cesspool. Furthermore, there just are not enough comets in our "neighborhood" to suffice.

Once again, to discover the truth, one needs to look no further than the book of Genesis. Check out what happened when God shut Noah and his family into the Ark.

*"And it came to pass after seven days that the waters of the flood were on the earth. In the six hundredth year of Noah's life, in the second month, the seventeenth day of the month, on that day all the **fountains of the great deep** were broken up, and the windows of heaven were opened. And the rain was on the earth forty days and forty nights."*
—Genesis 7:10-12

So here we are in the twenty-first century, searching outer space for the water deposited on the surface of the earth, and all the while Yahweh told us exactly where to look 5000 years prior. The water had been placed *inside* the earth all along. The Genesis account of the source of the flood waters is amazingly accurate. Couple the above revelation with Psalm 33 and a lucky prediction becomes an impossible piece of knowledge.

*"He gathers **the waters** of the sea **into jars;** he puts **the deep into storehouses.**"*
—Psalm 33:7

That is one incredible piece of foreknowledge. As I mentioned, science has just discovered (May 12, 2014) that the "fountains of the great deep" located deep inside the earth's mantle, contain a mineral called Ringwoodite. Each tiny piece of Ringwoodite contains roughly 2-3 percent water, which as I stated, exists in a previously unknown form. Folks, you can't make this stuff up! Can you see the incredible revelation you are gazing upon? Therefore, put two and two together.

Each piece of Ringwoodite is a tiny jar containing the the gathered waters of the sea God referred to in Psalm 33! A jar is a container. In their totality, these incredible little ringwoodite "jars" hold three times the amount of water contained in all of earth's seas combined. Each little heap, as many versions translated the word *"ned,"* acts as a tiny storehouse in preservation of the earth's water deep inside the mantle of the earth. Without these storehouses, the heat of the earth's core would surely evaporate the water and destroy the vital cycling mechanism that preserves life on earth as we know it. This incredible new discovery renders Psalm 33 to be completely accurate. The fact that the Word of God predicted the storehouses to be tiny little containers in the similitude of jars is beyond human comprehension.

As if that were not enough, the pressure caused by the movement of the tectonic plates is what causes the water to be "squeezed" from the Ringwoodite. In other words, tectonic plate movements break up of the deep and squeeze out the water. In the Genesis account of the flood, one can only surmise that the resulting pressure, which is how science has determined the water would be released, caused the water to burst fourth as fountains. For the first time in history it rained down upon the surface of the earth and the first sea vessel in history was the savior of Noah and his family.

Amazingly, the water that flooded the earth and created our oceans came from deep inside the earth, just as science has recently confirmed. It is still there and has been merely awaiting our discovery. God and His Word are real. They are infallible, and as science continues to progress, humanity continues to discover that the worlds were framed exactly as God so long ago proclaimed. (Hebrews 11:3)

Your Substance Yet Unformed

While we are discovering the wonders of the earth's depths, let's have a gander at the origin of the substance of man. You are about to discover that God's love is even deeper than the lowest parts of the earth and the greatest ocean depth. We will discuss the creation and nature of man shortly in the next chapter. Before we do, however, let's have a look at the physical substance of humanity. In the Book of Jeremiah, God makes an incredible statement to His newly called prophet:

*"**Before I formed you in the womb I knew you**; before you were born I sanctified you; I ordained you a prophet to the nations."*
—Jeremiah 1:5-6

As if that is not an awesome display of God's omniscience, through the Apostle Paul our loving Father takes us even further back in time.

*"Blessed be the God and Father of our Lord Jesus Christ, who has blessed us with every spiritual blessing in the heavenly places in Christ, just as He chose us in Him **before the foundation of the world**, that we should be holy and without blame before Him in love."*
—Ephesians 1:3-4

Did you know that God has always known you—and not just before you were born, but before He even created the earth? Your entrance onto the blue planet, made possible by the gateway into the physical realm known as your mother's womb, is merely a forgone conclusion of God's love for the spirit He created countless eons ago. Insert your own life into the following scripture.

*"In Your book they all were written, the days fashioned for me, **when as yet there were none of them**. How precious also are Your thoughts to me, O God! How great is the sum of them!"*
—Psalm 139:16-17

Psalm 139 contains a revelation that I had read past for many years, but my mind was torn open several days ago as I was meditating on the revelations I have found in the Book of Genesis.

Most of the people I meet, Christians included, have a hard time believing that God formed man *"of the dust of the ground."* Have you ever considered the implication? Creation is the foundation of faith. Either you believe God, or you do not. God is either all powerful, or He is not. The universe was either formed by God, or it was not. There is no in between. God either exists, or He does not.

To take this even further, consider what your children are being taught by the atheistic scientific community masked by the public, and in many cases, private, and even "Christian" educational systems of our modern culture. Our children are being taught that mankind was not created. They, and even we, are being taught, and the vast majority of the Christian community believes, that humanity evolved from a common single celled ancestor—even though there is absolutely no observable evidence to support evolutionary theory (which is taught as fact) as being anything other than the ability of God's manifold organisms to implement certain genetically predisposed adaptations within reproductively compatible species. There has never been observed, or found any change in kinds, as the Bible terms the variation of species.

In simple terms, there is no evidence that any organism has ever evolved into an unrelated organism, such as a paramecium to a blade of grass, or a cat to a dog. All science has is Mendel's experiments of E. Coli becoming other forms of E. Coli, fruit flies remaining fruit flies and stickleback fish magically evolving into . . . stickleback fish. In other words, garbage in (which is what evolutionary theory is) does not produce perfection out.

The ultimate goal of such a theory is to utterly destroy God in the mind of humanity. Yet Love, who is God, will have none of it. He left us the truth countless millennia ago in His Word. We just need to take the time to discover it while we are ultimately searching for Him.

Most people have no idea that the human body is made up of 59 trace elements. *All* of these elements are found either at, or just below the surface of the earth. These 59 elements, by the way, are also quite common in the composition of dirt. Let that sink in for a moment. Now anytime someone calls me a "dirt bag," I simply thank them and say, "I know, so are you!" Since they have no clue of what I am referring to, it usually does not end well, but hey, truth is truth.

Consider for a moment how God formed man. According to the book of Genesis, "*The Lord God formed man* **of the dust of the ground**, (From dirt) *and breathed into his nostrils the breath of life; and man became a living being.*" (Genesis 2:7)

In other words, God "scooped up" a portion of the earth's surface and formed man. If you have been indoctrinated by the modern educational system, there is no doubt that your main objection will be, "But man is comprised of about eighty percent water. Genesis says nothing about man being composed mostly of water."

Of course it does! What constitutes the makeup of water? The answer is hydrogen and oxygen. Remember, H_2O? Water is two parts hydrogen and one part oxygen, bonded together to formulate the miraculous substance that allows your body to absorb nutrition, cool itself by sweating, carry oxygen, and discard the blood's waste product, carbon dioxide, from your body.

Guess what two of the most abundant elements found at the surface of the earth are? If your answer is hydrogen and oxygen you have guessed right. In reality, before Love breathes into us the "pnuema," or spirit of life, we are nothing more than dust and ashes, as the Bible so eloquently categorizes us. We are merely compilations of inorganic matter, or as those whom were attempting to insult me as a child put it, dirt bags.

But wait—that is not quite enough evidence. God left us even more! If the above is true, we must be able to answer the question of, how did these elements get to the surface where God scooped them up? Think logically for just a moment and try to remember your earth science class. How was the crust of the earth formed?

As the earth was in its infancy, there was tremendous volcanic activity occurring that deposited the magma found in the earth's core onto the surface of the one and only blue planet. At the time, the surface of the earth was too hot to support carbon based life that breathes oxygen from the atmosphere. As the earth cooled, however, the crust cooled and hardened. It became what we know to be the earth's surface today. What does this have to do with the creation of man? To answer that, let's go back to Psalm 139. Remember, God formed man *"of the dust of the ground."* You are comprised of 59 of the earth's elements.

> *"For You formed my inward parts; you covered me in my mother's womb. I will praise You, for I am fearfully and wonderfully made; marvelous are Your works, and that my soul knows very well. My frame was not hidden from You, when I was made in secret, skillfully wrought* **in the lowest parts of the earth***. Your eyes saw my substance,* **being yet unformed***. And in Your book they all were written, the days fashioned for me, when as yet there were none of them."*
> **—Psalm 139:13-16**

Wow! God saw you. He saw your matter—your *"substance,"* all 59 elements that comprise your physicality *"being yet unformed,"* before you were ever conceived in your mother's womb. Perhaps, even, before Yahweh formed the earth. Can you guess where they came from? Just as Psalm 139 reveals, they came from *"the lowest parts of the earth."* Your substance, *"being yet unformed,"* was seen by God and deposited upon the surface of the earth. The elements to form your physicality came from the lowest depths of the earth. In your mothers womb God formed you *"of the dust of the ground"* (What do you think the nutrition is comprised of that entered your mother's womb through the umbilical cord. All food comes from the dust of the ground.) and "*breathed into you the breath of life, and man (you) became a living being.*" (Genesis 2:7)

That is the ultimate act of love! Time was never an issue. God never changed His mind. This, without a doubt, sheds new light upon Jeremiah 29:11. "*For I know the thoughts that I think toward you, says the Lord, thoughts of peace and not of evil, to give you a future and a hope.*"

Perfectly Precise

While we are on the topic, here is another really cool piece of information. Have you ever wondered why the sun and moon appear to be the same size in the sky? Here is an amazing truth that cannot possibly be a coincidence. The sun is exactly **four hundred** times larger than the moon. However, because the moon is exactly **four hundred** times closer to the earth than the sun, they appear to be exactly the same size in the sky. If this were not the case a total eclipse would be impossible, and by the way, this ratio does not exist anywhere else in our solar system, and as far as we know up to this point, in the universe! Could that possibly be a coincidence? When you add up all the additional coincidences necessary for life, the evidence becomes overwhelming in support of a lovingly creative deity whose name happens to be Yahweh.

Although the relationship between the sun and the moon will not last forever, (It will change in a few billion years or so as the celestial object continue to drift.) it seems that everything God created has been "*for such a time as this.*" (Esther 4:14) The universe and our exact location in it is precisely perfect for the creation and sustenance of life. Could this also be coincidental? I think not.

Why are these weird little scientific facts important? God has left His unmistakable signature upon the universe. It is so incredible that it causes your jaw to drop and declare that such an incredible act of random chance is absolutely and statistically impossible. It is the glory of God. Only God could have ordered so many events and processes in such a precise manner. God's method of creating and ordering the cosmos has been designed to lead His children right back to Him. Love is wooing you home. As the Bible clearly states, God speaks to mankind through astronomical events. The celestial objects are *"for signs and seasons."* (Genesis 1:14) As John Hagee states in his book, *Four Blood Moons*, the heavens are used by God as billboards. They confirm His sovereignty and proclaim His Word.

When you look up at the sky and at the world around you, you should see Love. Think about all the different colors, variations of species, differences in temperature and all the different faces of every person you will ever meet. Something as simple as the human face has an infinite number of variations. Yet we all look similar. The human face is unmistakable. So is the signature and love of Almighty God.

God could have created nature in complete visual uniformity. Something as seemingly insignificant as trees, for example, are unmistakable in the fact that one species varies from the other. Yet all trees look alike at the same time. They share the same characteristics. There is no mistaking what they are. Evolution on such a scale, if it were possible to happen even once, is beyond not just comprehension, but would require far greater spans of time— particularly when you consider the fossil records and when life began to prosper. From a cosmological perspective, life is a brand new occurrence in the observable portion of our universe.

God has created infinite variations to something as common as a color. Not all greens are the same. God could have made everything to be one color, one texture, and one species, but He did not. Love would never allow His children to live in a black and white world. He is extraordinarily radiant and He created the world to be so vastly astounding that it causes you seek the reason for its existence. Oh, the glory of God! God is Love.

Alien Life Forms

Let's take this even further. Although God had finished His work on the "seventh day," the laws of reproduction were set in motion and the universe follows these laws as well. Scientists now know that stars, galaxies, planets, solar systems etc . . . are still being produced today, but life and the conditions for it, seem to be unique to our planet. It seems that the earth is the epicenter of the universe in the eyes of God, and man is undoubtedly the center of God's attention. Every aspect of the universe was created for the purpose and existence of the ones God so loves and cherishes, His beloved children.

Of course we will never know for sure if life exists elsewhere until either we get to heaven and find out, or we find it on another planet. I personally do not think life exists in the universe outside of our planet. The Book of Genesis states (see Genesis 1:14-19) that everything in the heavens were created *"for the earth."* In other words, from God's point of view it is all about us. It is all about God's beloved. It is all necessary to support life on planet earth. God implemented immensely complicated processes to ensure that *you* would be here for *Him*. Just think about that concept for a moment. In His eyes, although He is perfect and has no need of man to support His existence, as He completes us we also complete Him. Perhaps you do not realize this. You are a part of the entire creation and God is one with it. What did you think omnipresence meant?

However, I will state this, because those of you who are particularly sharp should be asking the question, what about the angels? God *did* create life outside of the solar system but no matter how hard we look for it, and no matter how much technology we develop, we will never find it in this realm. It cannot be found in the natural, that is, the physical dimension in which we currently reside.

Before God created the physical universe, He created the heavenly realm, which does have physical properties. Remember, the

New Jerusalem will descend from it and reside on the physical earth. I do not pretend to understand the science of this, but I do understand that whatever God says is going to come to pass, comes to pass. Trust is the essence of faith.

Life does exist outside of our solar system. It exists in the heavenly realm. God created angels, seraphim and cherubim. Since we find Christ coming back to the earth on a white horse, (Revelation 19) there are quite possibly different types of animals residing there as well. If you are a person of faith you must also believe there are people there, but we will never find them in the space-time dimension in which we live.

They live in the kingdom of heaven which no telescope or space craft can ever reach. It has been set apart by God where no sin can ever impact its purity. Love has created the perfect place for you to reside for all of eternity.

"In My Father's house are many mansions; if it were not so I would have told you. I go to prepare a place for you."
—John 14:2

In fact, I personally believe the heavenly realm is somehow joined to us. How else could God and the angels interact with man, and in the case of God, actually reside within us?

Star Dust

Let's look at one final point in regard to the universe. When science looks for the origin of man they need to look no further than the following. Within the core of every star is the production of the elements that reside within the earth. The intense energy caused by the burning of Hydrogen followed by the burning of Helium, otherwise known as nuclear fusion, produces the elements necessary for the production of life as we know it. The stars have been spewing them throughout the universe since their creation.

In particular, it would be impossible for the heavy elements to exist if not for the production factories scientifically known as stars. Interestingly enough, contained within your body are all the elements which were deposited in the earth by the stars. Just take a look at your multi-vitamin bottle. Check out what it contains; zinc, magnesium, calcium, copper etc . . . It ought to be called a stardust pill, because that is what it really is.

As discussed previously, consider how God formed man. According to the Book of Genesis it was from the dust of the ground that has been deposited here by the stars. Therefore, until the Lord God Almighty breathes life into you, you are simply nothing but an inorganic pile of stardust. It is only His breath, His life and His love that gives *you* life. The entire universe as we know it, and all life therein, is an act of His love and His will. It is certainly of immense complexity, but that is all the more a testament to His greatness and power.

What's the Point?

I said all of that to bring us to the greatest and most precious act of all. You! In us, the Lord has manifested the pinnacle of His creation. The creation of man is the single greatest outpouring and manifestation of Love the universe has ever known. We see God's perfect will in the creation of mankind, as well as, the environment in which He placed us.

Many folks have asked me about God's purpose for creating human beings, especially in light of the chaos, and evil we see in mankind today. In seeing such horrific acts of sin manifested as child pedophilia, rape, murder, gang violence, the attempted genocide of entire races of people, famine, war, pornography, abortion, adultery, fornication, etc . . . I can certainly understand how a person can believe that even if there is a God, He cannot be the loving creator we claim He is. I used to feel that way myself.

What I must impart to you, however, is that if you feel this way you simply have a misunderstanding of who God is and the character and integrity He possesses. What we see on earth today *is not* and *never has* been God's ultimate will for mankind. Humanity is currently in the midst of God's temporary permissive will. God's ultimate will is never about the now. It is always in regard to forever, and as you previously learned, eternity is perfect.

Therefore, He has made a way to restore mankind. He will eventually take this earth back for Himself. Is there a purpose in what we see today? You bet there is. When viewed from the proper perspective, God's will is functioning perfectly. Everything God stated would occur in the Bible is coming to pass before our very eyes. As we now progress to the creation of mankind, you will discover that Love has manifested Himself in us, and believe it or not, His love is present even in the midst of this evil and perverse generation.

CHAPTER 4

Mankind

In God's eyes there is nothing like humanity in all of creation. Man is above every animal, every creeping thing, every fish, every bird—and being that God did not create the angels of heaven to be inhabited by Him, mankind is even above the angels created to dwell in heaven, who look at God's love for man with awesome wonder.

*"To them it was revealed that, not to themselves, but to us they were ministering the things which now have been reported to you through those who have preached the gospel to you by the Holy Spirit sent from heaven—**things which angels desire to look into**."*

Humanity is the pinnacle of God's creation. We are His wondrous work. Man is above everything you see throughout the whole of creation. Man is *the apple of God's eye.*" (Zechariah 2:8)

Why then, is man not the apple of *man's* eye? I find it to be absolutely amazing that we rarely, if ever, notice the greatness of humanity as a whole. While recently in Rome, I made a trip to the Vatican, which for many, is one of the holiest places on the face of the earth. It was simply stunning. Even my youngest son was impressed. That really says something.

However, in the midst of my exploration I noticed something that I found to be a bit strange. As the masses of humanity marveled at the architecture, sculptures, paintings, mosaics and multiple altars within the Vatican walls, very few, if any of the people noticed *each other.*

Walking amongst the Vatican in all of its glory was God's most incredible act of creation and for reasons we will discuss shortly, I think I may have been the only one who noticed. The vast majority would prefer to kneel before a lifeless statue than place a coin in the hand of the homeless man outside the Vatican walls. Do you realize that mankind, even in his perceived lowest state, is still the greatest of all God's creation? Need I tell you that God expects so much more than what we have become?

While at the Pantheon several days later I came to something of an epiphany. As we all marveled at this incredible structure that has been standing for umpteen thousand years, I came to the realization that it has absolutely no clue of its own existence. Although it has been standing for centuries and countless human beings have gazed upon its countenance, it is merely a lifeless pile of rocks and mortar.

This is not the case for the people wandering its grounds. We are acutely aware of our own existence, as well as, our own mortality. Mankind is the only "animal" in the kingdom with a stream of consciousness that is advanced enough to ponder both life and death, as well as, the afterlife. It is absolutely incredible when you think about it. We know we exist. We actually have the ability to love and to empathize with one another. Of equal majesty is the unique ability to ponder our own existence, our origins and the meaning of life. Your cat or dog cannot do this. Not even a chimpanzee that the atheists of the world think are their long lost cousin's can exhibit such unique abilities.

The beauty of the human condition is that all of these magnificent capabilities have been bestowed upon us intentionally. God created consciousness in order that we may discover and interact with Him. In addition, it is our God given gift of conscious that causes the vast majority of mankind to strive for harmony amongst the masses.

I do not believe Rene' Descartes got it right when he philosophized, "I think, therefore I am." When taken in light of how God revealed Himself to Moses, the famous philosophical principle should actually state, "I think, therefore *God* is." Do you remember the discussion from *God Culture*, when the Lord revealed Himself to Moses as "*I AM*," He was declaring, "Tell them I exist?" Furthermore, as I stood in front of the Pantheon I came to the realization that, "*Because* I can think, God is."

Thoughts are spiritual. Consciousness is spiritual. Because thought and consciousness is spiritual, having no physical properties, it could not have evolved. There is nothing in the genetic makeup to naturally select into, or out of existence. Perhaps you have never realized it, but we think in pictures. Thought pictures are not physical in their makeup. You cannot experience them with your five senses.

In my opinion, this, in conjunction with the preponderance of the evidence discussed earlier, is absolute proof that God created man. Humanity, nor any form of life, could have evolved from a less complex form of life. The genetic leaps, as well as, the sudden rise of consciousness do not allow for it. Other than mankind, no other animal ever has, or can, conceptualize and ponder the existence of

God, or even themselves, for that matter. Have you ever seen a chimpanzee pondering the meaning of life or searching for the existence of its Creator? They will eat your face given the opportunity, but they do not ponder the existence of either themselves or God. There are no chimpanzee philosophers, scientists or theologians. They simply do not possess the equipment to process that type of thought.

There is nothing concrete about a thought. Thoughts just are. Our brain, on a physical level is simply a series of billions, perhaps even trillions of neurons that produce a series of electrical impulses. So does a light bulb or an electrical socket, yet it does not contain any thoughts. Not even the most advanced computer has the ability to think and reason. A computer cannot emote. A computer does not long for the technician that built it.

This incredible ability has been set apart for the ones created in the image of their Creator. The ability to think, reason and understand has been implanted into our consciousness by God as a means of seeking after and communicating with Him. This alone demonstrates that there is Someone greater out there.

Still, and rightly so, we are fascinated by the cosmos. We love things such as horticulture, tropical fish, our pets, our possessions, money etc . . . and yet we ignore, abuse and perhaps even hate our fellow man. We see it consistently manifested in the form of racism, hatred, genocide and every act of evil and crime against humanity. Isn't that what racism and prejudice is, hatred of a different group of people?

For what reason, I might ask? It seems we have been mistaken about race. We view race in terms of color; white, black, brown, yellow and red. We even have different labels. We call them Caucasian, Negroid, Hispanic, Asian. The truth, however, is that God only created one race. He created the human race. Genetically speaking, we are all the same species. Our only true difference is whether we are redeemed or unredeemed. Are we "now" or are we "forever."

In terms of how God views us, apart from redeemed we are all equal. There is even evidence that our early American forefathers shared this view. "We hold these truths to be self-evident, that all men are created equal . . . " (Declaration of Independence, 1776) What happened to this idea? Did it ever really exist in the heart of man? I am sorry to say that I think the answer is no. Past history seems to confirm this reality. "*Watch and pray, lest you enter into temptation. The spirit indeed is willing, but the flesh is weak.*" (Mark 14:38) Unfortunately, as humanity drifts further from their Maker, the flesh is defeating the spirit.

Humanity has created the illusion of race based upon our fears and prejudice that one group of people will grow to dominate another. This was most certainly never God's intention. Mankind's differences, just like the rest of nature, were created to add flavor and beauty to all of creation. In unity, our differences are our greatest strength not our most precarious weakness. However, when separated by hatred, the perception of race is the cause of unbridled evil. Therefore, let's have a look at mankind from the point of view of Love. Let's learn God's true vision for humanity.

The Day After Tomorrow

Then God said, "Let Us make man in Our image, according to Our likeness; let them have dominion over the fish of the sea, over the birds of the air, over the cattle, over all the earth and over every creeping thing that creeps on the earth." So God created man in His own image; in the image of God He created him; male and female He created them . . . Then God saw everything that He had made, and indeed it was very good . . .
—Genesis 1: 26-27 & 31

Thus the heavens and the earth, and all the host of them were finished. And on the seventh day God ended His work which He had done.
—Genesis 2:1-2

And the Lord God formed man of the dust of the ground, *and breathed into his nostrils the breath of life; and man became a living being. The Lord God planted a garden eastward in Eden, and there He put the man whom He had formed. And out of the ground the Lord made every tree grow that is pleasant to the sight and good for food . . .*
—Genesis 2: 7-10

And the Lord God said, "It is not good that man should be alone; I will make him a helper comparable to him." Out of the ground the Lord God formed every beast of the field and every bird of the air, and brought them to Adam to see what he would call them . . . But for Adam there was not found a helper comparable to him.
—Genesis 2:18-20

And the Lord caused a deep sleep to fall on Adam, and he slept; and He took one of his ribs, and closed up all the flesh in its place. Then the rib which the Lord God had taken from man He made into a woman, and He brought her to the man.
—Genesis 2:21-22

Your Native Tongue

As stated earlier, whenever you translate a text from one language to another you lose certain nuances and intended meanings of the original text. The translation of the Hebrew/Chaldee text above is undoubtedly an example of this precept. I would like to point out that there seems to be a conflict in the Genesis account. On the surface, it appears as if there is a contradiction to the order of events. In one instance, Genesis states that God created everything, including the animals, prior to creating man. (Genesis 1:3-27) In another, it states that He formed man after the animals. (Genesis 2:18-20)

So which one is correct? Could God have gotten it wrong? Is this evidence that the Bible is flawed and is simply a book of legends and fables? Certainly not! If your native tongue were Hebrew you would find no conflict in this account whatsoever. The language would be as plain as day.

The potential conflict arises from the limitation of the English language as compared to Hebrew. In English, the words "make" or "made," and the word "form," have a very similar meaning with precisely the same connotation. Because English has no differentiating factors between its spiritual versus its physical applications, the same word "made" is used to describe both a concrete or physical act, and a spiritual or non-physical act. This is not the case with Hebrew.

Therefore, when we compare the creation account of chapter one to the historical record of chapter two, we are unable to distinguish between what is actually two separate events. If you read this text in the original language you would be reading two different Hebrew words with two very different meanings, thus avoiding the confusion we have heretofore been ignorant of. Because the majority of humanity is unaware of this fact, and let's be honest, too apathetic to even care, we have come to the incorrect conclusion that God is describing the same event in chapters one and two, when in reality we are looking at two separate, but *subsequent* events.

Made Men

In chapter one, when God creates the universe and in the process proclaims, "*Let us **make** man in Our image,*" the Hebrew word translated as "make" is, **asah**, pronounced, *aw-saw'*. It has a variety of meanings, but in its broadest sense it means, to accomplish, advance, or appoint. The very essence of the word is not something concrete which you can actually touch in a physical manner. It is like being given a promotion at work. Nothing physically changes, but you are instantaneously given, or appointed, to a position of authority which affects the environment around you.

Interestingly enough, in mafia movies you always hear the insiders being referred to as "made" men. They are not necessarily different in a physical sense, but everyone knows both the requirements and the authority associated with the title. The "made" men, by the way, have the authority to appoint people into various positions and give orders, thus creating certain circumstances which cause specific events to unfold within their organizations, all the while never leaving a trace of evidence of their involvement. Does that sound familiar? Are you catching on to where I am going with this?

You will not find their fingerprints at a break in or on a gun. They have not touched anything physically. Yet they caused the circumstance to unfold. They set it in motion. I guess that is a bad example, but it garnered your attention and you certainly understand my point. I am not trying to equate God with gangsters. He is way too holy for that. It is just a fun little illustration teaching how God differentiated the spiritual from the physical at creation. By the way, when you get "born again" you become one of God's "made" men—made in His image and given His authority to affect the world around *you* as well.

Now let's move into the physical realm of creation. In chapter two we read, *"And the Lord **formed** the man of the dust of the ground . . ."* In this instance, the word translated into English as "formed," is the Hebrew word, **yatsar**, pronounced, *yaw-tsar*. It means that something is molded into shape through squeezing. It denotes that God physically picked up the dust in His hands and just like an artist molding clay, He fashioned the man through the process of squeezing. God also "formed" the animals in the same manner.

Many people today find the above process hard to believe. Therefore, consider what happens to your physical body when you die. You decompose into what? As indicated earlier, we are all merely lifeless piles of fifty-nine element dirt, or as the Bible indicates, the dust of the ground, until God breathes life into us. Upon death we revert back into the same stardust from which we were created. The only thing keeping us alive right now is the love of God and the breath He breathed into us when we were separated from our mother's womb. The smack on the butt when you were born only made you cry, it was God who made you alive.

What we find in these two events; and this is the method by which you receive anything from God, is a **spiritual creation followed by a physical manifestation**. The former is more like an architect creating a blueprint than an artist spattering paint to canvas. It is not that the author of the Bible, who happens to be the Holy Spirit of God, could not remember the order. It is simply that God always creates in the spiritual realm before you can see or touch anything in the natural or physical realm. This is confirmed in the two different Hebrew words used to describe these two separate events.

Touched By Grace

When God created in Genesis chapter one, He never physically touched anything. It was simply, *"God said . . . and it was."* He appointed in the Spirit what was to manifest in the natural. However, when we move to Genesis chapter two and see the creation actually revealed, God physically touches it with His "hands."

When you meet with someone you love—when you actually greet them, what is the first thing you do? You physically touch them with either a hug or a handshake, sometimes even a kiss. The touching is personal. It is a divine act of love. That is part of being the image of Almighty God. God loves His creation. As the focal point of His affection, He longs to touch you as well—to be rejoined to you, and to pour His love upon you.

A Cut Above the Rest

However, "*God is Spirit.*" (John 4:24) So when God relates and communicates with man, it is your spirit that He interacts with. It is your spirit that He has penetrated and it is your spirit and your soul that He desires to save. That is how it is possible for God to "*choose us in Christ before the foundation of the world.*" (Ephesians 1:4) In terms of your physical body, do not even sweat shedding your fifty nine elements. In the resurrection we will receive a new and glorified, everlasting, physical body that is not subject to the second law of thermodynamics. Your eternal body will never break down nor grow old.

Why go through all this trouble? Perhaps you are wondering why God does not just "fix" us now. If God were to physically touch you in your current sinful state you would be annihilated. Therefore, He keeps it spiritual. One day, however, when sin is completely out of the way and the two realms are once again united, His touch will once again be personal. But for now, we wait.

Doesn't it make sense that if God were going to create or give anything to you He would do it in the realm in which *He* resides before moving it to your level? The blessings God has bestowed upon the Body of Christ are spiritual in nature prior to being physical in nature. (Ephesians 1:3)

A gentile (or non-Jew) cannot receive the blessings of Abraham, which do belong to us, and are material blessings, until after we receive Jesus Christ, who transforms our spirit, and joins us together with the Spirit of Yahweh. In so doing, we are grafted into and become part of the vine of Israel. (Romans 11:17) By receiving a new heritage as children of Abraham we become partakers of the covenant. Therefore, we qualify for all of the blessings associated with being a child of God. (Galatians 3:14)

This transformation allows us to carry the Spirit of God within us. With the Spirit residing in the natural or physical realm of a man's body, manifesting His blessing is a simple command. God just says the Word, "*Let there be . . .*" (Genesis 1:3) and it is done.

Once again we find this divine characteristic manifested in Jesus Christ. Take a look at the following incident taken from the life and times of Jesus of Nazareth:

> "*Now when Jesus had entered Capernaum, a centurion came to Him, pleading with Him, saying, 'Lord, my servant is lying at home paralyzed, dreadfully tormented.'*"
>
> "*And Jesus said to him, 'I will come and heal him.'*"
>
> "*The centurion answered and said, 'Lord, I am not worthy that You should come under my roof.* **But only speak a word, and my servant will be healed.** *For I also am a man under authority, having soldiers under me. And I say to this one, 'Go,' and he goes; and to another, 'Come,' and he comes; and to my servant, 'Do this,' and he does it.'*"
>
> "*When Jesus heard it, He marveled, and said to those who followed, 'Assuredly, I say to you, I have not found such great faith, not even in Israel! And I say to you that many will come from east and west, and sit down with Abraham, Isaac, and Jacob in the kingdom of heaven. But the sons of the kingdom will be cast out into outer darkness. There will be weeping and gnashing of teeth.' Then Jesus said to the centurion, 'Go your way; and as you have believed, so let it be done for you.'* **And his servant was healed that same hour.**'"
>
> **—Matthew 8:5-13**

Once again, we find Jesus implementing the Genesis process of creation to heal the centurion's servant. Just as God said, *"Let there be . . . and it was . . ."* Jesus implements the same process to heal the centurion's precious servant. He uses the authority of the spoken Word of God. Have you ever considered why? Healing is an act of creation. As such, it is the indwelling of the Father via the Holy Spirit that does the work. Healing is a spiritual act of empowerment. It is a blessing manifested into the natural realm. Like any other spiritual empowerment it must originate with the Father.

In Christ, we become like the "made men" in the mafia illustration I used. We ascend back to our original position of dominion. Therefore, the "made in God's image" men have the same authority as Yahweh to command the blessing. Why? Yahweh is conjoined to them. He has made His abode in the born again believer in Jesus Christ.

> *"Do you not believe that I am in the Father, and the Father in Me? The words that I speak to you I do not speak on My own authority;* **but the Father who dwells in Me does the works.**"
> **—John 14:10**

> *"In that day you will know that I am in my Father, and you in me, and I in you."*
> **—John 14:20**

Thus, the words of the Centurion ring true. Because the Father was in Jesus, Jesus merely needed to speak the Word and it came to pass. The same power resides within each and every one of us who are in Christ. When you are in Christ you are one with the Father, and thus, you are empowered by the Father.

The beauty of this revelation is that when we make Jesus Christ our Lord, we are indwelled, or anointed, by the same Spirit that Jesus was anointed with. Therefore, we have access to the same power and authority that was available to Jesus Christ. We simply need to understand and have faith in the process.

This is more than just an act of love on the part of the Father. It is absolute genius! It is eternal and as such, discloses the reason that the Spiritual blessing is infinitely greater than the physical blessing. The Spiritual blessing is filled with the resurrection power of Almighty Yahweh.

Unlike the Spiritual blessing, a *physical* blessing is limited to the natural surroundings of its existence. Once it becomes manifest it is subject to the same laws that govern our universe. Therefore, it is temporal.

> *"While we do not look at the things which are seen, but at the things which are not seen. **For the things which are seen are temporary . . .**"*
> **—2 Corinthians 4:18**

Not only is the physical blessing subject to change, (Because it is temporal, or temporary) it also cannot be manifested back to the Spiritual. It possesses the same limitations as human flesh. It is bound to only one dimension and is subject to the physical law of entropy. Any and all physical manifestation of the blessing will eventually decay into ruin. Even Lazarus died after being raised from the dead. Therefore, placing all your trust in any material possession, regardless of how you acquired it, is a house of cards. It will eventually fall.

This is not the case with the Spiritual blessing. Because it is not physical in its nature it is not subject to the governing laws of physicality. Therefore, it is not bound by space or time. Entropy is nullified. Decay is not a factor in its existence. The Spiritual blessing is not temporal. It has been granted to the believer for time everlasting. "*. . . But the things which are not seen are eternal.*" (2 Corinthians 4:18) The implanted Word of redemption is unchangeable, and thus, your salvation is eternal.

This is why "*it is easier for a camel to go through the eye of a needle than for a rich man to enter the kingdom of God.*" (Matthew 19:24) His trust is in, and limited to, a place that is decomposing. It is a temporary place where God does not dwell—the natural. God exists there, but He does not dwell nor operate there, except on certain rare occasions that we have come to know as miracles.

More Than Conquerers

It is also how and why we are able to overcome the world by faith in Jesus Christ. "*For whatsoever **is born of God overcomes the world**: and this is the victory that overcomes the world, even **our faith**.*" (1 John 5:4) Think about it. The world is passing away. Those who have placed their faith entirely in the natural world are trusting a temporary system. The natural realm is decaying and will eventually be deconstructed. Therefore, the tribulation of our natural lives is unavoidable. The world is wrought with perfect imperfection.

By placing our trust in Jesus Christ, we are trusting (having faith) in the highest spiritual authority available to man. "*These things I have spoken unto you, that in Me you might have peace. In the world you **will** have tribulation: but be of good cheer; I have overcome the world.*" (John 16:33) Why? Jesus Christ is eternal life. "*I am the way, the truth and the life . . .*" (John 14:6) "*Jesus said to her, 'I am the resurrection and the life. He who believes in Me, though he may die, he shall live.'*" (John 11:25)

The natural is man's realm, given to Adam upon his creation and as stated above, a spiritual blessing *can* be manifested into the natural. This is God's M.O. (Method of Operation) Because God is not just attached to it, but actually *in it*, the power is not just infinite. It is eternal. God never contradicts Himself. We simply need to love Him by taking the necessary time to get to know and understand Him.

The world, on the other hand, is perishing. In Jesus Christ, or stated another way, with the Spirit of Yahweh indwelling us, we become eternal. With eternity on the inside we overcome the realm of death surrounding us on the outside. Through faith in Christ we have overcome a perishing world. We have been resurrected to life. Permanence always defeats the temporary. Therefore, Satan is nothing more than a paper tiger. He too is perishing.

> *"Yet in all these things we are more than conquerors through Him who loved us. For I am persuaded that neither death nor life, nor angels nor principalities nor powers, nor things present nor things to come, nor height nor depth, nor any other created thing, shall be able to separate us from the love of God which is in Christ Jesus our Lord."*
> **—Romans 8:37-39**

Love Lost

To gain an understanding of God's love you *must* read and gain an understanding of the Word of God. This book series is simply a tool to help you do that. America and many other parts of the world have become inept at reading and understanding the Word of God. Therefore, movements such as New Age Mysticism, Yoga, and other campaigns devoid of salvation have taken root in man's futile attempt to fill the void intended for God to permeate. Ignorance of the truth has caused humanity to adopt movements such as Islam, Buddhism, Hinduism. Hari Krishna's, Mooney's and every form of mysticism, and even witchcraft, is nothing more than a vain and ignorant attempt to connect with the Creator of heaven and earth. If you have fallen prey to such deception you have been separated from the truth of true Love. Jesus Christ is the only name under heaven by which man can be saved. (Acts 4:12)

Therefore, I would strongly encourage all those reading this, the church included, to pursue gaining an understanding of God and His Word if we hope to save the lost—ourselves included. The Lord has loved us enough to provide deep instruction of His thoughts, intentions and will. Yet day by day we ignore His love and grace as our Bibles idly collect dust on the shelf—if we even own one.

I recently read that the hotels of the once great but rapidly declining American culture are removing the Gideon Bible from the drawers of hotel dressers. Interestingly enough, I have already found the Book of Mormon, as well as, the Q'ran in several hotel rooms which I have stayed. The Bible's other replacement is quite disturbing and is a manifest symptom of our sin sick society, as well—the television remote, chock full of pornography! Unfortunately, no one seems to mind. Perhaps the addiction is far worse than I have anticipated.

What is the world coming to when we allow the pornographers to usurp the Word and authority of God? Is it any wonder we have the social problems now facing this nation when our moral standards are being set by the LGBT (Lesbian, Gay, Bisexual, Transgender) movement, and sadly enough, national political leaders devoid of any moral character whatsoever, who will say or do anything for the sake of reelection. What did you expect to happen when we went down this road? Did you really think the eradication of traditional family values would strengthen our culture?

We are still feeling the moral decay of Bill Clinton's public affair with Monica Lewinsky et al, and his justification that oral sex is not really sex. Well what exactly is it? Does it really depend on the meaning of "is"? "Is" *is* what it is, and believe me he is not alone in his moral breakdown. Many of our religious leaders fall into the very same category. Ted Haggert was leading an entire Christian denomination all the while having homosexual extra marital affairs. Evil does not discriminate. Religion is not immune from sin. We are now reaping what had been sown in the past.

Sexual deviation and corruption are rampant upon world leaders, both in government and in the church. It seems that the god we call "self-gratification" has replaced the One and only.

> *"Nevertheless I have this against you, that **you have left your first love**. Remember therefore from where you have fallen; repent and do the first works, or else I will come to you quickly and remove your lamp stand from its place—unless you repent."*
> **—Revelation 2:4-5**

Yet in all of our deviance Yahweh has not forsaken us. Love is incapable of abandonment. How much farther can we fall before the Lord will be *required* to judge us? We must return to the Word of God for this world to remedy its social problems. To leave the Lord out of our affairs can only result in the spiritual death of our nations and culture, which will undoubtedly result in our physical deaths as well. Look around you, the "disease" has already begun to fester!

From Me to We

As previously stated, our *deadliest* wound is in the decaying of the marriage covenant, which is beginning to spread like a cancer throughout the world. In fact, marriage rates are down by nearly fifty percent. Abandoning the marriage covenant has become a government program. If you do not believe that check out your tax return. From a Federal Income Tax perspective, Americans are penalized for being married. You pay more in taxes for being married and filing jointly, or separately, than for being single and filing separate returns. Therefore, when God is removed from the picture, what is the benefit of marriage?

Divorce rates are at an all-time high; by some measures in excess of fifty percent in America, even within the walls of the church. Perhaps that is the goal of the Supreme Court of the United States in redefining marriage. The government fudges all the other numbers. Why not marriage as well? Same sex unions have made a joke of God's holy covenant. Therefore, judgment cannot be far off. "*Do not be deceived, **God is not mocked***; *for whatever a man sows, that he will also reap.*" (Galatians 6:7) When the marriage falls apart, the family falls apart. When the family falls apart, society falls apart and we are left with valueless children willing to shoot each other just for the thrill of it.

I am not being melodramatic. Thrill killings are actually becoming common place. I recently saw a statistic that for the first time in two years New York City went for an entire week without a murder. This statistic flabbergasted me! The prior streak was broken only due to a massive cold spell in the city. Perhaps all the guns were all frozen. I live forty-five minutes away from this incredible city. I never realized how common place murder actually is. If I were not intimately close to Yahweh I would be terrified.

Think about how far we have fallen since the birth of the radical liberalism of the 1960's. So what is the answer? Love is the answer— not lust and not appeasement. The "Me Generation" must set pop culture aside and learn to practice the love of Christ. Our culture must relearn to "*let nothing be done through selfish ambition or conceit, but in lowliness of mind let each esteem others better than himself. Let each of you look out not **only for his own interests**, but also **for the interests of others**.*" (Philippians 2:3-4)

The "Me Generation" must become the "We Generation." Such a radical transformation must begin within the hearts of each and every one of us—each individual and family. Morality begins at home. Its foundation lies within the marriage covenant, one man and one woman, that was instituted at creation.

> "*And the Lord caused a deep sleep to fall on Adam, and he slept; and He took one of his ribs, and closed up the flesh in its place. Then the rib which the Lord God had taken from man he made*

into a woman, and He brought her to the man . . . Therefore a
man shall leave his father and mother and be joined to his wife,
and they shall become one flesh.*"*
—**Genesis 2:21-22 & 24**

That, by the way, is God's definition of marriage! "*They shall*
become one flesh."

Why Marriage?

Did you know that when God created Adam he was both male and
female? It's true. He was not a hermaphrodite. He was one being,
created in the image of God, containing all the genetic components
of the two. It was not until God separated Eve from Adam that there
was a gender split and it is the act of sexual intercourse that causes the
return to "one flesh."

This is why adultery is such a heinous sin against God. The
actual marriage covenant takes place when a marriage is
consummated through sexual intercourse, which is intended to be an
act of love and not power. Sexual intercourse is the actual joining
together of the body, which momentarily creates one flesh both
physically and spiritually. This, even if only in small part (That is not
an insult guys!) or even symbolically, brings man back to the original
image of God in which he was created—one flesh.

Therefore, when a man or woman commits adultery they
become one flesh with another and break the marriage covenant with
the original partner. Sexual intercourse is actually God's true
definition of marriage. therefore, adultery is actually marrying
another. This is why Jesus stated that the only legal permission for
divorce is through sexual immorality. (Matthew 19:8) It is also why
homosexuality is sin.

The act of homosexuality attempts to join two men, or two
women, together in holy matrimony in both the physical and

spiritual sense. It is a perversion of God's original intention at creation. Since it was Yahweh who separated and created the genders, the attempted joining together of the same gender is an abomination of the will of God. It is the thrust of man's pride above God's act of creation. In essence, it is humanity injecting his own will in place of God's will. Whether you like that or not, by its very nature from both a physical and a spiritual standpoint, homosexuality is sin, just as adultery is sin, and due to the complete and total lack of commitment and covenant, fornication, otherwise known as casual sex, is sin as well. From a sexual standpoint, friends have no benefits.

The Liberation Movement

Let's take a look at God's will as He intended it to be. Pay attention to what follows because having an understanding of this information will eliminate a great deal of the problems which actually cause divorce. When you understand *how* God created you and your spouse, you will gain an understanding of how and why you and your partner think and act the way you do, and why men and woman are intentionally designed to play different roles in any and every healthy society.

It is no secret that men and woman think and act very differently. As you will now see, you were purposely created to be that way. Therefore, when a woman attempts to feminize a man, and vice versa, the result will almost always be chaos, usually resulting in divorce.

The proof is in the mere fact that half of all marriages have dissolved since the woman's liberation movement of the 1960's. Don't get me wrong, I am not against equality. I understand and am in agreement with equal pay for equal work, non-discrimination laws, etc . . . However, a woman's role was intended to be vastly greater than what it has been progressively reduced to in the name of equality. King Solomon, whom many consider to be the wisest man of all time, had quite a bit to say about the part a virtuous woman plays within society. If you dare, ponder the gender roles which are both implied and specified below.

"Who can find a virtuous wife? For her worth is far above rubies. The heart of her husband safely trusts her; so he will have no lack of gain. She does him good and not evil all the days of her life. She seeks wool and flax, and willingly works with her hands."

"She is like the merchant ships. She brings her food from afar. She also rises while it is yet night, and provides food for her household and a portion for her maidservants. She considers a field and buys it; from her profits she plants a vineyard. She girds herself with strength, and strengthens her arms."

"She perceives that her merchandise is good, and her lamp does not go out by night. She stretches out her hands to the distaff (part of a spinning wheel), and her hand holds the spindle. She extends her hand to the poor, yes, she reaches out her hands to the needy."

"She is not afraid of snow for her household, for all her household is clothed with scarlet. She makes tapestry for herself; her clothing is fine linen and purple. Her husband is known in the gates, when he sits among the elders of the land."

"She makes linen garments and sells them, and supplies sashes for the merchants. Strength and honor are her clothing; she shall rejoice in time to come."

"She opens her mouth with wisdom, and on her tongue is the law of kindness. She watches over the ways of her household, and does not eat the bread of idleness. Her children rise up and call her blessed; her husband also, and he praises her: 'Many daughters have done well, but you excel them all.'"

"Charm is deceitful and beauty is passing, but a woman who fears the Lord, she shall be praised. Give her of the fruit of her hands, and let her own works praise her in the gates."
—Proverbs 31:10-31

If you read this closely, you will discover that biblically speaking, the virtuous woman was not persecuted nor oppressed in the least, unlike the Q'ran where the exact opposite is true. By definition, a biblically virtuous woman had governance of her entire household. She was supremely confident without being arrogant. She was courageous while at the same time being compassionate, merciful, humble, and what seems to have been lost these days, pure.

Her responsibilities included, but were not limited to, the family's finances and personal business. In modern vernacular she held the family's "purse-strings." She contemplated and made financial investments into the family's future. She shaped their reputation, provided childcare, offered charity to the needy and the poor, along with a host of other vital and yet honorable endeavors, all the while never seeking to bring attention and fame to herself or usurp the authority of her husband.

In actuality, she did not have to seek fame. Fame sought her. God Almighty exalted her. Her husband exalted her. She was a woman of unspoken power and purpose, and her praise came directly from both her husband and Yahweh. Therefore, her fame and reputation proceeded her. She was the talk of the town, but not in an adulterous and dissolute manner, as is the case for so many modern women. She was a woman of virtue.

In truth, Yahweh had liberated women from day one. She was completely free to work both in the kingdoms of God and man. Her husband completely trusted and empowered her. God had bestowed *His* authority and influence upon her. She was the inspiration of her household and community, and when functioning properly within God's will, she still is.

Into the Void

As you can see, a virtuous and Godly woman *was* fashioned to be a liberated career woman, but not merely for the benefit of the corporate stock holder. Women were not created merely as sexual objects to be exploited on television and in magazines for the purpose of selling products and boosting corporate sales numbers. Yes, woman are intended to be sexy, intriguing, and whatever other adjectives you may want to use, but not for the pleasure of the multitudes. Her sex appeal is intended solely for her husband. Her role was to support him and the family in every endeavor. She was created to be the pillar of wisdom and kindness within her community and sphere of influence.

Does this sound like the female leadership we have plaguing society today? Particularly those who are in positions of political power, or the "role models" from MTV and Hollywood? How about the recent torrent of reality programs flooding our flat screens? Is virtue being portrayed anywhere within pop culture and the media? *Dating Naked*, along with a host of other abomination's gracing the airwaves is as far from virtuosity as heaven is from hell.

I am not saying all the famous are guilty, but it does appear that most have fallen into the Hollywood void. I *am* saying, however, that human beings need to take responsibility for the values they portray. If you are famous you are a role model by default. That is an obligation that comes with fame, and, by the way, is a major aspect of the career *choice* that those fortunate enough to achieve fame have made. Yet if this is you, you still have a choice.

Are you a virtuous woman? Do you even want to be, or do you believe virtue is dead? Whether we like it or not, people in positions of power and influence are shaping world culture. When viewed properly it is one heck of a responsibility.

Take note of the following example. One female member of Congress, who will remain nameless, but happens to be the former Speaker of the House of Representatives, formerly communicated her reasoning for wanting to attack another independent sovereign nation. Her rationale was communicated based upon a conversation she had with her *five year old grandson*! Are you kidding me? Can our nation's leaders really be that reckless?

This is merely one display of the complete and total lack of intellectual capability, coupled with the void of any business and moral acumen afflicting government today. With this type of logic plaguing government why not just consult Big Bird? At least there is an adult under the costume.

Unfortunately, this is no momentary lapse of reason. It is sad to say, that the five year old appeared to have more wisdom than the godless leader of American government and world culture. The power of life and death is in her hands. Her decision to reveal the consultation of her five year old grandson over the wisdom of Yahweh makes her a total fool. Unfortunately, she is not alone in her insanity and it is not limited to women. In my opinion, today's man has abdicated his spiritual responsibility and bears the brunt of the guilt and shame.

I recently watched a video of one U.S. Congressman who actually believes the Island of Guam can *capsize* due to overpopulation. He thought sending an abundance of troops to the coast of the island would cause it to tip over! Really? Does he think he can swim underneath it as well? In what world does an adult believe that an actual island is free-floating about the ocean like the raft in his pool? No wonder Al Gore was able to dupe the public with his global warming fantasy. Apparently, not even he believed his own charade. His personal residence was one of the worst offenders of carbon credits in the nation.

Where is the shame in such ignorance and hypocrisy? I watched with my mouth agape, as an elected official of the most powerful government in world history utterly humiliated himself, as he flaunted such callowness not just in front of the Admiral who unfortunately must take orders from him, but before the entire world.

How does such ignorance make its way into the halls of Congress? Even worse, how did we get to the point where the voting populace would elect such a fool to office? No wonder the country is collapsing under its own debt. The world has undoubtedly gone insane.

Although a multitude of world leaders carry around Bibles and make church appearances on Sunday, Godlessness has become the norm in government. Their voting records cry out to heaven against them, and as leaders who once *"knew God, they did not glorify Him as God, nor were thankful, but became futile in their thoughts, and their foolish hearts were darkened. Professing to be wise, they became fools and changed the glory of the incorruptible God into an image made like corruptible man . . . For this reason God gave them up to vile passions."* (Romans 1:21-23 and 26) How can the world survive such imprudence?

*"And even as they did not like to retain God in their knowledge, God gave them over to a debased mind, to do those things which are not fitting; being filled with all unrighteousness, sexual immorality, wickedness, covetousness, maliciousness; full of envy, murder, strife, deceit, evil-mindedness; they are whisperers, backbiters, haters of God, violent, proud, boasters, inventors of evil things, disobedient to parents, undiscerning, untrustworthy, unloving, unforgiving, unmerciful; who, knowing the righteous judgment of God, that **those who practice such things** are deserving of death, not only do the same **but also approve of those who practice them.***"*
—Romans 1:28-32

With this is mind, consider what the Supreme Court has just done in their decision to approve same sex marriage in all fifty states. The rainbow of judgment has illuminated the White House. Have you any idea how the mighty have fallen?

Thank God for Jesus Christ! I know how uncomfortable reading this portion of scripture is, especially the last couple sentences. However, change can only be accomplished when peering into truth. Have the minds of the masses been darkened, particularly in our debasing of the female image and the sexualization of our culture? I will let you be the judge, but my vote is a resounding, yes!

Many of today's movie and television stars achieve prominence only after releasing something as vile as a private sex tape. Most of the rest simply act out the same scenes in nearly every pornographic "R" rated movie and television show that has pervaded our failing culture.

Harlotry was once considered shameful and was shunned by society. Have you ever read, *The Scarlet Letter*? Today's culture not only encourages such lewdness, it rewards it with millions of dollars, fame and fortune.

*"Were they ashamed when they had committed abomination? No!
They were not at all ashamed, nor did they know how to blush."*
—Jeremiah 8:12

Who can resist such temptation? In truth, and without desiring to portray an image of self-righteousness, the vast majority of us are guilty. We watch and, therefore, support it. Myself included. I am the first to admit my guilt. Just like the rest of us, our role models, as well as, our world leaders are lost without Yahweh.

Modern Family

I have said all this in order to lead you to the following question. What have "modern" women been liberated from? Based upon what

I see in the Word of God, the answer appears to be that they have been liberated from being virtuous women. That is not a compliment, and, by the way, this does not mean that women should not have jobs or positions of leadership. It would be foolish and biblically inaccurate to believe so.

When reading the Bible you will discover that God has always had women in positions of leadership. In fact, the entire Book of Esther was written about one such virtuous woman, as was the Book of Ruth, and, by the way, the first person to lay eyes on the risen Lord Jesus Christ was Mary Magdalene—a woman. Additionally, since the Lord decided to bring the Messiah, the Savior of the world, Jesus Christ of Nazareth, through the womb of a woman, that undoubtedly leads me to believe the Yahweh has huge plans and immense respect for women.

However, it seems that the vast majority of today's female leaders and role models has abandoned virtue. They have bought into the gluttonous lust for power and money, as well as, the lie that there is no difference between the sexes, "a woman can do anything a man can do." No wonder Lesbianism runs rampant and modern women have usurped the role of their spiritually idle husbands. A woman cannot do everything a man can do, just as a man cannot do all that a woman can do. Is it any wonder that the modern family is falling into utter chaos?

God considers this information regarding woman to be so vitally important to mankind that there is no portion of scripture regarding men in the entire Bible that rivals Proverbs 31. In fact, the only thing even close is in regard to marriage and commands the husband to love his wife. "*So husbands ought to love their own wives as their own bodies;* (One flesh) *he who loves his wife loves himself. For no one ever hated his own flesh, but nourishes and cherishes it, just as the Lord does the church.*" (Ephesians 5:28-29) It is actually a guide for masculine conduct and for the protection of woman, "*the weaker vessel,*" (1 Peter 3:7) physically speaking.

Women are beautiful and they are powerful. They are unique beyond description and created by God to perform the function of binding together the family unit and the communities in which they reside. That is the message of Proverbs 31:10-31. A man is simply incapable of accomplishing such an incredible feat.

When you read the above description of a biblically virtuous woman it is clear that she was intended to play a vastly greater role than today's "liberated" woman. In fact, I would challenge any man to even attempt to perform the role of the virtuous woman. There is not a man alive who could succeed in the woman's *true* role. It is not man's nature and that is where a woman's actual power lies. It is not that one sex is superior to the other. True perfection lies when the two are unified together, seamlessly functioning as one flesh in God's intended roles and will.

Equality does not mean that we are to perform the same gender roles. Men were never intended to be "Mr. Mom," and woman, are not supposed to be the authoritarians of their household's, or fighting on the front lines of the nation's military.

The equalization, or perhaps even better stated; the elimination of gender roles is resulting in the breakdown of both our culture and our society. It is producing confused and angry children with no regard to what is right and wrong. Unfortunately, this behavior is unwittingly being learned from the equally confused progressive parents who purport to want what is best for their children but leave Yahweh out of the equation. If our true desire is to correct society's problems something has to change. So with that in mind, it is time revisit the creation of mankind.

Venus is Mars

We already know that when God physically formed man, He did it through the process of squeezing together the dust of the ground.

Think just for a moment about the personality and physical nature of most men as compared to woman, Rhonda Rousey not included, and no disrespect intended. I love MMA, and in my opinion Rhonda Rousey is pound for pound the most dominant fighter on the planet. I am a huge fan and outside the ring she is a very attractive woman.

With that said, however, a top level male fighter would absolutely annihilate her in the cage. A man is physically stronger than a woman and that is by design. On the same front, men and women follow a radically different thought process. A man is very straight forward in his thinking, "If it's broke, fix it." Period the end. Let's move on to the next task.

This is consistent with the way a man was formed. Squeezing is not a very complicated process. I am sorry to say men, you are not a very a complicated individual. Most likely, you are pretty well satisfied as long as you are not hungry. They say, "The key to a man's heart is through his stomach." It is basically true and in many cases life seems extraordinarily simple until a more complex individual enters your life and complicates things. That is definitely not one your drinking buddies!

*"And the Lord God caused a deep sleep to fall on Adam, and he slept, and He took one of His ribs, and closed up the flesh in its place. Then the rib which the Lord God had taken from the man He **made** into a woman, and He brought her to the man."*
—Genesis 2:21-22

Let's first look at the "rib" taken from Adam in order for God to "make" Eve. There is another misunderstanding within the translation to English here. The English language uses the word "rib," but the Hebrew word is **Tsela**, pronounced *tsay'law*. Because the connotation of this word is something curved, the translators used the word rib, which is a curved bone in your side.

The literal meaning of the word tsela, however, is "a side." Although the connotation is something curved, curved is not the actual meaning of the word. Keep in mind, that the shape of the human body is much more curvaceous than straight, particularly from front to back, and not up and down. I would venture to guess that since we are the same species yours is similar to mine.

The truth is that God did not just remove one of Adam's ribs. In fact, He didn't remove a rib at all. He actually removed *half* of Adam—an entire side. As I mentioned previously, I am sure that you have heard of your spouse being referred to as your "better half." Although mine is, I do not know if one half is necessarily better than the other. I do, however, know that one is certainly more complex than the other. I also know that we are stronger together than apart.

$$Eve = -YX^2$$

If you are having a little trouble believing this, it is because you are mistakenly thinking that God separated Adam and Eve the way a surgeon would separate a pair of Siamese twins. That is simply not the case. Consider the following. What is it, biologically speaking, that makes a man different than a woman? It is your chromosomal make up that determines your sex, as well as, the ratio of testosterone versus estrogen in your body. Gender is determined by the presence or absence of the Y chromosome. This is what determines the chemical make-up of a man verses a woman.

Amazingly, if you break down the chemical ratio of men and women you will find that a woman has about the same percentage of estrogen in her body as the man has testosterone in his. If you look at the percentage of estrogen within a man's body, you will find that a woman has roughly the same level of testosterone. Why is that? These two hormones are a part of what God separated in forming the "half" (tsela) He utilized to build the woman.

That is not all, however. It gets even better. Remember, in the beginning Adam was both male and female. God created one man, Adam. He then built Eve from a part of Adam's body. Thus men have both the X and the Y chromosome. It is the possession of the Y chromosome that makes a man male and determines the male sexual organs which produce sperm, excess testosterone, etc . . .

Therefore, it appears to me that in the gender split only half of the chromosomes were used to build Eve. That is the true meaning of tsela, which has been translated as "rib," but actually means "a side" or "half." Is it possible that the tsela God used is not a rib bone, but is the X chromosome? Hear me out. Women are composed simply of two X chromosomes. They do not have a Y chromosome. Therefore, X-Y is the tsela value (1/2) of the substance taken from Adam to manifest Eve. A woman's chromosomal make up is XX, as opposed to their male counterparts who are XY. Technically speaking, women have half (tsela) the chromosomal variation of men.

Amazingly, however, science has discovered that the X chromosome has a much larger "instruction manual," and thus, God used the X to "banah," or build the more complex woman. With two X's her nature is much more elaborate than her male counterpart. God did not "yatsar," or squeeze her into shape as He did the man.

Science has also discovered that one of the X chromosomes has actually been deactivated in women. Women have two X chromosomes, but only half (tsela) of them function. (X) + X = X, or half of 2X. How incredible is that? Do you still believe it is remotely possible for humanity to have evolved from a single cell? I certainly do not. The two really were one flesh. God took Eve from Adam.

Let me be clear. It appears that the tsela, or rib, that God took from Adam was not a bone located in his thorax. God replicated the X chromosome to build Eve. Men are composed of XY and women are composed only of X. Although we each have two, (chromosomal pairs are a requirement of the human species) only one X chromosome is functioning in women. X-Y=X. X is the tsela value

(1/2) of the "rib" from which Eve was taken. Yes, the Bible *is* correct. God *did* use the tsela from Adam to create Eve. Is that incredible or what? Stand up and take a bow Yahweh! There is none like you.

By the way, the connotation of something curved is also correct. The strands of DNA that contain your chromosomes are curved. Tsela!

Remnants

Do you want to see living proof that we were once one? Through hormonal therapy modern science has allowed us to manipulate the human body. We cannot create a human from dirt, but we now have the ability to change the chemical makeup, and thus, seemingly alter the sex of the individual. Can you say Caitlin Jenner?

When a man or woman wants to "change" gender, how do doctors accomplish this, surgery notwithstanding? If it is a woman wanting to live as a man, they pump her full of testosterone. In essence, they fill her with what the Y chromosome would instruct the body to produce. The introduction of excess testosterone causes the body to function as an XY.

What happens as the process progresses? She begins to grow hair on her face, arms and legs. Her voice deepens and her physical appearance including her bone structure, even in the face, begins to become more masculine. Her clitoris actually begins to extend and resemble a small penis. Conversely, when a man wants to live as a woman they fill him full of estrogen and he begins to feminize, even to the point of growing breasts. Chemically speaking, the doctors are deactivating the Y chromosome and causing his body to function as an XX.

Why does this work? It works because each sex still contains the remnants of each-others physicality. In the beginning the two were one flesh. In the consummation of the marriage covenant (which is sexual intercourse) the two return to one flesh.

> *"Therefore a man shall leave his father and mother and be joined to his wife, and they shall become one flesh."*
> **—Genesis 2:24**

Moving Parts

That is some incredible stuff, is it not? However, the question still remains, why do men and woman act so differently? In the English language the word "made" is used to describe the construction of the woman, as opposed to "formed" when regarding the man. These two words do not do justice to the process God used to separate them. When God "made" the woman, the Hebrew word **banah**, pronounced *baw-naw*,' is used. It literally means "built." Think about the process of building something. It is a detailed and intricate process that requires planning and patience. It is usually, but not always, more delicate than something without many moving parts.

As a result, a woman is much more complex than a man in her thought process and she is infinitely more delicate in her emotional makeup. Guys, your emotional make up does not have any moving parts. That is why you are so miserable when your wife tries to feminize you. Let's face it, you are really not that far removed from being a caveman. "Man want woman. Man grab woman by hair and drag woman home . . ." I know what you are thinking. I just heard on the radio that such behavior would be considered rape today. C'mon, have a sense of humor. We can still joke around with one another . . . can't we?

Guys, I am just kidding about your make up. Well . . . not really. Ladies, that is fairly important for you to understand when dealing with your husbands. I was not totally kidding. It is the truth in something that actually makes it funny. Just don't tell your husband. Let him think he is smarter and deeper than you. It's good for his ego . . . but you and I both know the truth.

Perfect Together

When the two are joined together as one, and when the woman submits to God and her husband as "helper" and not "ruler," you have in God's eyes, perfection. Are you beginning to understand what great depths God has gone through to create you? Only Love could drive such an intense desire.

To God, perfection does not mean without flaw. When God created mankind, we were perfect in God's sight. Perfect, meaning exactly as God intended us to be. Therefore, when relating to your mate, do not look for man's definition of perfection, which is someone without fault. You will never find it. We need to discover our partners God given qualities and gifts. With very few exceptions, but they do exist, this *requires* coming together in the marriage covenant. It is what makes mankind whole.

For a woman, it is the reunification of her origin. This is why the woman has such an intense desire for marriage, much more so than a man. Without ever being taught, a little girl will dream about and plan her wedding almost from the time of her earliest memories. Men dream of being sports stars and soldiers. One sex dreams of conquest. The other dreams of bonding and settlement. Did you actually believe that was cultural?

Yet modern cultures are attempting to stifle the course of nature through so called "gender equality." It is not our gender's that God has created to be equal. No one can argue that men and woman are unalike, sometimes even polar opposites in their thought process and physical make up. Five minutes in the presence of one another will confirm this truth. It is our love for one another and our treatment of one another, regardless of gender, that God has intended and purposed to be equal.

That's Your Downfall

Being that most of us have never had this information our relationships often result in chaos. The man is expecting his partner to act and think like a man, while his female counterpart is expecting her mate to act and think like a woman. It does not take a genius to figure out that this does not work for very long. So what is the result? A fifty percent divorce rate, broken homes, chaotic children, and a complete breakdown of a society resulting in the eventual downfall of a nation. "There seems to be a terrible misunderstanding on the part of a great many people to the effect that when you cease to believe you may cease to behave." **Louis Kronenberger**

In studying the Word of God, you will always find that before Israel is judged, there is a moral breakdown within the society. Then God judges them. If Israel is God's chosen nation and people and God judges them, what is the future of America and the rest of the world if something does not change? The answer has to be judgment. America, and the world for that mater, must change spiritually before it can change in the physical realm. We must repent. That must happen in each individual heart of a man or woman, one at a time. You must *be* the change that you want to see.

How can we possibly accomplish such a task? We cannot—not without God. Not without Love perfected. It is imperative to do it God's way. We must adopt righteousness which is exactly that, doing things God's way. It is not perfection. It is simply accepting Him and His way.

You may ask, "Why should I accept God and His way? I have suffered my whole life and He has ignored me. I'm better off on my own," or as **Ann Gaylor** proclaimed, "Nothing fails like prayer." The truth is, He has never ignored you. God has not abandoned humanity. Humanity has abandoned God.

You simply need to know where to find Him. You are looking for an Ogre when it is a Father who is calling you. Love is diligently pursuing you as a Father desperately searches for a lost child. Are you ready to come home? In the following chapter you will discover the essence of love. You are about to meet your heavenly Father.

CHAPTER 5

Abba, Father

In the previous chapter we learned of the essence of God's love and began to experience what we have lost in the modern world. We have also discovered what great lengths the Lord went through in creating the world in which we live. We also learned that without ever realizing it, mankind has all but abandoned Yahweh. Yet through it all, God has never left nor forsaken us. Yes, God is love and even more, He is our Father. With that in mind, let's visit a very familiar scripture that you will most likely remember from Sunday school. In it, you will discover the heart of our Father. Therefore, hold on tight, you are about to find that your holy Father is calling you, His precious prodigal home.

A Tale of Two Sons

"A certain man had two sons. And the younger of them said to his father, 'Father, give me the portion of goods that falls to me.' So he divided to them his livelihood. And not many days after, the younger son gathered all together, journeyed to a far country, and there wasted his possessions with prodigal living."

"But when he had spent all, there arose a severe famine in that land, and he began to be in want. Then he went and joined himself to a citizen of that country and he sent him into his field to feed swine. And he would have gladly filled his stomach with the pods that the swine ate, and no one gave him anything."

"But when he came to himself, he said, 'How many of my father's hired servants have bread enough to spare, and I perish with hunger! I will arise and go to my father, and will say to him, 'Father, I have sinned against heaven and before you, and I am no longer worthy to be called your son. Make me like one of your hired servants.''"

*"And he arose and came to his father. But when he was still a great way off, **his father saw him and had compassion**, and ran and fell on his neck and kissed him. And the son said to him, 'Father, I have sinned against heaven and in your sight, and am no longer worthy to be called your son.'"*

*"But the father said to the servants, 'Bring out the best robe and put it on him, and put a ring on his hand and sandals on his feet. And bring the fatted calf here and kill it, and let us eat and be merry; **for this my son was dead and is alive again**, he was lost and is found.' And they began to be merry."*

"Now his older son was in the field. And as he came and drew near to the house, he heard music and dancing. So he called one of the servants and asked what these things meant. And he said to

him, 'Your brother has come, and because he has received him safe and sound, your father has killed the fatted calf.'"

*"But he was angry and would not go in. Therefore **his father came out** and pleaded with him. So he answered and said to his father, 'Lo, these many years I have been serving you; I never transgressed your commandment at any time; and yet you never gave me a young goat, that I may make merry with my friends. But as soon as this son of yours came, who has devoured your livelihood with harlots, you killed the fatted calf for him.'"*

*"And he said to him, 'Son, you are always with me, and all that I have is yours. **It was right** that we should make merry and be glad, for your brother was dead and is alive again, he was lost and is found.'"*

—Luke 15:11-32

You obviously recognize this as the story of the *Prodigal Son.* Have you ever considered the relevance of the allegory in regard to the personality and nature of Yahweh? Most likely not, as even the recognized title of the story diminishes the most prominent character of all. This is not simply a tale of two sons. It is the story of our Father.

There are several things that jump out at me right away when I read this. As stated above, the story is not simply about one lost person. There are actually three main characters in the story: the prodigal son, the obedient son, and the father. Secondly, and what stands out the most is the unconditional love, affection, and compassion of the father. It is also obvious that these are not real people and that this is a parable to illustrate a principle regarding the true nature of God. Its beauty is in the absolute truth regarding the compassionate heart of Yahweh.

So who are these characters patterned after? Think before you answer. Things are not always as they appear. Let's start with the prodigal. Whenever we think of the prodigal son, we dig up images of folks we know who have completely fallen off the deep end. Perhaps they are drug addicts, alcoholics or prostitutes. Maybe they are children who have run away from home. May I say, however, that at one time or another, perhaps even now, *you are the prodigal!* We are all born prodigal. We are born separated from God. Until you come to Christ you will remain prodigal, that is, away from God, no matter who you are or how many good deeds you have done or continue to do.

Secondly, we have the brother, the seemingly obedient son. I want to spend a little time talking about this brother. Many of us wind up the same way. He is a different kind of prodigal. Many of us have been "saved" forever, but never quite realize who we are or what belongs to us. Perhaps even more importantly is that we never come to the realization of who God is. We never submit to the fact that He is our Father and that He wants what is best for us. Therefore, we remain in bondage and slavery when all the while we have been sons and daughters of the Almighty.

Take a look at his reaction to the return of his brother. In his discourse he reveals the misunderstanding of his true identity, as well as, the affliction of his parched spirit. First of all, he becomes angry. Why is he bitter? We very quickly find out that his anger is derived from envy. He feels the father is showing partiality by celebrating the return of his disobedient brother. Additionally, as is revealed by his answer, his anger is also due to materialism over what he feels is owed to him.

The father tells the obedient son that all he has belongs to him. Certainly, the obedient son knew this as he watched his little brother take half the family possessions and walk out the door. However, he never came to the truth of knowing what was rightfully his. He had access to his father's resources all along. Then out of the blue his little "loser" brother comes home after wasting all of dad's money on hookers and booze—and dad *celebrates* his return? To make matters worse, he gives him the fatted calf, which is the best and most valuable calf they own. It also happens to be *his* calf by rights of inheritance. His whacked out little brother already spent his half of the money—remember? Talk about piling on! No wonder he was pissed. I don't blame him.

Be Still and Know

Is the young man justified in his anger? Maybe. That is for you to decide. The truth, however, is that the father has the right to use his estate in any manner he chooses. It does not really belong to either son until after the death of their father. Keep that in mind for future reference. Unless given prior, the death of the testator is the point in time after which one receives their inheritance.

An even greater truth is that if the obedient son wanted something from his father all he had to do was ask. It is no different with our Father in heaven either. "*You lust and do not have. You murder and covet and cannot obtain. You fight and war.* **Yet you do not have because you do not ask.** *You ask and do not receive because you ask amiss, that you may spend it on your pleasure,*" (James 4:2-3) rather than on the will of God and just like the prodigal son.

James, the brother of Jesus, addresses quite a few issues in these two verses of scripture. Whenever you meditate upon scripture do not just pull out one or two verses and apply their meaning as stand-alone phrases. You must always derive the meaning from how it harmonizes with the passage as a whole and with the Word of God in its entirety.

We see this mistake made all too often in organizations such as the Jehovah's Witnesses, for example. They have lost the true meaning of the Word of God because they rarely look at the entire context of a particular scripture, in addition to molding the text into what they *want* it to mean. It is quite easy to find single sentences in any book, let alone one as large and complex as the Bible, and twist it to mean whatever you want. Do not fall into this trap whether you like what it says or not.

James says something rather profound here, particularly when looking at it in light of the story of the prodigal son. James says, "*You do not have because you do not ask, and when you do ask you ask amiss that you may spend it on your pleasures.*" That describes the two sons to a tee. In other words, you cannot receive because you will waste it on yourself rather than use God's blessing to further His kingdom.

> "And **you shall remember** the Lord your God, **for it is He** who gives you **power to get wealth**, that **He may establish His covenant** which He swore to your fathers, as it is this day."
> **—Deuteronomy 8:18**

Or perhaps even worse, most of us do not even know God well enough to realize we have the right to ask. When you finally "come to yourself," you realize that Yahweh is Lord of all. If your request falls within the will of God, He will not only answer, He will provide whatever it is that you requested, and oftentimes even more.

Sometimes, however, and just like we see with the prodigal son, He will even provide to our detriment. In the aforementioned allegory, the father gave his prodigal son exactly what he asked for. Is this because God is cruel and He wants to see you suffer? Did God feel a sense of satisfaction and utter a divine, "I told you so," as his precious son lay in the nightmare of gentile pig slop? Of course not. That goes against everything Love is and stands for.

Unfortunately, many of us need to hit bottom before we will bend our knee and cry out to God. Often times, the things we desire most are the things we can least afford to have. In other words, God does not always need to save you from the wiles of the devil. He needs to save you from the wiles of yourself. God, more often than not, needs to save you from *you and your own twisted will!*

That is how God salvaged my life. It is also how He rescued the prodigal son. What is required to save you? Only you and Yahweh can answer that question. Finding out requires you to submit to His will. It requires you to "come to yourself," or as we say in modern day vernacular, to "come to your senses," and cry out to the one and only living God. More often than not, this requires us to experience some sort of pain. If you are honest, you will find that your suffering is usually self-induced.

It is not that God does not want you to experience pleasure. He certainly does. He is the creator of pleasure. God will give you the world if you are responsible and obedient to Him. God always allows us to benefit from serving and obeying Him, but you must seek *Him* and not the material. All too often, because of our misunderstanding of His ways, we seek Him through busyness when He desires to meet us in unengaged calm.

Like the obedient son, we become so busy being a *servant* of God that we never take the time to develop the relationship of being a *child* of God. The obedient son was so busy working in the fields that he never realized his father's aspiration was to fulfill his needs and desires. His father just wanted to hang out with him, but he was too busy and too bitter to make merry. I see this throughout the body of Christ continuously. In essence, the obedient son reduced himself to being just another servant. When his brother finally came home he grew envious of the blessings and attention bestowed upon his "newborn" and "newly found" brother. Is that really obedience?

In actuality, it is a contagion that we see ravaging the body of Christ today. We have folks so busy with the *work* of the church that they forget about developing a relationship with the *people* in the church. Perhaps even more importantly, we seem to have forgotten the masses of humanity outside the church. In other words, the goal of the institution takes precedence over the work of the gospel. The resulting power struggle causes a disconnection between the Spirit of God and the child of God. When someone truly blessed comes upon the scene they are often times met with envious territorial disputes. What is the result? The vicious circle continues when all the while God had intended to love and to bless both in the same manner according to each individual's gifts.

Jealousy is the manifestation of a terribly infectious disease. It is a sick and twisted spirit that must be met with aggression in its expulsion. It always leads to isolation, strife and ultimately division, when God's will for your life is unity with the brethren and unity with the Spirit of God. Both the pulpit and the people must guard against this malevolently twisted, sin sick spirit.

Arms Wide Open

Finally, we become familiar with the most beautiful character of all, the father. Let's make sure we recognize what precedes the father's reentry onto the scene. After all of the prodigal living, the scripture states that the young man *came to himself*. In other words, he was out there living a fantasy that nearly destroyed his life.

How many of us are living this same type of fantasy? We are striving to become something or someone we are not because the world dictates what we are supposed to be. When you "come to yourself," you realize the promises of the world—the fun, fortune, fame, men, women etc... were nothing but a bunch of lies and deception. When you wake up in the slop of life you realize that all you ever received from the world were *pigs*!

No disrespect to us gentile (non-Jewish) believers in Jesus Christ, but just imagine the horror of being a prominent Jewish man reduced to living as a filthy gentile and eating the slop of life with pigs. Could anything have been worse for him? It would have been diametrically opposed to everything his culture practiced and believed. He had become an outright social outcast, as far away from his Father as any man, woman or child alive.

However, he comes to an epiphany. The displaced run-away states, *"I will arise and go to my father."* As you are reading this I would like to assure you that your Father is calling you to do the same. If you are feeling the call of God I would encourage you to simply arise, confess your sins and your shortcomings, just as the young man did in the story, and receive forgiveness. Your Father's arms are wide open.

If you never have, you are about to encounter the true nature of the God we love, serve and live for. The scripture makes it perfectly clear that you do not need to clean yourself up before coming to Him. It does not matter how far you may feel you have drifted from God. It also does not matter how the media, or perhaps, even, how the church has falsely portrayed Him. Yahweh is not a punishing ogre. He desperately awaits your return.

> *"But when he was still a great way off, his father saw him and had compassion, and ran and fell on his neck and kissed him."*
> **—Luke 15:20**

Within the millisecond second that you turn to Him, the Lord begins running toward you—arms outstretched, seeking to hug, kiss and fall all over you no matter who you are or what you have done. Therefore, *"draw near to God and He will draw near to you."* (James 4:8) No sin is too great to receive His forgiveness. He is not looking to just make you a hired servant. You do not need to perform for Him, attempt to deceive Him, or as some religions portray, die for Him. He is seeking to receive you back into the family you were created for, as a son or daughter of the King of all kings. Watch how He treats His precious prodigal son.

The Ring, the Robe and the Shoes

"But the father said to his servants, 'Bring out the best robe and put it on him, and put a ring on his hand and sandals on his feet. And bring the fatted calf here and kill it, and let us eat and be merry; for my son was dead and is alive again, he was lost and is found. And they began to be merry.'"

Notice that the father did not just greet his son, nor did he judge him. As incredible as it may seem, he fully *restored* him! In doing so, he gave his son three very significant gifts each having its own representation of prestige. It did not matter that the prodigal son had already wasted what was previously given him. It did not matter that he was covered in pig slop. There was no chance of mistaking what was implied by these gifts among anyone residing in the home.

First, he *commanded* that a robe be put on his son. A simple servant did not wear a robe. The robe was consecrated for those members of the household related *by blood*. So what is the significance of the robe?

*"I will rejoice greatly in the Lord, my soul shall be joyful in my God. For **He has clothed me with the garments of salvation, He has covered me with the robe of righteousness,** as a bridegroom decks himself with ornaments, and as a bride adorns herself with jewels."*
—Isaiah 61:10

The robe represents salvation and righteousness. Salvation means he has been welcomed back into the kingdom of his Father. He now enjoys all the covenant rights associated with that position. He is right with his Father. Only the blood of Christ can restore your position of righteousness. You simply need to accept it and come home.

> *"After these things I looked, and behold, a great multitude which no one could number, of all nations, tribes, peoples, and tongues, standing before the throne and before the Lamb, **clothed with white robes**, with palm branches in their hands, and crying out with a loud voice, saying, '**Salvation belongs to our God** who sits on the throne, and to the Lamb!'"*
> **—Revelation 7:9-10**

Notice that there is no requirement to be of a particular race, tribe or creed. Country does not matter. Neither skin color nor ethnicity matters. Religion does not even matter. Believing that Jesus Christ of Nazareth is the Messiah and making Him both your Lord and Savior are the only prerequisites. When you belong to Christ you belong to God. Your inheritance is the "snow white robe" of salvation. Nothing else is needed. No one else compares.

The second gift was a ring. *"Put a ring on his hand."* In nearly every society rings are used to symbolically commemorate or represent a specific event. A wedding ring signifies that you belong to another. The endlessness of the circle represents the unbreakable marriage covenant between husband, wife and the Lord. We use rings to commemorate our high school graduations, achievements in our careers, and sports victories, such as the highly coveted super bowl ring.

I have a wonderful friend who possesses two super bowl rings. I must tell you that they are something to behold. Just their presence on his hand brings him favor from nearly everyone gazing upon their majesty. Yet even in all of its glory it cannot compare to the ring placed upon the hand of the redeemed which represents the authority given to the believer.

"Then a stone was brought and placed on the mouth of the den, **and the king sealed it with his own signet ring and with the signets of his lords,** *that the purpose concerning Daniel might not be changed."*
—Daniel 6:17

A signet was a personal and unique seal engraved into a ring. It represented the authority of the dignitary it belonged to. The owner, often times a king or his lords, would dip the signet in wax which made a mark identifying the owner. His signet, just like the the Presidential seal of the United States, was a symbol of power and authority that fixed the matter decreed and rendered it to be unchangeable.

We see the permanent restoration of authority given to the prodigal son when his father commands the ring to be placed upon his finger. He regained his place of authority in the home along with the unmistakable signet of his household. Spiritually speaking, so have we. Our Father is Yahweh, the King of all kings, whose everlasting signet is Jesus Christ crucified. The eternal nail marks engraved into His palms have rendered the redemption of humanity to be an everlasting decree. When you possess Christ all the authority given to Him in heaven and on the earth is placed into your care. You become a household and mansion bound member of the kingdom of God. Once you learn how to use and not abuse this authority, the entire world belongs to you.

Finally, we see sandals placed upon the prodigal's feet. The shoes meant that he was no longer a slave. A slave was prohibited from wearing shoes in his master's house. The shoes represent the fact that the son once again belongs to his father. His rightful place has been restored. Keep in mind that both sons believed they were slaves. One left to *escape* it, but the other remained to *endure* it. The father let both of them know their true place of freedom in the house and now I have let you know as well.

*"Sigh in silence, make no mourning for the dead, bind a turban on your head, **and put your sandals on your feet**, do not cover your lips, and do not eat man's bread of sorrow."*
—Ezekiel 24:17

When you belong to God there is no need to mourn as an unbeliever mourns. You have hope because you know where you and those in Christ dwell in the forever. Your rightful home for all of eternity has become heaven with the Lord. The sandals signify that you belong in the mansion of God and you are willing to let others know their rightful place as well. You have entered God culture. You can now serve the Lord in complete and un-condemned righteousness. (Romans 8:1)

"How beautiful are the feet of those who preach the gospel of peace, who bring glad tidings of good things."
—Romans 10:15

Stay Inside

Do you still question God's love? This chapter has been designed to set you free. Do you want to be free—truly free? Then you *must* know and understand the truth. *"Then Jesus said to those Jews who believed Him, 'If you abide in My Word, you are My disciples indeed. And you shall know the truth, **and the truth shall make you free.**'"* (John 8:31-32) What truth was Jesus referring to? *"Jesus said to him (Thomas), "'I am the way, **the truth**, and the life. No one comes to the Father except through Me."* (John 14:6)

Freedom is in the Father, and the Father is found in Christ. The world brings you into bondage through sin. Just as the prodigal son was seduced by the world and enslaved by its passions, when you obey the lust of your flesh and walk in darkness outside the will of God, you become enslaved to Satan through sin.

*"Most assuredly I say to you, whoever commits sin is a slave to sin.
And a slave does not abide in the house forever."*
—John 8:34

Jesus says something profoundly revealing and instructional here. He says, *"A slave does not abide in the house forever."* What is implied here is that a slave *can* be in the house for a time, but he will not remain. Eventually he is going to be put out of the house. He does not belong there. He is not part of the family. The slavery Jesus is referring to here is sin and, unfortunately, our family, the body of Christ, is seeing this embodied all too often in our churches and pulpits.

Look at the sins of pedophilia and homosexuality within the Roman Catholic Church. Although many of the crimes had taken place years ago, it has been revealed! Sin will always be revealed at some point.

*"For there is nothing hidden which will not be revealed, nor has
anything been kept secret but that it should come to light."*
—Mark 4:22

Do not believe for a minute that you are getting away with sin. Countless preachers, whose secret sin ultimately came to light, have been found out. If left un-repented, your sin will come to light as well.

Do not be fooled. The slave does not remain in the house forever. Sin will destroy you. There is a time when he/she will be put out of the house. Your sin *will* be revealed, particularly, if you are a leader of the people. According to the Word of God, leading carries a greater responsibility (James 3:1).

This makes perfect sense when you realize you are leading people down the paths which lead to either heaven or hell. For many, God may have commended you with the responsibility of spiritual life and death over your flock. In essence, you are performing and have been entrusted by God with the role of spiritual father in their life. Did you realize it was that serious? Did you comprehend that God is not playing a game and, therefore, neither should you?

Do you realize if you are merely a husband or a father, that you have the responsibility to lead your family down the path of righteousness? They are your flock. Consequently, Jesus said, "*There is nothing hidden that shall not be revealed.*" (Matthew 10:26) Resist sin. No one ever said it would be easy but you have the Holy Spirit to strengthen you, and Jesus Christ to forgive you if and when you fail. From time to time we all do. If you refuse, however, you will eventually be caught up to.

Walking Backward

Hopefully that scared the "hell" out of you—literally. It does me. The fear of God should scare hell out of all of us. It does if you truly fear and revere Him. How could it not? Don't you respect and perhaps even revere your earthly father? Many people actually fear their earthly father's, even as adults. Some, even long after his passing.

Your heavenly Father is unique though. He treats us differently. He is without condition in His love for us. He never has and never will disown even one single child. He sacrificed for all and His sacrifice frees all who come to Him. "*Greater love has no one than this, than to lay down one's life for his friends.*" (John 15:13) God laid down His life for you.

To make sure that you understand all that Jesus sacrificed, and the immense love required for Him to do so, take note of the following scriptures. "***But we see Jesus,*** *who was made **a little lower** than the angels, **for the suffering of death** crowned with glory and honor, that He, by the grace of God, **might taste death for everyone.**" (Hebrews 2:9)

First and foremost, we must see Jesus and not just with our physical eyes. We must see Him with our hearts and with our minds. Remember, *no one* comes to the Father except by Him. Can you see Him or are you still blind? Perhaps you are holding your hand over your eyes and hoping He will not see *you*.

I will never forget what my cousin did one day as a child. He was about four or five years old and had committed some sort of transgression. I do not even remember what it was, but I do remember how he responded. As my Aunt scolded him, Jimmy covered his eyes and attempted to leave the room backward. Taken aback, one of the adults exclaimed, "Jimmy, why are you walking backwards?" He put his finger to his lips as if to shush the crowd and quietly stated, "If I can't see her she can't see me . . ."

How many of us treat God in this exact manner? We believe that because we cannot see Him, He cannot see us, *or* our disobedience and sin. Here is a revelation that I pray you never forget. God *can* see you. However, when you make Jesus your Lord and Savior He no longer sees your sin. It is not as if He turns His eyes away from it either. He does not have to. He does not see it because it no longer exists.

> *"As far as the east is from the west, so far He has removed our transgressions from us."*
> **—Psalm 103:12**

The beauty of this scripture is the fact that the East never meets the West. The two directions continue into perpetuity with Jesus firmly implanted in the middle. As you read what follows think about how much He has sacrificed for you.

Jesus, the King of all kings, and Lord of all lords, seated at the right hand of God and in perpetual oneness with the Yahweh, was made a little lower than the angels. Just imagine being made lower than that which you have actually created. Have you ever known a business owner to voluntarily step down and take a position lower than his employees, apart from doing a television series such as *Undercover Boss*? People actually commit suicide over losing their money and their place in society. Jesus did exactly that, and although His purpose was death, this was no suicide mission.

Jesus, possessing the power and glory of almighty God, submitted to becoming lower than the angels in heaven He commands on a daily basis. In order to save humanity Jesus *chose* to do lower Himself. Everyone residing in the heavenly realm is immortal. Angels do not die. Cherubim and seraphim do not die—at least not until the Lake of Fire imparts the second death upon the rebellious. Furthermore, God cannot die—unless, that is, He *becomes* a little lower than the angels, and a part of the decaying physical realm where entropy is the norm.

In other words, Yahweh chose to step out of the glory of the heavenly realm and into the natural realm of man where death reigns. Because of His love for you, the Lord stepped into death. His death brought Him a crown of glory and honor and it brought favor from the Lord to you. That is what grace means. It means unmerited, unearned, favor.

Dead Man Walking

You may be wondering how death could bring a crown to Jesus and favor to humanity. Earlier, you read regarding Yahweh, *"For my thoughts are not your thoughts, neither are your ways my ways,' declares the LORD."* (Isaiah 55:8) Thank God for this and Jesus is certainly a prime example. It was not Jesus' death that differentiated Him from the rest of mankind. Death was merely the "now" plan that any man can see.

God's "forever" plan was to resurrect Him. That is what differentiates Jesus from every other prophet—the not so simple fact that God raised Him from the dead. No other prophet can lay claim to this miracle, and, therefore, all those reading this from religions other than Christianity need to take note of this incredible truth. Jesus is alive and remains active in your life! He is not a religion. He is the resurrected Lord who *"ever lives to make intercession for us."* (Hebrews 7:25) Jesus is eternal and immortal. He *"was, and is, and is to come."* (Revelation 1:4, 1:8, 4:8 and 11:17) No other prophet surpasses Him in glory because no other prophet is divine.

Who is the greatest? Undoubtedly, the One who tasted death for all of us. He is the One God poured His glory upon. He is the one who performed the loving act that only a father would perform. Jesus is the only one who died for His "brethren."

Jesus is the only one whom was restored back to His rightful place of glory in heaven and oneness with the Father. Jesus *is* the Father. In Christ, God demonstrated His power over death as only God possesses the power to make alive, or as in the case of the resurrection, to *once again* make alive.

"Now see that I, even I, am He, and there is no God besides Me; I kill and I make alive; I wound and I heal; nor is there any who can deliver from My hand."
—Deuteronomy 32:39

Therefore, it is His Spirit dwelling within you that gives you the everlasting life you so desperately seek. Without Him, you are the walking dead—nothing more than a spiritual zombie returning to the dust of the ground from which you were taken.

Before Jesus sent the Holy Spirit, which occurred *after* His death, He was the only human alive filled with the Spirit of God from within. Over the course of history, the Lord anointed many prophets to perform miracles. Their power, although originating from the same Source, was poured upon them from without, not raised from within. Only the Spirit has the ability to resurrect and make alive. Only God can create life. Now that Jesus has conquered sin and sent "the Helper," the Holy Spirit, to make His abode within you, the same power is a part of you as well.

This truth is demonstrated by the fact that Jesus was not the only one in history to raise the dead. I can name three others from the Word of God, Elijah, Elisha, and Peter, all of whom were anointed with the Spirit of Yahweh. They were not anointed with the power of Allah, Buddha, nor any of the thousands of Hindu gods. Only Yahweh can resurrect the dead because only Yahweh can breathe life into the lifeless dry bones. (Ezekiel 37: 1-14)

Did you know that when you become one with Him you possess this same power as well? Consider that when you wake up for work tomorrow, or go to church, temple or the mosque this weekend. If you dare, think about that next time you go to a funeral.

He's My Brother

No one can possess this life giving power without God's Spirit within them. Therefore, by being created in His image, God can place His Spirit, which is life, within you. He did the same with Jesus when He roamed the blue planet, and as a result, He can bring you into eternity as one with Him. You now fit through the key hole, or as Jesus put it in Luke 13:24, "*The narrow gate.*"

That emptiness that you feel inside is the hole bored into your spirit by sin. It is the remnants of the severed umbilical cord that connects you to the Father. His goal is to fill it. That could only be accomplished through the life, death and resurrection of Jesus Christ, who alone has the power to defeat sin. He is the only one with the power to "*kill and to make alive.*" (Deuteronomy 32:39) His killing of sin allows you to become spiritually alive and dwell where sin cannot, in oneness with God.

Do you see why you were created in God's image? The creation was the "now," the resurrection is the "forever." The image is the means to God's end. Have you ever had someone in your life who you loved so much that you would do anything within your power to be with them? Have you ever loved someone so deeply that you desired to be with them every second of the day? Maybe to you that means a spouse, a child, a parent or grandparent, or perhaps even that one special friend. For God, that person is *you*! His love for you is immeasurable.

Believe it or not, after all of that we are not quite finished with this topic. There is still more pertaining to the subject of God coming to us as one of us. I must say that Hebrews chapter two is one of the great chapters in all of scripture. I think I said that before about other biblical passages, but the truth is that when you begin to understand the Word of God and begin to receive revelation from it, it is all amazing. Yet I still believe that this chapter of the Bible is unusual in both its revelation and ability to inspire.

> *"For it was fitting for Him,* **for whom** *are all things, and by* **whom** *are all things, in bringing many sons to glory* (that is us), *to make the captain* (or leader) *of their salvation perfect through sufferings."*
> **—Hebrews 2:10**

It is important to note that Jesus was made perfect through sufferings. You are not. You are made perfect, meaning restored to His image, through accepting the sacrifice of His sufferings.

Although experiencing spiritual growth requires trials and tribulations, they are not what perfects or saves us. Only Christ is our perfection, meaning our righteousness. God did not create you to suffer. He does not receive glory in your sufferings. He receives glory in your deliverance, or the deliverance of others, *through* your suffering. He receives glory when you are freed from the curse of sin, sickness and spiritual death. When viewed form the reference point of eternity, nothing else matters.

> *"For both He who sanctifies (which means to be set apart to and for God) and those who are being sanctified are all of one, for which reason He is not ashamed to call them brethren . . ."*
> **—Hebrews 2:11**

If you look closely at this scripture you will see exactly what we were discussing above. As a result of our being one with God, and adopted as sons, that makes Jesus and us brethren. Can you imagine? It's true, and not only does the author of Hebrews proclaim this, but Jesus Himself proclaims it in the gospel of Luke 8:21, *"My mother and my brethren are these who hear the Word of God and do it."*

Back to Hebrews chapter two: *"Inasmuch as the children have partaken of flesh and blood, **He Himself likewise shared in the same**, that through death He might destroy him who had the power of death, that is, the devil, **and release** those who through the fear of death were all their lifetime subject to bondage."* (Hebrews 2:14) This right here clearly states God's purpose for coming to the earth as a man. It is plain as day.

Because we are flesh and blood we are subject to the bondage of both fear and death. There is just no escaping it. Therefore, and in order to deliver us, **God decided to adopt our same nature**. He put on an earth suit, flesh and blood, so He might die. It is only in death that we are released from our sin and our greatest fear . . . public speaking! Gotcha, I am just kidding. Contrary to what many believe our greatest fear is not public speaking, it is death.

Jesus in the natural realm put an end to the devil's reign. In Him, you are translated from death to eternal life. Only the love of a Father would go to such extraordinary lengths to rescue His children and only the God of the universe possesses the power to do so.

"For indeed He does not give aid to angels, but He does give aid to the seed of Abraham (Who are all those who believe in the name of Jesus Christ through faith). *Therefore, in all things HE HAD to be made like His brethren, that He might be a merciful and faithful High Priest in things pertaining to God, to make propitiation for the sins of the people. For in that He Himself has suffered, being tempted, He is able to aid those who are being tempted."*
—Hebrews 2:15-18

The more I learn about God the more I am amazed at what a gift death actually is, but only in its proper time. Beware of the bridges over troubled waters. They are a cross-over into a better life, not a platform to jump from.

John 3:16

Is there any other god who has gone through so much to save His people? Is there any other god who has actually done anything to save his people? How about Allah, did he suffer to deliver you from the scales? Does he love you enough to put off his own "glory," that you may live forever? Does he even possess the power to do so? What has Buddha done, or Jain, or even Satan for those of you he has deceived into bondage? Did he suffer for you? Would he?

You will find out just how evil he is and who is actually doing the suffering if you stand before him in hell. Do you think it will be fun there? Do you think all of your friends will be there with you? Is it politically correct to say that they may be, but you will never know it? You will have decided yourself into darkness, fire, torment, and worst of all, eternal destruction. Take the first exit off the *Highway to Hell.* In hell you will be forever Fatherless.

In my years I have studied quite a few religions. I have read the Q'ran cover to cover, twice, along with the Hadith. I have read the

Book of Mormon, searched the Jehovah's Witnesses version of the Bible along with having read quite a few of their Watch Tower publications. I have debated with Atheists, been to Hindu Cremation ceremonies . . . all in search of salvation, and I must tell you the truth. It does not exist outside of Christ. All you get is bondage and a scale that cannot be overcome—weights against good and bad deeds that can never tip in your favor due to your fallen nature and endless ceremonies devoid of true power. Every impure thought, deed, or even omission weighs against you. It is all designed by Satan to keep you in bondage. False religion is not accidental.

Allow me to ask you a question and I want you to answer honestly. How much good have you really done? If you truly want to be honest and if you truly want to search for the truth, the answer is probably not much, especially when it is compared to your impurity. Think about your thoughts, about your envy and/or jealousy, sexual fantasies, thoughts of revenge, anger etc . . . How many times have you passed that poor person on the street, lied, or had that "me-first" attitude. Think honestly about your sin.

Now tally up how many people you have actually helped. If you are a good person you can count them on your fingers. If you are really good you might have to include your toes. Now weigh that against the scale of sin. I am sorry to inform you that you cannot win. If you are like me you have probably blown it in one day. It is time for a change.

Jesus is the only solution to the battle. Your loving Father who is one with Jesus became flesh and blood in order to save you! You cannot earn it. It is free but it must be chosen.

*"For by grace you have been saved through faith, **and that not of yourselves**, it is the gift of God, not of works, lest anyone should boast."*
—Ephesians 2:8

You cannot work for it and you cannot die for it. It is priceless. When you realize all that it entails, no one would ever be willing or can afford to pay the price of its cost. Only God could and would.

"For God so loved the world that He gave His only begotten Son, that whoever believes in Him shall never perish, but have everlasting life."
—John 3:16

Nobody can afford to live without the priceless gift of Jesus Christ. Yahweh gave His all to redeem you and there is only one way to reach Him. Therefore, let's pass through the narrow gate. It is time to travel down the road of faith.

CHAPTER 6

Faith

No dialogue regarding the nature of Yahweh could ever be complete without discussing the chief cornerstone of faith. "We may seek God by our intellect, but we only can find him with our heart," – **Cotvos**. Since "*God is Spirit*" (1 John 4:24) the only access we have to Him is through the spirit. Apart from the thirty-three year period that ended roughly two thousand years ago, we cannot communicate with God in the flesh. Take note of what follows. It specifically details where our access to the Almighty is:

*"Therefore, having been justified by faith, we have peace with God through our Lord Jesus Christ, through whom **we also have access by faith** into this grace in which we stand, and rejoice in hope of*

the glory of God."
—Romans 5:1-2

Before we discuss faith as being our access point to the Almighty, I want you to take notice of the first half of the above Scripture. It is confirmation of where our true peace lies. I am sure you have heard the recent cliche that states, "No Jesus, no peace—Know Jesus, know peace." It is true. There is no peace without the Prince of Peace. In light of the recent developments unfolding in the Middle East, which has actually been going on for thousands of years, the world is undoubtedly in the process of discovering this.

Earlier we discussed the ministry of angels. Do you remember the declaration they made regarding the birth of Christ? They proclaimed, *"Peace on earth and goodwill toward man."* Here we see it again, in plain English or whatever language you may read your Bible in, that *"we have **peace** with God **through** our Lord Jesus Christ...."* Christ *is* the access point of faith. The Messiah is humanity's point of entry into the kingdom and presence of God.

Reverse Engineering

There are times, however, that we must understand the implication of the opposing point of view in order to gain clarity on what the Lord is communicating to us. In this instance, the Word of God says, *"We have peace with God through our Lord Jesus Christ."* What if we do not have Christ in our lives? What if I am an Atheist, a Muslim, a Buddhist or perhaps simply Agnostic? What if I am anything besides a disciple of the Lord Jesus Christ? What are the implications if our faith is not in the Messiah?

It is quite simple. According to the Word of God, we have not made peace with God. It implies that we are vainly continuing our struggle against Him. We are resisting the grace, goodness, and most importantly, the will of God Almighty. Therefore, since our loyalties lie elsewhere we remain in opposition to Him. We are denied access to His grace.

The Word of God is quite clear in regard to this topic. Denying Jesus Christ equates to carnality, and *"the carnal mind is enmity **against** God, for it is not subject to the law of God, nor can it be."* (Romans 8:7) Why do you think God feels this way? It is simple. God is holy. He cannot, and will not be in fellowship with sin. Looking the other way would make Him an accomplice with both sin and Satan. If that sounds as absurd to you as it does to me, then you understand that He will not support your ultimate demise. Spiritual death is the choice you have made when you stand in opposition to Jesus Christ. Although this decision grieves God, and He *will* allow you to make it, He will not support it by equating the unbeliever with the believer.

Therefore, He cries out, *"adulterers and adulteresses . . . !"* (James 4:4) This is how God views our rebellion, which is often manifested in our choice to follow the world's manifold religious systems over the kingdom of God.

> *"Do you not know that friendship with the world is enmity with God? Whoever, therefore, wants to be a friend of the world **makes himself an enemy of God.**"*
> **—James 4:4**

As all you Star Trek fans know, "Resistance is futile." Even the mighty Borg are no match for Yahweh. How ill-equipped are *we* to stand in opposition to the majestic King of the universe?

Carefully consider the following statements: If you have refused to accept the sacrifice of Jesus Christ, you are not only out of fellowship with God, you have actually waged war against Him. You have declared that His blood is unworthy of your acceptance. In essence, You have made a personal declaration of independence apart from the governmental rule of the Maker of the universe.

That is the same decision Lucifer made! Are you okay with Lucifer being your partner? Keep in mind that you cannot win the battle against Yahweh. God was, is, and always will be, the preeminent power in all of creation. Satan tried to overthrow Him and we know *his* end lies in the Lake of Fire. Those of us who resist God's will are doomed to suffer the same fate.

Come to Papa

Quite simply stated, entering the presence of Yahweh requires us to cast off our sin by making peace with God *through* Jesus Christ. Only then can we experience both His friendship and His covenant of grace. We seem to have lost this vital truth. As a result, we never truly seek the Father, Yahweh. We unknowingly abandon Him at the front door of Jesus Christ (John 10:7-10) and never actually step through and into the kingdom of Yahweh.

We sing the song, "*It's all about you . . . Jesus. And all this is for you . . . .*" Well, you get the gist of the song. There is nothing wrong with the song in and of itself. In fact, it is a wonderful song which glorifies the Lord Jesus Christ and that is good, holy, and necessary.

The problem, however, is that we love to play games and be "buddy, buddy" with Jesus without ever making a true commitment to Him. Contrary to the lyrics of the aforementioned song, and what most of us do not realize, is that it is not only about Jesus. It is all about the Father and His will. Jesus Christ, manifested in flesh and blood, (in addition to existing as the eternal Word of God) is an extension of God's glory. He is a manifestation of God in the natural realm. In other words, He is a protraction of Yahweh whose purpose for becoming flesh and blood is to unite us to God's perfect will for humanity. God's ultimate, perfect and eternal will for mankind does not include the presence of sin.

Therefore, as you haphazardly sing the song, *"Friend of God,"* keep in mind what being a friend of Jesus consists of.

*"You are My friends **if** you do whatever I command you."*
—John 15:14

That is one big "if!" Most of us are so unfamiliar with the Word of God that we have no idea what Jesus commanded. In fact, we have drifted so far from the truth that we believe Jesus abolished the law and does not command anything of us. Let's take this even further. What does Jesus *demand* of us? Contrary to what you may believe, both grace and salvation are free, but becoming a disciple of Christ is costly. Jesus commanded that we love God, love our neighbors, and thirdly, and this is where most people run for cover, that we make disciples of all nations. In order to be His friend, Jesus demands that you keep these three ordinances.

Don't get me wrong, I am not belittling anything that Jesus is or did. Jesus is worthy of all praise, and He is, without a doubt God and worthy of equal honor with the Father. (John 1:1) He is, and always has been, an equal part of the eternal Godhead. He has completely and perfectly fulfilled the purpose for which He was sent, and He continues to perform His function in complete and total perfection. However, in truth, it is all about Yahweh. Jesus Himself said so. The "reason for the season" is to bring you back into a "right," or better stated, a "righteous" relationship with Yahweh for the purpose of obtaining eternal life.

Before you call me a blasphemer and throw this book into the fireplace, consider the purpose of Jesus' mission. Many other religions point to the distinctions between Father, Son and Holy Spirit and claim that we worship three Gods. Nothing could be further from the truth. I will touch on the trinity in detail in a later chapter. Most simply do not comprehend Yahweh's nature. The point I am making, however, is that *"in Jesus dwells all the fullness of the Godhead **bodily** *and that you* (we) *are complete in Him,"* (Colossians 2:9) and only in Him.

> However, *"God is Spirit, and the hour is coming, **and now is,** when the **true worshippers** will worship **the Father** in spirit and in truth, **for the Father is seeking such to worship Him.**"*
> **—John 4:23-24**

Take note of Jesus' continual emphasis is on the Father.

The Apple of His Eye

Therefore, let's break down Colossians 2:9 a little deeper and have a look at the following two points. First, Jesus (Yeshua) is the bodily form of God, and second, without Him we cannot be complete, or better stated, one with God.

Did you notice the word, *"bodily?"* Christ is the fullness of the Godhead bodily, meaning when it comes to the flesh, or better stated, the realm of our physical universe, there could be no one more complete than Christ. He alone is divine. In fact, there could be no other divine flesh period. *"God is one!"* (Deuteronomy 6:4)

However, Christ in bodily form is not the complete nature of Yahweh. Just as the skin of an apple does not encompass the entire apple, Jesus, manifested in flesh and blood, is merely a part of Yahweh. To discover Jesus place in the Father, let's have a look at the Shekhinah glory (Pronounced, shi-**kee**-n*uh*) that used to manifest itself as a cloud filling the temple.

Most gentile (Non Jewish) believers who speak of the Shekhinah glory of God have no idea what it (actually, He) is. That is understandable when you consider that very few gentiles speak Hebrew, nor are most gentile believers familiar with Yahweh. Therefore, it becomes just another meaningless religious idiom. We know there was the manifestation of a cloud but have no clue of what, or who, the cloud represents, or better stated, manifests. The Shekhinah glory is not just smoke.

Furthermore, we miss the why. What is the purpose of the glory? As a result, the true meaning of something as valuable as Jesus transfiguration on the mountain is all but lost. (Luke 9:28-36 and Matthew 17:1-7) If you think back, you will recall that the cloud showed up on the Mount of Transfiguration as well? Therefore, let's check out the definition of Shekhinah. The Shekhinah glory is: **The presence of God on earth**, or a symbol or **manifestation of His presence.**

With that in mind, let's take a look at the following scriptures from the gospel of John in regard to the identity of Jesus Christ:

> "*. . . As You Father are in Me, and I in You, that they may also be one in Us, that the world may believe that **You sent Me.**"*
> —**John 17:21**

Jesus made the following statement as well, "*For I have given to them the words which You have given Me; and they have received, and have known surely **that I came forth from You.**"*
> —**John 17:8**

To make sure there is no identity crisis in regard to our Lord, we find the following scriptures which prove beyond any shadow of a doubt who the Bible is claiming Jesus to be:

> "*In the beginning was the Word, and the Word was with God **and the Word was God** . . . And the Word **became flesh** and dwelt among us . . .*"
> —**John 1:1 and 14**

> "*I and the Father **are One.**"*
> —**John 10:30**

Now put two and two together. According to the above definition, Jesus is the Shekhinah glory of God. Why? He is a manifestation of God in the natural, or physical realm. Once we understand this, Jesus' words make perfect sense. Jesus is a manifestation of God on earth, just as the Angel of the Lord was a manifestation of God on earth. That is the reason many biblical scholars consider the Angel of the Lord to be the pre-incarnate Christ.

The Shekhinah glory is a manifestation of God on earth, as well. They are all one. God is one. Each is a manifestation of the access point to our holy Father given to humanity to satisfy the purpose of the dispensation to which He was sent. As you are about to see, because of sin, Yahweh always has to mask Himself. No one can see His face and live. (Exodus 33:20)

Think about it in terms of the apple we discussed above. When you peel away the skin of an apple, you find the flesh. When you cut through the flesh, you find the core, which contains the seeds. Let's not even discuss all of the nutrients, minerals, enzymes, molecules, and even further down to the genetic, atomic, and even sub atomic level of all that comprises the makeup of an apple. All are components of the apple. Separating them does not make any one piece less of the apple, nor does it make it multiple apples.

Keep in mind that God is infinitely more complex than the most circuitous creation you could possibly find on earth, which just happens to be you, me, and every other human being roaming the blue planet. Therefore, Yahweh can manifest Himself on earth in any manner He chooses. This is why the manifestation of the trinity is not idolatry. Each is a part of the essence Yahweh.

In reality, human beings being formed in the image of God are composed in the same manner as the apple I just spoke of. Your physical body of flesh is not all that you are. It is your spirit and your soul that will ultimately and eternally be joined together with the Lord, thus making your spiritual body complete upon the resurrection. Until you are resurrected, your natural body, and all that it is composed of will ultimately perish and return to the dust from whence it was taken. This imperfect body, which will one day be perfected, is temporarily along for the ride.

Point number two, and of utmost importance, is that Colossians 2:9 is referring to *our* completeness and not the completeness of Jesus and/or God the Father. As previously stated, Jesus is the fullness of the Godhead *bodily*. Bodily is not the only aspect of the Father. It is not even the complete nature of Christ. He is the fullness of God in bodily form. There are numerous aspects that encompass the Father's nature. We know of three, and we refer to this as the trinity.

Jesus Christ is one aspect of the Father. The Holy Spirit is another. I do not know exactly all that encompasses Yahweh's complete and Almighty nature. Neither does any other human being alive, but the Shekhinah gives us a clue that there is much more to God than meets the eye. He is way too awesome for mere human beings to fully comprehend.

> *"And I looked, and behold, in the midst of the throne and of the four living creatures, and in the midst of the elders, stood a Lamb as though it had been slain, having seven horns and seven eyes, **which are the seven Spirits of God** sent out into all the earth."*
> **—Revelation 5:6**

His Spirit alone contains seven characteristics for lack of a better term. Consider the above definition of the Shekhinah glory which is a manifestation of God on earth. Revelation 5:6 alone contains seven different Shekhinah's being sent throughout the earth. What exactly encompasses His complete nature? I have to believe that He alone can answer that question.

Therefore, it is important to keep in mind that the *bodily* aspect of Jesus Christ completes *us*, not God. Why? Through the natural, or physical death, and supernatural resurrection of Jesus Christ, we are reunited with our life source, Yahweh. We are restored back to the image of God in which we were originally created.

Colossians 2:9, says *we* are complete. The origin and unitary nature of Christ has no derivation in time and space as we know it. It has been reconciled by the Father through the resurrection and restoration of Christ to the right hand of God. In truth, Jesus' separation from the Father only lasted for a very short period of time and for one purpose only; the destruction of sin. Never before, and never again, will there ever be any separation whatsoever of the glory of God nor any of His attributes.

> *"And the Lord shall be King over all the earth. In that day it shall be—'The Lord is one,' and His name one."*
> **—Zechariah 14:9**

The work has been completed. *"It is finished."* (John 19:30) The prerequisite of death was only required one time and for one single purpose—redemption.

Not as They Appear

We catch a small glimpse of Jesus' glory on the Mount of Transfiguration when Christ shines like the sun before Peter, James and John. For a brief moment, He discarded His "earth suit"— flesh and blood. The aforementioned disciples beheld a peek of His true and glorious nature. We are also told the following; *"Beloved, now we are children of God; and it is not yet revealed **what we shall be**, but we know that when He is revealed* (referring to His true and glorified nature, not when He became *"a little lower than the angels"* [Hebrews 2:7 and Psalm 8:5] to redeem us on the cross), *we shall be like Him, for we shall see Him **as He is**."* (1 John 3:2)

I do not believe any human being has ever seen all that Jesus truly is. We can never comprehend Him in our presently sin stained state of being. Our carnality will not allow it. Furthermore, no one has ever returned from heaven to explain all that He is, but I can tell you that your present eyes could never fathom such beauty and multiplicity.

According to the above Scripture, we do not even have an inkling of *our own* true spiritual nature, let alone the spiritual completeness of Christ. How much more perfect and replete is the nature of God the Father who encompasses Christ, the Holy Spirit, the Shekhinah glory, the entire universe, and the heavenly realm, wherever and whatever that is?

Yet, through Christ we have access to God's mercy and grace.

Therefore, *"let us therefore come boldly to the throne of grace that we may obtain mercy and find grace to help in time of need."*
—Hebrews 4:16

Jesus humbled Himself to restore our image and to personally escort us to the holy throne of God. He came to reunite us with the Father. Why would I not want to submit my life to such an incredible and loving God?

Our Father

Moreover, what was Jesus' primary mission? Why was it so important for Jesus to die? Think about it; so we could regain access *to the Father* in heaven through the power of His resurrection. Jesus' reason for entering the realm of death was about the Father's will. *"Father, if it is Your will, take this cup away from Me; nevertheless not My will, but Yours, be done."* (Luke 22:42)

Therefore, from Jesus' point of view, it is all about Yahweh. Hence, that must be our primary consideration as well. We have changed Jesus' mission into a religion, which He never intended, and have essentially forgotten about the Father in the process. Listen carefully to Jesus' prayer from the gospel of John:

"*I have manifested* **Your name** *to the men whom You have given Me out of the world.* **They were Yours,** *You gave them to Me, and they have kept* **Your** *Word. Now they have known that* **all things** *which You have given Me are* **from You.** *For I have given to them the words which You have given Me; and they have received, and have known surely* **that I came forth from You;** *and they have believed that* **You sent Me.**

"*I pray for them. I do not pray for the world but for those whom You have given Me,* **for they are Yours.** *And all Mine are* **Yours and Yours are Mine,** *and I am glorified in them. Now I am no longer in the world, but these are in the world,* **and I come to You** *Holy Father. Keep* **through Your name** *those whom You have given Me, that they may be one* **as We are.** *While I was with them in the world, I kept them* **in Your name** . . .

"*I do not pray for these alone, but also for those* **who will believe** *in Me through their word; that they may all be one, as You, Father, are in Me, and I in You; that they may also be one in Us, that the world may believe that* **You sent Me** . . .

"*Father, I desire that they also whom You have given Me may be with Me where I am, that they may behold My glory* **which You have given Me;** *for You loved Me* **before the foundation of the world.** *O righteous Father!* **The world has not known You** *but I have known You; and these have known that* **You sent Me.** *And I have declared to them* **Your name,** *and will declare that the love with which You loved Me may be in them, and I in them.*"
—Excerpts from John 17:1-26

According to Jesus, who is it all about? Clearly it is about the Father! Through faith in the death and resurrection of Jesus Christ, we gain access to the Father. It is Jehovah (YHWH), the Father, who actually does the all work. Yahweh *is* the resurrection power that works through Jesus Christ.

This is why Jesus instructed us not to pray to Him directly, but to pray in His name. It is through Jesus Christ that we tap into the power of the Almighty. Yahweh is our *"ever-present help in times of trouble."* (Psalm 46:1)

> *"In that day **you will ask in My name**, and I do not say to you that I shall pray the Father for you; for the Father Himself loves you . . ."*
> **—John 16:26-27**

Jesus actually took it even further, *"And **in that day you will ask me nothing**. Most assuredly I say to you, whatever you ask the Father **in My name** He will give you."*
—John 16:23

All too often we unwittingly look for Jesus to fulfill our every need when in reality He is pointing us directly to Yahweh. Jesus *is* our advocate with the Father, but it is the Father, Yahweh, who actually does the work we so desperately desire. It is Yahweh who answers our prayers.

Why is this important? The majority of Christian people, in direct contradiction to Jesus' instruction, pray directly to Jesus and expect Jesus to answer their prayer. Some even to the saints, but I will not even go there at this point. That is just outright paganism and rebellion against God.

The truth, however, is that in Jesus Christ *"we have an advocate with the Father."* (1 John 2:1) An "advocate" is someone who pleads a case on behalf of another. Jesus is our Savior, but it is Yahweh whom we need to cry out to with Jesus as our advocate. Don't worry, Jesus *"ever lives to make intercession for us."* (Hebrews 7:25) When praying directly to Jesus we are targeting the wrong power source. That is like expecting your agent to pay your insurance claim. It is the company that cuts the check. The agent simply assists with the claim and delivers the check.

Jesus, as Lord of all, is a conduit to the physical realm. He has the authority to plead our case directly before the throne of our heavenly Father. Our access to the Father is the benefit that His blood purchased.

Do you think it was a coincidence that Jesus was manifested in the flesh, and not the Father or the Holy Spirit? John 1:14 was not a random act. The Word becoming flesh was an act of laser-like focus. Of course God perfectly thought it through! That is the purpose of the Shekhinah glory who is as ageless and timeless as God Himself. The Shekhinah glory is God, and, therefore, being an advocate to the natural realm is a major part of Jesus' function within the Godhead. Together, they created everything in existence. (John 1:3) In knowing this, why would you want to operate differently. Everything pertaining to humanity goes through Jesus.

Therefore, as our agent before the King, we pray only in His name. Because He is directly connected to Yahweh as a part of the eternal Godhead, Yahweh always hears. Therefore, you can be confident in knowing that our friend and advocate Jesus Christ, will take it from there. When you trust Him and act according to His will and His ways, in other words, when you enter God culture, you can truly call Him friend. In Him, we are friends of God. Therefore, out of love we worship, praise, fellowship, and sometimes just bear our souls to our friend and Savior, Jesus Christ of Nazareth, the King of all kings and Lord of all lords.

"Therefore humble yourselves under the mighty hand of God, that He may exalt you in due time, casting all your care upon Him, for He cares for you."
—1 Peter 5:6-7

To be effective, our prayers must be directed to the Father *in the name* of our advocate Jesus Christ. Once in His hands the Holy Spirit will lead you and guide you to whatever actions you must take to produce the desired outcome.

This is how the Bible teaches prayer. It is what gives us true access to the Father through faith. Think about it, when the disciples asked Jesus to teach them to pray, He instructed them to say, "*Our Father who art in heaven . . .*" (Matthew 6:9) Jesus taught us to pray and cry out directly to Yahweh. Therefore, "*this is the confidence that we have in Him, that anything we ask according to His will, He hears us.*" (1 John 5:14)

If we have prayed according to the Father's will, we can be confident that He has heard our prayer. In knowing this we can confidently rest assured that contrary to how we may feel our prayer has gone farther than the ceiling. In fact, we can be assured that it has made its way out of our range of audibility and directly into the throne room of God. In Christ, your prayers go directly into the ear of Yahweh. Having this confidence is the essence of true faith.

If it is in His will, and/or when the time is right, He will have one of three answers—yes, no or not yet. No simply means He has something better in mind. Therefore, by faith, believe He has your best interest in mind and seek His perfect will for your life. We can have peace in knowing that because He loves us it is simply a matter of our prayer being fulfilled in God's time.

Pleading Together

While we are on the subject, I always encourage people to pray according to scripture. Scripture is the foundation of everything pertaining to God. It is where both faith and the will of God are found. You may not realize it, but prayer is simply communicating with God. It is really nothing more than having a conversation during which time we make our requests known to our Father. The concept of prayer is quite simple to grasp once you recognize you have been communicating this way with your naturally born parents from the day you were born.

Praying scripture simply means that if you are believing God for a particular request, find scripture that pertains to the issue and recite it back to God. In the natural, your earthly parents set the household rules and when viewed from the Spirit, so did God. When you obey (or obeyed, if you are an adult) your parents rules you are rewarded. So it is with your heavenly Father as well.

> Isaiah 55:11 proclaims, *"So shall My word be that goes forth from My mouth;* **it shall not return to Me void,** *but it shall accomplish* **what I please,** *and it shall prosper in the thing for which* **I sent it.***"*

This is what gives us the faith and confidence to know that when the time is right, our scriptural prayers will be answered. His Word will not return to Him void. The Word of God *is* faith because the Word of God, and I am not talking about the ink on a page, but the logos (The Greek translation of "word.") that went forth from Yahweh, does not just come from God, it *is* God. (John 1:1)

When we pray according to scripture we are acknowledging God. We are agreeing with Him and the rules and regulations governing His kingdom. It is actually a form of worship, which is an act of reverent honor and submission to Him. Therefore, we know we have prayed according to, and have asked for something within God's will.

This is the beauty and the benefit of being familiar with the Word of God. It allows you to partner with Him. Did you know that God's desire is not just to provide for you? God's will is to work together with you.

*"Put me in remembrance: **let us plead together**: declare thou, that thou mayest be justified."*
—Isaiah 43:26

Scripture is the direct access to the power of our Holy Father, Yahweh. When recited back to Him, it is a prayer that comes directly from the mind of God and not the self-centered heart of man. Thus, you can rest assured that *"His will be done on earth as it is in heaven."* (Matthew 6:10) Ignoring this principle just may be the reason so many prayers go unanswered. In the name of Jesus Christ, who is the Word of God, (John 1:1) we are directly connected to the power of Yahweh.

Access to Heaven

That leads us to the question of why Jesus—why must we go through Jesus? As stated earlier, Jesus is our conduit to the heavenly realm. He was born as a man and died as a man for the remission of our sin. Jesus' death and resurrection is all about fulfilling the law. In just a bit you will learn both how and why. For now, suffice it to say that without a sacrifice it would be impossible for us to gain entrance into the heavenly realm and into the presence of God. Why? Quite simply, there is no sin where the Father dwells. Without Jesus's blood a sinful humanity has no access to heaven.

*"According to the law almost all things are purified with blood, and **without shedding of blood there is no remission.**"*
—Hebrews 9:22

Therefore, keep in mind that no religion, no amount of works, and no level of performance can grant you access to the Father. You simply fall short. All of man's religious systems fall short. Even the laws of Moses, also known as the Pentateuch, and the entire Torah fall short. That, by the way, is not meant to be blasphemous or disrespectful. It is the truth of God. It is the purpose of Christ crucified.

This deficiency is why salvation, as well as, the power of the Almighty is only attainable in Christ. Salvation cannot be found in any religious system including the religions of Christianity and/or Judaism. It may only be obtained through faith in the life, death and resurrection of Jesus Christ. Only Christ can reconnect you to the Father. Under the New Covenant, entering the presence of God through rules, regulations and traditions is not feasible.

> *"For Christ is the end of the law for righteousness to everyone who believes."*
> **—Romans 10:4**

In fact, it was not feasible under the law either. Only the High Priest was permitted to enter the holy of holies and he often times never made it out. Legend has it, that the priests would tie a rope to the High Priest to pull him out should he meet his ultimate demise behind the curtain. Think about it. Under the law, the rituals needed to be performed in a precise manner. Any mistake or even the tiniest deviation would cause God to drop the High Priest in his tracks. His body would thump to the ground and the bell tied to his hip or ankle would stop ringing.

Although that illustration may only be legend, what a picture of sin and the death of our High Priest, Jesus Christ, it paints. Consider the dilemma. They could not even go in to drag the body out. Due to man's sin, only one person, the High Priest was permitted entrance. This was true of Christ as well until in death He tore open the veil, thus allowing all who believe to enter God's presence. (Matthew 27:51) Without Christ, the presence of God is deadly. Judgment is instantaneous.

It is not that we no longer need to follow the law. We are not permitted to murder, steal, covet and so forth. Freedom is not lawlessness. Freedom is having an advocate to release us from the penalty of our imperfection.

One of our greatest misunderstandings is that Jesus came here to convert Judaism, or every other religion for that matter, into Christianity. Perhaps more clearly stated, many believe Jesus came here to make all men Christians. Jesus never uttered the term. Jesus did not come here to start a religion. He came here to save us, regardless of our race, color, creed, social status and, yes, *even* our religion.

Jesus is the resurrection and the life, but God is the power behind Him and in Him. Through the aforementioned miracle-working power, Jesus removes the sin that separates us from our Father and chaperones us into the heavenly realm. He escorts us into the presence and oneness of the everlasting Father. Without Him, we would be hopelessly lost and thrust eternally into the Lake of Fire. Therefore, it is truly Jesus who completes us. As He conjoins us to the Father, He gives us life. Therefore, through and in Christ, it is Yahweh whom we genuinely seek because that is who Jesus truly is in the glory of eternity. Yahweh is not just the origin of our faith, He *is* our faith.

Seek and You Shall Find

In truth, we seek a relationship with Jesus Christ so we may have a relationship with the Father. If that sounds disingenuous, it is not. That is why God sent Him. It is not as if God is jealous of Himself. In the Garden of Eden, Yahweh used to walk with Adam and Eve in the "cool of the day." (Genesis 3:8) Without sin, the manifestation of the Shekhinah glory was unnecessary. There was no need to mask His power. There was no need for an intermediary. The earth was paradise for both God and Adam. However, sin ruined that for all of us, Yahweh included. Since that time, we have been separated from Him. We have continuously drifted further from His presence. In the process, we have lost sight of His will and have relinquished His mighty power.

Ever since, God has been patiently biding His time and awaiting His opportunity to be reunited with you. That is not just His will, it is His desire. His moment of fortuity has come through the person of Jesus Christ. Christ has fulfilled the hour and the law.

However, you cannot access Christ or the Father in any manner you desire. He can only be accessed one way. We must enter through the "*narrow gate,*" (Matthew 7:13) which is the power of faith in Jesus Christ. Ignorance of this truth has left us adrift. The resulting void, or perhaps even worse, the pains of apathy, has left us meandering through the storms of life—aimlessly wandering through the vicious gauntlet of sin that is no place for a man without a paddle or a "life preserver." Sin never ends well. We all must answer to eternity.

Time for a Change

I find it ironic that faith has been the subject of countless sermons, books, as well as, both secular and Christian music. Even George Michael got in on the act as he so eloquently opined the refrain of his hit song, "*I gotta have faith.*" I am pretty sure he had no clue of what he was actually cantillating. Therefore, let's talk candidly about this infinitely important topic.

If you are seeking faith in order to gain material possessions, or positions of power and authority, or if you are seeking faith for any purpose other than salvation, the knowledge of God and a relationship with your holy Father, you must change your paradigm and your motivation.

You must, *"seek ye first the kingdom of God, and His righteousness, and all these **things** shall be added to you."*
—Matthew 6:33

Not too long ago I was having a conversation with a friend of mine. Although I dearly love and respect him, we do not always see eye to eye on matters of spirituality. He has some "New Age" beliefs commingled with his roots in Judaism.

At the time he was experiencing financial trouble. During the course of our visit he asked me if I read the Bible every day. My reply was, "Yes, as often as I can. For the most part, that means daily." His response surprised me a little. He exclaimed, "Yeah, I gotta get in on some of that prosperity."

Do you see where he has gone astray? His motivation for seeking is wrong. His efforts are directed toward God's wallet and not His face. The Word of the Lord tells us exactly what our priorities must be. We are to seek the giver not the gift.

If you want to be a person of faith you must heed His command. It is not written as a suggestion. We are instructed, first and foremost, to seek the kingdom of God, which as stated earlier is God's way of doing things. It is His realm of government and it is not a tedious chore. Trust me, once you get to know Him you will fall madly in love with Him. Thus, seeking will no longer be cumbersome. It becomes a heavenly visitation that leaves you empty when your appointment is unkept. Voluntary submission to the will of God is evidence that we trust Him. It is confirmation of our love, respect, and yes, even our fear of Him.

If you are not quite there yet—if you are feeling a bit disingenuous, don't worry. God is not condemning you. He is calling you. The guilt means you are yet to enter His presence. You have not yet developed a relationship with Him. In time, if you continue to seek Him this feeling will fade. You will come to know your Father and your love will grow over time.

My friend, love does not just happen. Love is developed through relationship. Relationships take time. Relationship is not a feeling. The feeling we experience, also known as desire, is most often lust. True love always includes joy. It is the supernatural ability to place the best interest of the object of your affection above your own. That is what God did in Christ. Are you willing to do the same for Him? Just like any marriage true love evolves as it grows. For humanity, love of God can only be found in Christ. "*God is love.*" (1 John 4:8) Because of sin there is simply no other way to enter His presence. Therefore, there is no other means of getting to know Him.

Consider the vital truth that Jesus Christ *is* God's way of doing things. He *will* rule over the Lord's government in eternity. In other words, the Scripture is telling us that we must seek the Lord first by submitting ourselves to His way of doing and being right and not *our* way of doing what *we think* is right.

We must be willingly governed by the Lord. That is what "righteousness" is. It is God's way of doing, thinking and being. It is not the appearance of false religiosity or following a set of man-made rules. It means doing and being what is right in God's eyes and not man's eyes. If you are wondering what that means the definition is contained within the Word of God. It looks somewhat different for every one of us, however, it follows a common set of guidelines— namely, being a *seeker* and a *doer* of the Word of God. (James 1:22)

Am I Holy?

To gain perspective on what a disciple of Jesus Christ looks like, let's have a look at righteousness. Have you ever considered what it means to be holy? Holiness is a prerequisite of faith. Does it mean you must attend every church function or dress and act a certain way so everyone can look and see your righteousness? Is it merely a religious idiom that no one can define, let alone become? Of course not!

Holiness simply means that you have allowed God to separate you from the way the world acts and functions. It means you have committed to being and doing what God wants you to become and do. Righteousness means you have become a part of God culture. In other words, you are allowing yourself to be governed by the Almighty and living your life according to His ways and purpose.

That is what made the utensils in the tabernacle holy. It was not what they were made *of.* It is who they were made *for,* and by whom and how they were to be used. You are no different. You were made *for* God, *by* God. Submission to God's truth is what makes you holy. That is where our motivation to serve the Lord should begin. The utensils in the tabernacle were not common objects set aside for anyone who wanted to use them in any manner they chose. Neither are you. They were set apart for the service of the Lord and were not to be used in any other manner. Period! The same is true for God's children. You are holy to God. You were created by Him and for Him.

As human beings we are not common objects good enough for any Tom, Dick, or Harry that comes along. I suppose I dated myself by using that old cliche, but the point is, you are a son or daughter of the King of all kings. You have been specifically chosen to accomplish the will and purpose God has for your unique life. Regardless of your age, sex, or ethnicity, God created and *"knew you in Christ before the foundation of the world."* (Ephesians 1:4) Therefore, His plan for you is perfect. You simply need to access the power of faith and holiness in order to find and accomplish it.

Understand On Purpose

The blessing of God is also accessed by faith. In order to live in the blessing, which is "living by faith," when expressed in modern day "Christianese," we must actually know what the blessing is. Many folks have sworn to me that they want to be blessed. When I ask them what living a blessed life means their reply, more often than not, is a blank stare. It is certainly understandable to want to be blessed or holy. After all, there is a tremendous amount of hype surrounding it, particularly in religious circles.

However, you cannot walk in the blessing or in holiness if you do not know what it means to be blessed, or what it means to be holy. It is nearly impossible to be something in the world when you do not know what it is. Blindly walking through the kingdom of God is an impossibility. *"The light shines in the darkness."* (John 1:5) One must be able to see to pass through the narrow gate.

The same holds true with your faith. How can you walk in faith if you do not know what faith is? It becomes nothing more than a religious exercise, and a source of frustration and mystery if you attempt to connect with God in this manner. You must accomplish what you want, and be who you want to be, on purpose and with understanding.

The word "blessed" in its most common use means "empowered to prosper." Interestingly enough, it may also mean, "happy and fortunate" as less commonly used in Jesus' famous Sermon on the Mount. Personally, I do not object to being either. Empowered, happy, fortunate—whatever. I'll take them all. You know the old saying, "Sometimes it's better to be lucky than good." That is fine with me. Only there is no luck involved when God is present. The blessing *makes* you good. Nevertheless, here is the example that I always give, which folks inevitably seem to have previously misunderstood.

Let's say your light bill is due for $50 but you do not have fifty dollars. You go out to your mailbox and, lo and behold, out of nowhere you find an anonymous check for $50. Is that the blessing of God?

Almost everyone I propose this question to, religious people included, answers in the affirmative. "Yes, John, that is the blessing of

God." I then always have the unfortunate appointment as some sort of "Grim Reaper," or as the always unpopular bringer of bad news, to inform them that they are wrong, their concept of God and His blessing is wrong, and that is why they have been continually frustrated and unable to walk in the goodness of Almighty God. Understandably, many religious people are not real eager to accept the insight I have just shared. It can be quite difficult to unlearn a lifetime of bad, or perhaps even, erroneous habits—especially religious ones.

Their idea, and perhaps even yours, of both faith and the blessing of God is Him simply materializing "things" from thin air and raining them down upon whomever He randomly chooses. Furthermore, an even more twisted idea of the blessing is the belief that God just arbitrarily answers one prayer over another. Perhaps He likes you more than me. Really?! All this produces is envy, jealousy, and the misconception that God "works in mysterious ways." Have you forgotten that God works according to covenant? Receiving the blessing through faith is one of the major aspects of being in covenant with God. We must learn the rules of God culture.

Even worse, is the continual misperception and individual condemnation that I must not be praying right. That used to be my misunderstanding. With that as our misguided perception, it is no wonder that many of us may become dismayed and frustrated, unable to receive anything from the Lord. Apart from what we discussed earlier there are really only four rules to prayer, (1) Ask, (2) Ask in Jesus' name, (3) Ask according to scripture, and (4) Until the answer either materializes, or God says, "No," keep on asking. Everything else is a matter of God's timing.

In truth, the person receiving the $50 check in the above example has just experienced "grace" and not "blessing." Grace actually means "unmerited favor." The word "unmerited" means, "of no merit," which broken down even further means you did not have to *do* anything to obtain it. It was not performance-based. You did not earn it. It was simply given as an act of kindness, mercy and love. At most, it could have been a *result* or manifestation of the blessing, but in this instance it is most certainly grace.

Grace, by the way, is the only means of obtaining salvation.

> *"For by **grace** you have been saved **through faith** and that not of yourselves; **it was the gift of God**, not of works, lest anyone should boast."*
> **—Ephesians 2:8-9**

Your salvation is free. It is the gift of God's grace and is unmerited except for the saving work of Jesus Christ. He earned it. You cannot. Your only obligation is to believe that God and His Word are truthful. Salvation can only be obtained by faith.

I would encourage you to remember this principle: Your salvation is free but you must *work* for your blessing. If the Scripture says that you are saved by grace *through faith*, but you do not know what faith or grace is, how can you be saved? What is there to stop you from falling away? How would you even know that you fell away if you don't know what you don't know? Without first understanding these concepts of grace and faith, you will be like chaff blown by the wind. You will waiver in whatever direction the winds of the world blow you. This is why people backslide, which means you have abandoned God culture, albeit sometimes unknowingly.

In truth, you can be saved without much understanding at all. God is infinitely merciful. The breakdown occurs in living a life of righteousness and leading others to the way of salvation. How can you fulfill the Great Commission of making disciples of all nations if you yourself are not one?

Drilling Down

Let's move on to a second example so that you may gain understanding. Let's go back to the light bill that was due. You still have the same issue. The lights are still out. You still do not have the money to turn them back on and there was no check in the mail. This time, when you get to work your boss asks you to help him with a project and you are the only one with the skill-set to do it. Your reward will be, voila, fifty dollars in cold hard cash. Was this the blessing?

By now people are usually beginning to catch on and answer, "Yes, that's definitely it!" They often times begin strutting whimsically with *Moves Like Jagger*, believing they have the problem licked. By the way, that is not necessarily a compliment. I once heard the late great comedian George Carlin equate Mick Jagger's "dancing" to a chicken on acid. If you watch him closely it is a pretty accurate description.

Anyway, so while seeming to have a bit of a mean streak and not wanting to let people off the hook too easily, I begin to test their understanding by replying with that dreaded one word question that no student ever wants to hear, "Why?" Once again I am greeted with blank stares and deflated egos. Testing one's understanding, by the way, is of eternal importance.

> *"When anyone hears the word of the kingdom, **and does not understand it**, then the wicked one comes **and snatches away** what was sown in his heart. This is he who received seed by the wayside."*
> **—Matthew 13:19**

Understanding is what determines whether or not you are a "wayside" Christian. In Matthew thirteen's version of Jesus' famous *Parable of the Sower*, Jesus describes four incidents that will occur in the lives of all those hearing the Word of God. In one of the instances, the hearer gladly receives the Word but fails to gain understanding. Immediately that Word, and the grace and blessings within it, is snatched away by the enemy of our souls, Satan. For those unwilling to pursue understanding, being snatched away is the result one hundred percent of the time.

Most of us, however, have a somewhat instinctive understanding of faith and either cannot quite define it or simply feel that I am trying to trick them—and oftentimes I am. It helps people learn. So hands slowly and reluctantly ascend. I, without a doubt, am enjoying the discomfort as voices sheepishly toss out the reply, "Because God gave you the ability?" Yeah, it is usually in the form of a question and not a definitive reply as it should be. Like many of you, confidence is the first hurdle upon entry into God culture. That is understandable.

I then slap the podium or triumphantly declare into the microphone, "Yes, because God gave you the ability!" That is what the blessing of God is. It is God-given ability, talent, or however you may want to categorize it, but it is an ability to get the job done.

Sometimes it is ingrained within you as a "gift," so to speak, like a "gifted" athlete or musician, and sometimes it is a temporary ability, or something acquired through learning in order to accomplish the needed task at that specific moment in time. It may be a talent that you have always known about but have never acknowledged, like my innate ability to play the drums, or you may even be left wondering, "How did I do that?" Like my innate ability to play the drums under the influence, or "anointing," of the Holy Spirit. As Rush Limbaugh so boldly declares, the blessing is "Talent on loan from God." Can you now see the difference between grace and blessing? Excellent, let's move on.

Evidence of God

That leads us back to the issue of faith. This is the big one because it is your faith that allows you to operate in every area of God's kingdom. Without faith, you cannot walk in the blessing, obtain the favor of God, please God, or be holy and righteous. You cannot even receive salvation.

Let's continue our discussion of faith by looking at one of my favorite faith passages in all of the Scriptures. I will begin with this one because it is what I most often hear quoted, or more accurately stated, misquoted. I also believe it is one of the most confusing because, without understanding, it leaves us looking for something we can never find.

Let's say I am speaking with someone regarding their faith. Quite often people are struggling in this area, so I ask the question, "Well, what is faith?" After the blank stare and stammering lips, I am most often graced with the following response, "Brother John, '*Faith is the substance of things hoped for . . ..*'" Someone who really knows the Word of God will promptly add, "*..it is the evidence of things not seen.*" (Hebrews 11:1)

Most people think they have nailed this one because they have quoted me a Scripture passage that has the phrase "faith is," attached to it. They naturally believe they have grasped this one fully without ever truly analyzing what they have just regurgitated. Yet they are still struggling mightily in this area. How can that be?

The answer is that in reality all they have done is quote me a Scripture passage, because when I ask, "So what does that mean?" I am greeted with the same stammering tongue followed by a blank stare as I was when I asked about being blessed. Believe me; their lips are not quivering because they are speaking in tongues either. I am talking utter confusion here.

Here is the real problem; as human beings, we like to naturalize everything. That makes sense. God created us to live in the natural realm. It is our domain. Of course we feel comfortable here. Therefore, often times our beliefs never progress past what we can see, taste, hear, feel, smell or touch. This Scripture is quite easily naturalized because of the terms "substance" and "evidence." Therefore, we begin looking for the natural substance of something that may not exist in our natural domain. "Just because you can't see it doesn't mean it isn't there. You can't see the future, yet you know it will come; you can't see the air, yet you continue to breathe."
—**Claire London**

Have you ever tried to find the substance of God here on planet Earth? You may have a better chance of finding Big Foot! Heck, I don't know if *he's* real or not. He might be. At least we have a few foot prints, a couple questionable video's and some unidentified DNA—and don't forget about *"Finding Bigfoot,"* which although is completely mindless, can be a pretty darn entertaining television show.

God, however, has left us no natural substance at all. Have you ever tried to provide someone with the *evidence* of God's existence? Good luck with that one! Try converting someone to Christianity from evidence. I have been trying for years. Both the atheist and the religious simply throw their hands over their ears and cry, "blah blah blah!" Entering the kingdom of God requires faith. Evidence alone will not cut it.

Yet, we still try. We search for Noah's Ark, the Ark of the Covenant, the spear that pierced Jesus' side, biblical cities, the family of Jesus, and all sorts of artifacts so we can just have some tangible evidence. We need some substance. We look to and continuously test the Shroud of Turin. We even search for evidence of ancient aliens.

When we do not find anything we turn to so-called "evidence" that God is a hoax. We begin believing novels such as *The Da Vinci Code* to be factual works of history rather than the deceptive fictional nonsense they truly are, and are intended to be. We turn to the gospel of Thomas as evidence of inconsistency, while we are totally and completely ignorant of how to genuinely authenticate a document for accuracy. Don't forget the big lie. Evolution. Believing that nonsense requires even more faith than believing God.

Scientifically speaking, meaning the scientific method must be observable, testable and repeatable, there is no evidence of Darwinian evolution. Firstly, we cannot observe what occurred millions of years ago and the so called evidence of the fossil record is fragmented. We do not even know if there was a primordial stew. It is merely a guess—and an uneducated one when you look at the real evidence.

If you take an honest look at it, and where and when life began to prosper, and how species appear and disappear, the fossil record provides far greater evidence for creation than evolution. Similarly, there has never been an observation of the type of species change that results in a new "kind," to use the biblical terminology, meaning an unrelated and sexually incompatible organism or species. Think about it, grass only produces species of grass, flowers produce flowers, trees produce trees.

Similarly, when we observe animal reproduction, dogs produce dogs, cats produce cats, and even when you think about primate species, chimps only produce other chimpanzees. Have you ever witnessed the birth of human from a chimp, our "closest relative?" Never has any primate produced anything other than its interrelated and sexually compatible kind—and all that from a single cell that crawled out of a primordial stew that no one can claim ever existed? With that in mind, who is really operating by blind faith, the worshipper of science or the worshipper of Yahweh?

What *has* been observed, tested and repeated in experiments such as Mendl's E-coli and the fruit fly, and even in natural situations, such as the isolation of the Stickleback fish, is that kinds can only reproduce with, and thus, produce similar kinds, just like Genesis chapter one states. Mendl's E-coli has merely evolved (adapted is the more appropriate term. The incredible ability of adaptation has been implanted by God within the DNA of every organism.) into another related species of E-coli. The fruit fly experiments have only produced other fruit fly's and the Stickleback fish have remained Stickleback fish. Therefore, the scientific method only and always observes, tests and repeats what we find in the Book of Genesis. The scientific method points right back to God.

In reference to religious artifacts, a quick search of the Scriptures will confirm that the Shroud of Turin, for example is a hoax. Don't get mad at me, especially all of you Roman Catholic folks out there! I know you want to believe, but the Word of God proves it is fraudulent, meaning that it cannot be the image of either the crucified or the risen Christ. What is more important to you, the truth or a lie? Here is some truly substantive evidence for you.

*"Then Simon Peter came, following him, and went into the tomb; and he saw the linen cloths lying, **and the handkerchief that had been around His head, not lying with the linen cloths**, but folded together in a place by itself . . . ."*
—John 20:6-7

Now read that one more time and then picture the Shroud of Turin. Hmmm . . . how many pieces is it? That is correct; it is one long piece. There is no separation between Jesus' head and torso. Yet, the above scripture clearly states that there were at least two pieces: one wrapped around His head and at least one more for His body. ("Cloths" can be either singular or plural.)

Now you are faced with a choice and *you* must decide what to believe. Do you believe in the shroud or do you believe the Word of God? Do you believe the natural evidence or do you believe the Spiritual evidence? That is the real issue.

You will find shortly that this is a pivotal question in your faith walk with God. Do you believe what you can see or do you believe the Word of God? The substance of God and the physical evidence of God do not exist in the natural realm. He will never leave His fingerprints at the scene. We cannot test Him for DNA. Therefore, the unconverted man has been, and will continue to search forever with no avail. It is only in the realm of His Spirit that you can ever find God. Once you believe that *"He is,"* (Hebrews 11:6) you will find that the processes of nature, as well as, the natural order, can only have been implemented by Him.

Hence, there *is* overwhelming evidence of God's existence, but you must train yourself as to where and how to look for it. Once you have confirmed your faith, you will find Him every place you look.

True Faith

Let's return to this popular faith Scripture.

> *"Now faith is the substance of things hoped for, it is the evidence of things not seen."*
> **—Hebrews 11:1**

The problem is that this makes you *feel* like you should be able to see, taste, feel or touch it. Let's focus for a minute on the words "substance," "things," "hope" and "evidence." It is here that we will find true faith.

The word "substance" is translated from the Greek word *hupostasis*. It means a "setting under," meaning a support. Let's build this out. Let's insert the true meaning of the translated words. Now we have, *Faith is the setting under*, or, *Faith is the support of . . .*

The next word of importance is "things." It comes from the Greek word *pragma*. It is most of the English word pragmatic which means to be practical. We must learn to be practical, that is, to develop the ability to put into practice, or apply our faith. In that, I mean that we must learn to actually use it.

This does not mean we are to reduce our expectations. In fact, we should raise them because practical faith means applied faith, and, perhaps better stated, active faith in practice. This begins to give you something of real substance, which can be counted on no matter what the situation says.

The Greek word *pragma* means "a deed," "an affair," or "an object." Now we have *faith is the support of your deeds, affairs and /or objects . . . .* As you can see, understanding breeds tangibility.

Let's move on to the word "hope." It is from the word *elpizo*. It means to "expect or confide" and/or "to trust." "Hope," no matter where you find it in the biblical text, always has this same meaning. It is a trusted expectation. Now we have: *Now faith is the support of the deeds, affairs, and/or objects you are expecting and/or trusting for . . . .* Trusting who for?

Finally we have the word "evidence." The Greek word is *elegchos*. Elegchos means "conviction." So what is faith? Let's put it all together. *"Now faith is the support of the deeds, affairs, and or objects, you are expecting and trusting for, it is the conviction of receiving those deeds, affairs and/or objects you cannot yet see."*

Do not forget that what we are discussing is Spiritual, and, therefore, such things can only be recognized and understood in the realm of Spirit. Earlier we discussed how God always appoints in the Spirit before He manifests in the natural. This is your direct application of how God creates in your own personal life through the process known as faith. Faith is a process, not an instant microwave oven. Let's continue.

We are left with one last word, "Faith!" The word "faith" only appears twice in the Old Testament. In Deuteronomy, it refers to *"children in whom there is no faith."* You will see in a moment why that is accurate, and in Habakkuk, it refers to *"the just living by their faith."*

Note that the usage of the word faith is virtually the same throughout the entire New Testament with the exception of four incidents in the gospels where it refers to those of little faith. It comes from the Greek word *pistis* and it means "persuasion." Think about your atheist friends in that regard. Because they are those of little faith (atheism requires a lower form of faith than being persuaded by Yahweh) they are persuaded only by what they can wrap their natural minds around.

If you put it all together, you have "*Now what* (or Who) *you are persuaded by* (or believe) *is what supports the deeds, affairs and/or objects you are expecting* **and** *trusting for, it is the conviction of receiving those deeds, affairs and/or objects which you cannot yet see.*"

The million dollar question is, are you persuaded by God and His Word, or are you persuaded by the circumstances of life? If you answer honestly, you will discover where your faith lies. Immersing yourself in His Word will rectify the problem.

Crystal Blue Persuasion

Abraham had a similar problem. To solve it, God completely immersed Abraham in Himself. Check out the fruit of God's labor:

> "*Therefore it is of faith that it might be according to grace, so the promise might be sure to all the seed, not only to those who are of the law, but also to those who are of the faith of Abraham who is the father of us all (as it is written, 'I have made you a father of many nations') in the presence of Him whom* **he believed—God***, who gives life to the dead* **and calls those things which do not exist as though they did***; who contrary to hope,* **in hope believed***, so that he became the father of many nations,* **according to what was spoken***, 'So shall your descendants be.'*
>
> *And not being weak in faith, he did not consider his own body, already dead (since he was about a hundred years old), and the deadness of Sarah's womb. He did not waver at the promise of God through unbelief, but was strengthened in faith, giving glory*

*to God, **and being fully persuaded** that what He had promised He was also able to perform."*
—Romans 4:16-21

As a result, a baby was born to a one hundred year old man and a ninety-year old woman, and later on, the Messiah, the Lamb of God who takes away the sin of the world, was born from his lineage. All because Abraham believed that what God said was true. He was fully persuaded by God (Romans 4:21) and God's Word became the support of Abraham's life. That is faith in its most simplistic form.

Born Again Believers

Therefore, think about it this way. The Word of God is your substance. It is your support, and you must make it your conviction in order to enter it as evidence. To live by faith you must be persuaded by God. Do you remember a little earlier I stated faith is what allows you to walk in the blessing? It is also what allows you to obtain favor, to be righteous, and to be holy.

Isn't that exactly what we see in Abraham in the above Scripture? Since God shows no partiality (Acts 10:34), when you sell out to God the same way Abraham did, and you become so fully persuaded that you will do anything He tells you and stop wavering in unbelief, He will do the same for you. However, that requires work. It requires diligence in learning, living and doing the Word of God.

I know what you are thinking and you are wrong. "I could never be like that. There is no way that I could have faith like Abraham. I do not even know if I believe God *did* all those things." I understand completely. I used to be the same way.

Let me encourage you with this: we are not *born* believers in God's Word. We become *born again* believers through God and His Word. It is a process that takes time, patience and diligence, but it always produces faith. We are all born with the ability to believe. In fact, I would submit that it is impossible for a human being not to believe in something. Heck, the fact that you do not believe in anything actually means you have the ability to believe. Denial of God is the belief that He does not exist. You cannot help but believe even when you do not believe. We were created as believing beings.

Believing the Word of God is a skill that must be acquired. It is a decision that must be made and one must be willing to diligently pursue the Word of God in order to develop faith. To believe or not to believe, that is the question? You can have the faith of Abraham. You can have the faith of Jesus Christ of Nazareth if you truly desire it. God shows *no* partiality, not even to Jesus.

In fact, Jesus' fate was even worse than yours. God held Himself completely accountable for your sin. That is just who He is. Remember, Abraham's faith did not only deliver him from a crisis in the "now." By siring the future generations that led to the Messiah, his faith delivered *you* from the crisis of "forever!"

CHAPTER 7

More Faith

As a child one of my favorite games was Cowboys and Indians. Oh wait—quick—back space! I don't think I can say that anymore. Whew! I just nearly blew my budding career as an author. Nowadays it's "Cowboys and Native Americans." I suppose I should have learned that from all the controversy over the Washington Redskins? I find it comical that the liberal watch dog groups have such an immense problem with the Washington Redskins nickname and logo. As they say on ESPN, C'mon man! It's a football team for goodness sakes. For seventy years it was harmless, and now all of a sudden the name of a football team is the cause of society's woes?

Is a football team the reason our Native American brothers and sisters are struggling so intensely with poverty, alcoholism and drug abuse? Or is it the fact that the same leaders who cry foul, hide the fact that the reservations have relegated them to a miserable existence—cut off from society and unable to assimilate into the nation whose forefathers brutally stole their land and killed their people. But that's okay. The government provides them with cheese and a host of other processed foods that ravage the parts of their body's the drugs and alcohol have left behind. Is it okay to say that? It it too offensive and politically incorrect? Perhaps you are unwilling to even believe it.

Here is a message to all you wolves in sheep's clothing, I mean political activists. Reparations are not the answer. Wrongs need to be righted by encouraging unity with our Native American brethren while providing them with equal opportunity through hard work and education. The same holds true with our African American brothers and sisters, and with whomever the hateful illusion of race has trampled upon. Division only perpetuates racism and let's be real, changing the logo of a football team is not the answer. It is simply fueling a fire that was previously dormant. The emblem on a football helmet is not the cause of what occurred in Ferguson, Missouri or Baltimore, Maryland. Isolation never leads to prosperity—just prolonged chaos, suffering and pain.

Bombs are blowing up all over the planet. Children are starving and ebola, along with a multitude of other drug resistant diseases are on the verge of wiping out the world's population— the masses are going to hell, literally, and the name of a football team is what people are worried about? Is it just me or can you too see the lunacy of the new insanely politically correct normal?

So what is it now, Cowboys and Native Americans? Early American Law Men and Sacajawea? Try fitting that on the team jersey. I'm confused! Can I say cowboy? Does it now have to be Cow-man or Cow-woman—is it Cow-person? Thank God I didn't forget the dash. Is Cowgirl disparaging? How about Cowpoke?

Then there are the Cowboy's cheerleaders . . . How degrading is that? Women who actually cheer for men? Is that even legal anymore? I am amazed they can still brandish the costume. Actually, with the direction American culture is heading, I am surprised they are still wearing a costume. Nudity, pornography and adultery seem to be just fine with the new breed of morality. Just don't say Redskin or label immoral behavior as sinful.

Ah, the heck with it! It was Cowboys and Indians, and yes, we carried a cap gun, perhaps even two—in a holster—with pretend bullets. We even had the audacity to point them at each other and pull the pretend trigger. Can you imagine? We would even throw rocks at one another on occasion. As stupid as it is, we would probably be charged with felony assault in today's world— and be charged as adults. Don't even get me started on Roman Candles, fire crackers and M-80's. That is where the real fun was. Have you ever seen an M-80 blow the lid off a garbage can? To a twelve year old it is simply glorious.

Nowadays, and since children cannot have pretend guns, they buy the real ones and shoot each other over a pair of sneakers. Meanwhile, the kids who actually learn to shoot with their parents seem to lack this deviant behavior. Hmm, maybe having two traditional parents is not such a terrible thing after all.

To make matters worse, we called each other paleface. That might land you in court today. I wonder if today's children have ever heard the term, "paleface." I bet they know the word "lawsuit" though. Just ask the Redskins. The smart ones might even know the word "litigation."

Hold on—back space again . . . I can't say that either—that some kids are smarter than others. Little Johnny might need therapy due to the resulting inferiority complex he develops when he hears he is not the smartest child on the planet. Then the government will have to pay for his Xanax, or his girlfriends birth control—*and* the out of wedlock child born into the vicious circle of welfare due to daddy's debilitating mental illness caused by keeping score in a little league baseball game.

Think about it, little Johnny has never lost a baseball game. They have stopped keeping score. If he knew he lost his two daddy's would sue the little league for causing his depression. My goodness! How will our nation's young people ever learn how to handle adversity? I have news for you, little Johnny most likely is not going to make it to the European Soccer League either. Then what will you tell him?

Excuses, Excuses!

Anyway, I did not mean to digress but I had to get that off my chest. To begin this chapter, lets use our God given gift of imagination and take a short trip back to the good old day's of childhood. What was the appeal of Cowboys and Indians? As children, we had this glorified perception of "The Old Wild West." What made it so appealing? Wasn't it the shootouts, duals and bank robberies? Is it just me, or was it the excitement of the nearly lawless Wild Western society?

I can still hear the spurs jingling and the clapping of hooves on the dusty ground as I rode into town atop the saddle of my trusted steed. I can feel and smell my imaginary leather or suede vest and Cowboy boots. I can hear the spinning of the gun barrel and the shuffling of the cards as the bartender slides a glass of whiskey down the bar. In my imagination it all seemed so free.

There was a major problem with this paradigm, however. As appealing as it may have seemed it was misguided. It implanted the wrong ideas into my psyche. Some of which I unconsciously attempted to live out.

Whoops! Hold on for just one more second. I have to back space again. I must apologize because that was an excuse. Do you see how modern culture has taught nearly all of us to shift the blame? It could not have been *my* fault, could it? I didn't really want to smoke that joint. The peer pressure got the best of me. It must have been a childhood game that caused me to err. Perhaps my mom did not love me enough.

In truth, I did not even realize I was shifting the blame until quite some time after I had originally written that introduction. Such a misguided perception of reality is nothing new. Humanity has been blinded by sin. Adam did the same thing when he blamed Eve for giving him the forbidden fruit in the Garden of Eden. Certainly it was not his fault that he disobeyed God and ate it.

> *"Then the man said, 'The woman whom **You gave to be with me**, she gave me of the tree, and I ate.'"*
> **—Genesis 3:12**

Can you imagine blaming God for your self-induced quandaries? As silly as Adam's statement sounds, we do it all the time. We act as if God rescinds our free will and forces our hand. That is the other guy, folks. Satan is the bully, not God. Yahweh patiently awaits our return, even as we continually turn our backs on Him. I guess some things never change—the blame-game being foremost on the list.

In truth, I can only blame myself and my licentious nature for the "issues" I encountered early in life. The sad reality is that before I made Jesus the Lord of my life, *I was Lord of my life*. I was quite simply a "normal" human being corrupted by sin—no different than every other human being born of a woman, with only one exception.

I had not yet experienced the regeneration of my spirit, resulting in my becoming the righteousness of God in Christ. Therefore, it was, and quite honestly sometimes still is, my corrupt and rebellious nature to turn from God. And, yes, I actually *did* mean to digress earlier. In an effort to cover up my tirade, I lied and said it was not my intention to rant. But it was. My intention was to jump atop my soap box and rant and rave until someone, somewhere, somehow is willing to listen. Thank God for Jesus Christ. As you can now see, just like you, I am hopelessly lost without Him.

Transparency

I had to let you peer into my soul in order to broach this vital topic. Therefore, I would like to ask the following question. What is it that defines right and wrong? Our society, in particular the younger generations, does not seem to know anymore. Not only are we are back to sex, drugs and rock n roll, we have recently added rampant homosexuality accompanied by the normalization of transsexuality to the list of debaucheries! To make matters worse, we do not just condone it, we glorify it.

As recently as the day before this chapter was penned, my then sixteen year old daughter came home with the latest news from her high school. It was not how well her track team had done in the meet, although they had qualified for the national tournament. That is quite a feat in itself. Her relay team ultimate went on to finish third in the nation. Unfortunately, this incredible accomplishment was immediately overshadowed by the news that a young girl had performed oral sex on a young man in the athletic training room. For many of you, this may not seem so unusual, which in itself is a symptom of how far gone our culture is, but guess how they got caught? The young *woman* was overheard bragging about what has now become a shameless act.

In my day it was the guys doing the bragging . . . and usually lying about it. These days, many young woman are obtaining their "good" reputation based upon what they "put out." My how we have fallen!

I was shocked to learn that one of the high school's in a neighboring town of mine is now known as "Heroine High." Really? I thought that drug went out in the sixties. Sadly, it is back with a vengeance along with a host of new drugs as well. I actually heard very recently that some folks actually smoke embalming fluid! How desperate must one be to smoke embalming fluid?

As a father I need not tell you how sad and twisted society has become, especially if you have ever seen such incredible potential annihilated by drug addiction, prostitution or even teen-age pregnancy. God's laws on morality are out the window and strewn about the ground by the god we call progress. Just solve your "problem" with the abortion pill. All it takes is a dollar, a dream and an Obama phone. What ever happened to hard work, integrity and morality? What happened to Chastity? Oh, never mind, she's Chaz now.

As young children, however, and perhaps even still as adults, we seem to fall on one of two sides. You were either the law man or the outlaw. The appeal of Cowboys and Na . . . I mean Indians, was its inherent good versus evil message. Although many of us wanted to be the outlaw, we understood the line it drew in society, both legal and moral—laws that define what is right and wrong within a civilization.

As we begin this second chapter on faith, it is imperative for us to gain an understanding of God's law. Without it we have no basis for faith. In it, we find the definition of what is right and wrong in God's eyes. In essence, we learn both the definition and truth of sin. That seems to be the crux of our modern day dilemma. The better part of humanity seems to have excused their way out of truth.

This beautifully powerful, seemingly insignificant one syllable word, sin, has been deleted from Western culture. As a result, the disease known as deception has begun to fester. It is actively spreading all over the globe. In order to overcome this ailment we must peer into the purpose of God's holy law. Although we will not do an extensive study on the law, let's at least lay the foundation.

Foundations

What purpose then does the law serve? It was added because of transgressions, **till the Seed should come to whom the promise was made**; *appointed through angels by the hand of a mediator. Now a mediator does not mediate for one, but God is one.*

Is the law then against the promises of God? Certainly not! For if there had been a law given which could have given life, truly righteousness would have been by the law. But the Scripture has confined all under sin, that the promise by faith in Jesus Christ might be given to **all those** *who believe.* **But before faith came** *we were kept under guard by the law,* **kept for the faith** *which would* **afterward** *be revealed. Therefore the law was our tutor to* **bring us to Christ**, *that we might be justified by faith.* **But after faith has come** *we are no longer under a tutor.*
—Galatians 3:19-25

Wow! This is one of those sections of scripture that absolutely blows my mind. As mentioned in the previous chapter, there is a reason the word "faith" only appears twice in the Old Testament. Before we go there, however, let us have a brief discussion regarding the foundation of the three major world religions, the law.

Have you ever noticed how difficult, if not impossible it is to keep the Ten Commandments, let alone the whole law, which is commonly known as the Pentateuch, or the first five books of the Christian Bible or Jewish Torah? Make no mistake; "*Whoever shall keep the whole law, and yet stumble in one, he is guilty of all.*" (James 2:10)

The phrase, "*keep the whole law,*" refers to being bound to it. In other words, you have based your spiritual justification upon upholding the law. Think about the following question; In your entire life have you ever broken the law? Have you ever not loved the

Lord with your *whole* heart? Have you ever placed something in your life ahead of Him? I think we have all been guilty of that at some time or another, perhaps even right now as I pen this composition. Well guess what that means? You have placed another god before Him. We cannot even get past commandment number one without falling into judgment.

Have you ever stolen anything? Not even a pen, or a paperclip? Perhaps you have even justified yourself by believing you were entitled to it. What is a couple of pennies to such a grand corporation anyway? Or, my parents will never miss it, it is only a couple dollars. If you have, even just once, you are guilty.

Have you ever lusted after a man or woman other than your husband or wife? Guilty! How many lies have you told in your life? I guarantee that you can not even count them all. We are only on commandment number four and we have already obliterated them all. In just four commandments we have discovered that left to our own devices we are nothing more than a bunch of lying, thieving, adulterous, idolaters! This, in case you are wondering, takes up less than a half a page of the Bible. The law contains the entire first five books which encompass about two hundred-fifty pages. Can't you see that you are hopelessly lost?

Defining Sin

So where does that leave us? Are we all tragically condemned to hell? Certainly not! Just like Congress, God left a loophole in the law, for lack of a better term. In order to find it we must understand the purpose of the law and why it was implemented. The law was never intended to save mankind. It does not have the power to do so. All any law can do is define right and wrong behavior.

"Therefore by the deeds of the law no flesh will be justified in His sight . . . for by the law is the knowledge of sin."
—Roman 2:20

The law was given simply to define what sin is and is not. The law was designed to bring you to the point of knowing you need a Savior. The law only has the power to condemn. It cannot save. Therefore, by peering into our own frailty through the law, it becomes abundantly clear that we are dead in our trespasses without Jesus Christ.

That is why Lot's two daughters were able to get away with seducing him, their own father, and not be judged guilty of sin. Since the law had not yet been delivered to mankind there was no definition of sin, and, therefore, no transgression or condemnation.

That is not to say that sin was not present. We know sin was present from the very beginning—even in the Garden of Eden. Adam and Eve had their own version of the law in what God had commanded them. I am not saying that Lot's daughters did not sin by committing such a heinous act. They certainly did, but since the law had not been defined they could not be held accountable. That would be akin to not telling your children the household rules and spanking them every time they broke one.

Furthermore, since I do not want you attempting to place yourself in this same category of ignorance, they had no way of obtaining God's law. It was yet to be dictated. Therefore, they did not have access to the knowledge contained in the Bible, or Torah.

The law brings definition to what is right and wrong in God's eyes. It defines sin. In essence, it brings sin to life.

*"I was alive once without the law, but when the commandment came, **sin revived** and I died.*
—Romans 7:9

Therefore, the law does not have the power to bring eternal life or to forgive sin. To the contrary, since *"the wages of sin is death,"* (Romans 6:23) it can only produce the opposite effect. The law produces the knowledge of sin, which procreates accountability, which judges one guilty, and thus, effectuates death. (Romans 7:13) So what is its purpose?

> *"Therefore **the law was our tutor** to bring us to Christ, that we might be **justified by faith.**"*
> **—Galatians 3:24**

Just like everything else contained in the Word of God the ultimate end of the law is to bring us to faith in Jesus Christ. In other words, it was designed to show us that we can never be justified on our own, and that it is impossible for us to be righteous in God's eyes according to our own power or perceived goodness. *"There is none who does good, no, not even one."* (Psalm 14:3) Therefore, it was to teach us, since that is what a tutor does, that we all need a Savior.

Self-Righteousness

When we read the law we should never see our own righteousness, or feel justified in ourselves and our works. This was the problem Jesus had with the Pharisees. They never peered into the mirror of the law and applied it to their own lives. They judged themselves superior in the sight of God since the law had been given to *their* ancestors. After all, they were God's chosen people weren't they?

They believed the abhorrent lie that the spiritual authority, or so called Godly social status of their ancestor's was a free ticket to their justification. Do not judge them for this. We do the same thing when believing whatever ignorance our parents, priests, mullah's, rabbi's or any so called "spiritual authority" jam down our throats—when we just swallow whatever we are spoon-fed without ever peering into the truth of God's Word to discover where such doctrines originated, or if they are even based upon the law of God.

That is the difference between Jesus Christ and every other prophet who has ever walked the face of the Earth. Not only is Jesus Christ the basis of the law, He is the fulfillment thereof. I challenge you to name one other prophet that can make this claim.

In turn, the Pharisees, just like we, never judged *themselves* upon breaking not only their own rules, but God's rules in spirit and in deed. They had learned the letter of the law but never came to its true spiritual meaning that they, just like we, are a bunch of filthy rags, and are forever lost unless God is, or was, to do something about it. Therefore, they plunged into the sins of arrogance, apathy and hypocrisy. They chose to remain blind to the true purpose of God's holy law. Now, right now, hold your place, put down the book and go look in the mirror. Without Christ peering back at you, you are no different than the person described above.

> *"Let not your heart be troubled. You believe in God. Believe in Jesus also."*
> **—John 14:1**

Thank God that He understands our dilemma. In fact, it is even better than that. He experienced our dilemma first hand. He is acquainted with every temptation, every thought, and every sin your flesh can conceive of.

Therefore, as an act of love and mercy, He made a way to deliver not just the the Pharisees, but the whole of mankind, you and I included. All we need to do is believe. However, we cannot believe in any old thing, or in any manner we choose. The Lord went through great pains, literally, to pave the way to salvation. Therefore, we must enter through *"the narrow gate,"* (Matthew 7:13-14) according to His way and in agreement with His plan of salvation. That, of course, is through faith in Jesus Christ.

Fulfilling Faith

As I began to touch on earlier, there is a reason the word "faith" only appears twice in the Old Testament. Jesus Christ is *"the author and finisher of our faith.* (Hebrews 12:2) Therefore, before Christ came in the flesh, true faith was still a mystery which was yet to be revealed. That is why we read above that, *"**before faith came** we were kept under guard by the law."* Belief in Jesus Christ is where true faith begins.

In the previous chapter we defined faith as believing that what God has already said is true. According to His Word, which is the only place we can find what was said, and in turn the only place we can find truth, He proclaimed Jesus Christ to be the Messiah, and the only means of salvation. Without believing this eternal truth there is no faith. In fact, all you have is, "A false expectation of the wrong information." —**Kenneth Copeland** Jesus Christ *is* our faith because He is the living embodiment of the Word of God. *"In the beginning was the Word, and the Word was with God and the Word was God . . . and the Word became flesh and dwelt among us . . ."* (John 1:1 and 14)

In actuality the letter "f" should be capitalized in Hebrews 12:2 as Jesus is our faith. Hence, before the manifestation of Christ on earth, and thus in our personal lives, there is no other true means of obtaining faith. He *is* the Word where our faith lies. Both the Old and the New Testaments agree and witness of Him. We find the manifestation of Jesus walking in the Garden of Eden, in Messianic prophecy, and manifested as both the Angel of God and the Shekhinah glory within the Old Testament. The New Testament simply fulfills these typologies. Therefore, the truth of Jesus Christ is authenticated by the law of witnesses required by Jewish law.

A Ravenous Wolf

The principle of witnesses states, "*One witness shall not rise against a man concerning any iniquity or any sin that he commits; by the mouth of two or three witnesses the matter shall be established.*" (Deuteronomy 19:15)

Additionally, "*Whosoever is deserving of death shall be put to death on the testimony of two or three witnesses; he shall not be put to death on the testimony of one witness.*" (Deuteronomy 17:6)

It would be a mistake to consider this only in regard to sentencing one found guilty of physical murder. It is also the basis of judgment. God will hold you spiritually accountable to the same law. Those pronounced guilty will be sentenced to spiritual death as well. The reason this is not just important, but eternal, is that of the three major world religions, only the Q'ran disagrees with the witness of the identity of Jesus Christ. Judaism, which is based upon the Old Testament, foretells of the coming Messiah, and in Jesus Christ we find its fulfillment.

Since the result of denying God is sin, which we have already learned can only lead to death, whoever denies the true God will be deserving of spiritual death. Remember though, according to the law referenced above, there must be at least two witnesses to establish the truth. Therefore, of the religions based upon Mosaic law, it is only the Q'ran that denies the deity of Christ. According to Deuteronomy 17 and 19, Jesus Christ alone is the laws fulfillment leading to eternal life, and Islam can only produce spiritual death since it is in denial of the aforementioned law.

Therefore, if you are a Muslim reading this, or you are a Christian in the Muslim world, disregard your fellow Muslims who are telling you that you will go to hell if you leave Islam for Jesus. They have no basis for truth according to their own law, but even more importantly, it is according to Gods law, which has been revealed within the laws of Moses. In it, only Jesus Christ qualifies as the fulfillment of the law and, therefore, only in Jesus Christ can humanity obtain eternal life. So stand strong, no matter what the consequences! (Ephesians 6:14) In the end we will rise again.

Think about it, if Allah is Jehovah and he denies the truth of Jesus Christ, he would be in denial of Himself. Since, "*a house divided cannot stand*, (Mark 3:25) it leads us to the truth that Allah cannot be Jehovah since his existence is not based upon the Word of God which testifies of, and is truly in oneness and harmony with Christ the Word. (John 1:1 and 14)

Consequently, faith leading to salvation cannot be obtained through the Q'ran. Islam is ultimately rendered to be devoid of salvation. If this is true, it cannot be denied that Mohammed is a false prophet. Therefore, if Allah ultimately leads us away from Jesus Christ, who is God's only path to salvation, what else can Allah's true identity possibly be? In order to keep my opinion out of it, let us allow the Word of God to answer that question.

> "*Beware of false prophets who come to you in sheep's clothing, but inwardly they are ravenous wolves. **You will know them by their fruits.** Do men gather grapes from thorn bushes or figs from thistles? Even so, every good tree bears good fruit, but a bad tree bears bad fruit. A good tree cannot bear bad fruit, nor can a bad tree bear good fruit. Every tree that does not bear good fruit is cut down and thrown into the fire. **Therefore, by their fruits you will know them.**"*
> **—Matthew 7:15-20**

I am going to ask you a series of questions based upon the above scripture and let you be the judge. This may make you uncomfortable but that is okay. In fact, it is intended to annihilate your comfort zone.

If the fruit does not lead to salvation, and thus the only possible harvest being hell, is it good or bad fruit? If its author only leads us to hell thus producing bad fruit, who must the author be? Now be honest, who can Allah possibly be if he and his prophet can only bear bad fruit? Remember, based upon the above scripture, and what we see as being a natural physical law, you cannot do, or be, both the bearer of good and bad fruit. A bush cannot produce both poison and edible berries. It is either one or the other. So be honest, who is Allah? I submit to you that he is a ravenous wolf. That is my final answer.

Developing Faith

With that settled I will end with this. If you desire to be a person of faith and you aspire to be a person who bears good fruit, you must consider Jesus Christ. He is the Word. He is our faith and "*without faith it is impossible to please Him, for He who comes to God must believe that He is, and He is a rewarder of those who diligently seek Him.*" (Hebrews 11:6-7) Therefore, without Christ it is impossible to please God and without the Word it is impossible to please God.

If you want to develop faith you must develop the Word in your heart. You will never hold on to Him, Christ, the Father, or the Holy Spirit without firmly implanting the Word of God in your heart. Therefore, if Christ is our faith, then the following must be true. No Christ, no faith. No Word, no Christ. No Word, no faith! As stated earlier, without the Word your hope is a false expectation based upon the wrong information. You may have heard it said, "the path to hell is paved with good intentions." Think about that truth. Well intended people will still lead you to hell.

So where does your faith lie? If you said the Word of God you have surmised correctly. Your faith lies within the pages of the Bible.

If that does not motivate you to open it nothing will. You will never recognize His voice without knowing what He might say.

"Now faith comes by hearing, and hearing by the Word of God."
—Romans 10:17

Hearing God

Romans 10:17 has been a widely misunderstood scripture. In fact, I have never heard its true meaning properly interpreted. Faith does not come by hearing the Word of God preached, as nearly every preacher has interpreted it to mean. In order to make that work you have to delete the phrase "and hearing by . . ." so that it simply reads, "Now faith comes by hearing the Word of God." That is not what it says, however. It says, *"Now faith comes by hearing, **and hearing by the Word of God.**"* Additionally, if this interpretation were true, every person that goes to church and hears a sermon every Sunday would have incredible faith. We both know this is not the case.

To the contrary, faith comes by hearing *the voice of* God and seeing His goodness work in your life. No one builds faith by simply going to church on Sunday or by going to Christian conferences and listening to sermon after sermon. All this is good and necessary, but it is not the method for building faith. It is merely an assistant to learning the Word of God.

This distinction must be understood to avoid falling into condemnation. Faith is built by learning the Word of God and then hearing God speak it back to you. *"Faith comes by hearing"* God's voice, obeying what He said, and experiencing victory over your present circumstance. It is knowing the Word of God that empowers you to recognize God's voice when He speaks to you.

God will never contradict His Word. In order to follow His direction you must recognize and understand what He has already spoken and commanded. Do you remember how we defined faith?

Once you have heard, understood, obeyed, and had success, you begin to believe . . . and that is how faith is built, through experience and time spent in God's presence.

Therefore, let us break this scripture down. *"Faith comes by hearing . . ."* By hearing what? Faith comes by hearing God's voice in your heart . . . *"and hearing,"* God's voice, *"by the Word of God,"* which is what He already said. According to this, it is the Word of God that allows you to discern, or hear, Who, or who (small 'w') is speaking to you. Most of us believe it is the voice of God that allows us to discern what is being said. While this is true, it is only the *Word* of God that allows us to discern the *voice* of God.

Consequently, without the Word of God firmly implanted in our hearts it is only a matter of time before someone else speaks to us and we fall into deception. This is fundamentally what became of Eve in the Garden of Eden. She was deceived into responding to a voice that did not belong to God. Her ignorance, coupled with the disobedience of Adam, resulted in the disease of sin being spread to all of mankind, which ultimately lead to death. It was the exact opposite of the fruit produced by faith.

Game Changer

If you want to change the world it is imperative to learn the Word of God. Elections cannot change our current world's circumstances. Political will and political ideology has only been proven to divide mankind. The fruit of sin present in every man is too powerful. Politics can only corrupt. To effect change we must bring Spiritual anarchy to the world's political systems. Change must be Spiritual in nature. In fact, it must be of and by the Spirit, who is love personified. Neither nations, governments, religions, nor even a single human being can be changed through political ideology. Only faith can change the world.

If you would like to have the faith of Abraham, the Apostle Paul, or even Jesus Christ, learn the Word of God. Twelve ordinary men who followed one extraordinary Savior have brought billions to salvation and influenced every cultural aspect of the entire world . . . and we are not yet finished. Time has not run out.

Over the past two thousand years Jesus has called His disciples one at a time. Each disciple has accepted their responsibility by faith one at a time. Now He is calling you. Do you want to show your faith? The Son is up and the fish are biting. The true disciples have cast there lines and faith in Jesus Christ and the Word of God is the chosen bait—but there is blood in the water. The *"Angel of Light"* is circling. (2 Corinthians 11:14) The stench of death reaches the four corners of the globe. Since you are reading this I must assume that our Messiah has not yet come. Therefore, you must make a decision. Are you willing to fish with us? Are you willing to catch the dead back to life? Can you feel the tug on your line? If so, through the power of faith set your hook. Together we will catch millions into forever.

CHAPTER 8

Sacrifice or Investment?

Sacrifice, **sac-ri-fice** 1. The offering of animal, plant, human life, or some material possession to a deity, as in propitiation or homage. 2. The surrender or destruction of something prized or desirable for the sake of something of *perceived higher value.* 3. To surrender or give up, or permit injury or disadvantage for the sake of something else.

Investment, **in-vest-ment** 1. The investing of money or capital in order to gain profitable returns, as interest, income, or *appreciation in value.*

In my day job as a Financial Advisor, I have spent the last twenty five years analyzing whether a client's sacrifice of their hard earned money into our business is a worthwhile investment. In most cases, achieving ones stated goals requires both sacrifice and investment. One may sacrifice their time, the current purchase of an item, a relationship or any number of items to build an investment toward obtaining that which is of a *perceived higher value*, such as a house, retirement or whatever the object of their affection may be.

How about our pursuit of the Almighty; is He a worthwhile investment? Take a minute to review the above definitions, in particular, numbers two and three of the word "sacrifice," then answer the following question. Do you believe serving God is a sacrifice or an investment? The unfortunate truth is that too many of us believe that coming to God is a sacrifice, which means we must lose something, perhaps even everything, in order to serve Him.

In the following pages you are about to encounter a couple of truths. **1)** It was God who made the sacrifice in order to save us, and **2)** In order to come to God you will only be required to sacrifice one thing—yourself, that is, your sinful nature. That is all He wants you to give up—your sin. Sin is the only thing coming between you and God, and, therefore, it is the only thing that God wants to take *away* from you. Everything else that you offer to Him is an *investment* into your future, not a sacrifice.

Many of you will say, "No way John! That is absolutely untrue. In order to serve God I have to sacrifice my time, talent, money etc . . . perhaps my entire lifestyle. God has called people to give up their jobs, their homes—yeah even their homes. If God calls me to go to China or Africa, I have to sacrifice my home, my family, my comfort . . . *that's* a sacrifice! There is no doubt about the fact that that is a sacrifice."

Greater Value

This perception is exactly where we get tripped up. In fact, it had plagued me for years until I came to understand God's will for my life, as well as, the true purpose of the incredible evangelistic act He instituted when birthing the good old USA. Amazingly, God does not need to call anyone to China or Africa, or wherever your worst nightmare may be. In America, all you need to do is walk down the street, or go to the mall. Queens, New York, for example, is represented by 142 different nations. Any public park, or even street, for that matter, in the city of Queens is a world mission field. Think about that the next time your political bent drives you to despise immigration. You just may be setting yourself in opposition to the will of God.

In truth, most of us do not understand sacrifice *or* investment. God is not sacrificing you. He is investing in you. Take a look at definition two in the above word, "sacrifice." It reads, "*The surrender or destruction of something prized.*" That is your sin, and yes, many of us take pride in, or even prize our sin. Part two reads, "*For the sake of something of perceived higher value.*" That would be God.

You are not losing something in your sacrifice. You are gaining something of much greater value. You will profit from your relationship with God whether it is here, in eternity, or both. That, by definition is an investment. With any investment you must give up something for the short term in order gain a greater future value. Take a look at the following scriptures:

> "*Give and it will be given to you: good measure, pressed down, shaken together, and running over will be put into your bosom. For with the same measure that you use, it will be measured back to you.*"
> **—Luke 6:38**

You must admit that sounds like an investment. By definition, an investment consists of contributing some sort of capital with the expectation of having your original principle returned to you, plus a profit. *"Good measure, pressed down, shaken together, and running over,"* certainly qualifies as a hefty profit if you ask me. Running over means there is more than can be contained.

No one can deny that America is running over with the blessing of God. Although America, just like any country, has a multitude of past and present sins, it is undeniable that we are reaping the harvest of our investment into the gospel of Jesus Christ, as well as, our support of the Promised Land that is Israel. God will always honor your commitment of whatever resource you invest into His kingdom and return more than you could possibly imagine. You cannot out-give Him. I dare you to try.

Capital Gains

With that in mind, let us have a look at an incident from the life of Isaac, the son of Abraham, in which it appeared that God was going to require a great sacrifice from him. I want you to take note of who ultimately benefits from the arrangement.

> *"There was famine in the land . . . and Isaac went to Abimelech king of the Philistines in Gerar. Then the Lord appeared to him and said, 'Do not go down to Egypt; live in the land of which I shall tell you. Dwell in this land and I will be with you and bless you.'"*
> **—Genesis 26:1-3**

Isaac's plan was to head down to Egypt, but as you will see, that was definitely not God's plan. Who can blame Isaac? Egypt was the most prosperous and technologically advanced civilization of the ancient world. If there was any place on earth where one could survive a famine, certainly Egypt was the place. After all, Egypt had survived famine in the past. Surely this would be no different. Egypt had experience in dealing with all types of problems. They had irrigation systems, the most modern farming and engineering techniques—Egypt was the Mecca of the ancient world. Who would not want to live there? However, God had a different idea in mind. From Isaac's point of view it did not seem to make sense.

Just like Isaac nearly did, it is inevitably in the following principle that we continuously miss the will of God. *"Behold, to obey is better than sacrifice."* (1 Samuel 15:22) Learn from Isaac. He was faced with a life and death choice. Do I follow human logic or do I stay here with the notorious Philistines? Do I obey my instincts or do I obey the God of the universe? "Well . . . now that you put it that way, it seems sort of simple," is often times what I hear. Trust me, it is not. Diving headfirst into unseen waters always comes with reservation.

As you might guess, Isaac quite astutely decided to sacrifice his own logic and invest everything into the wisdom of God. Here is the result. *"Then Isaac sowed in that land, and reaped in the same year a hundredfold; and the Lord blessed him. The man began to prosper, and continued to prosper, until he became very prosperous,"* (Genesis 26:12) just like his father Abraham. They both followed the same God culture principle of investing, *"To obey is better than sacrifice."*

Here is the question. What was it that Isaac was asked to sacrifice? What would he be required to give up? The answer is his earthly "wisdom," which in addition to a man's education and experience, is most certainly founded upon his pride and ego. Isaac, however, had become adept at following the will of God. Do not forget that he was the one who willingly laid his life down upon the altar on Mount Moriah. Obedience to Yahweh was a part of his culture. God culture was an investment into Isaac's future and it is an investment into yours as well.

In fact, that which he offered up was replaced with that of much higher value; one hundred times greater. He replaced his wisdom with the wisdom of God. In other words, he sacrificed his pride on the altar of God. He invested into an act of worship. That is what submission to the will of God is. It is recognition of God's supremacy above your own.

The result was the very first "hundred bagger," resulting in a huge capital gain. By today's standards it would have been considered a short term gain as well, being that all of the gains were incurred in one several month long growing season. God does not mess around. When you obey Him, He will uphold His end of the bargain.

In stock market investing, we are always looking for those "ten bagger" stocks, which are those that will increase ten-fold in value. Rarely, and for most, if ever, do you invest in a "hundred bagger." Ten baggers are rare enough. Keep in mind also that Isaac's return occurred in the course of less than a year. It occurred in one growing season.

I would venture to say there have probably only been a handful of stocks in history that have increased one hundred fold in a matter of months. I am not talking one hundred percent. That is a doubling, a two-fold return. This multiplied one hundred fold. That means it doubled ninety-nine more times. It became nearly impossible to contain.

How could this occur? Most people never come to the realization that there are no limitations when you value the wisdom of God above the wisdom of man.

"Jesus said to him, 'If you can believe, all things are possible to him who believes.'"
—Mark 9:23

Invest in God

Wouldn't you say the God who knows the outcome of every possible situation before it occurs is certainly worth obeying? Don't you agree that this was no sacrifice at all, but an investment into Isaac's future? In the opinion of most, a stock that increases one hundredfold is a pretty spectacular investment. So why are we constantly sacrificing to God when He is really trying to get us to invest in Him?

When you give an hour to God you are not sacrificing that time. You are investing it. You are not losing that hour. You are gaining the Almighty. If in that hour the Lord gives you one idea that solves a problem, starts a business, or a ministry etc... What did you give up? The answer is nothing. You did not lose, you have profited— with a guarantee! You received something of greater value. God *always* causes us to prosper when we make the decision to invest in Him. *He is the greatest value!* Therefore, stop sacrificing your time to God. Stop sacrificing your money to God. Stop sacrificing whatever you are holding onto and begin investing it.

"So let each one give as he purposes in his heart, not grudgingly or
of necessity; for God loves a cheerful giver."
—2 Corinthians 9:7

Trust Me

"'Bring all the tithes into the storehouse that there may be food in
My house. And try Me now in this,' says the Lord of hosts. 'If I will
not open for you the windows of heaven and pour out for you such
blessing that there will not be room enough to receive it. And I will
rebuke the devourer for your sakes, so that he will not destroy the
fruit of your ground. Nor shall the vine fail to bear fruit for you in
the field,' says the Lord of hosts. 'And all nations will call you

blessed, for you will be a delightful land,' says the Lord of hosts."
—Malachi 3:10-12

Let me begin by stating that God does not need your money. In fact, the issue here is not the tithe at all. As believers in Christ, we are no more bound by the tithe than we are bound by any other part of the law. We have been freed from it and the yoke it possesses.

Furthermore, this segment of scripture was not even written with the gentile in mind. It was written to the Levitical priests who are the descendants of Levi, Joseph's brother who did not receive a portion of the Promised Land. The Lord made it clearly known to Aaron, Moses' brother, and a Levite, that *He* was their portion. (Numbers 18:20) Therefore, the concept of the tithe was implemented to meet the needs of the Priesthood. Otherwise, they would have gone hungry.

Understanding this concept provides the freedom that allows us to be relieved of the *burden* of the tithe and move into the higher calling of the *investment* of the tithe. The principle of God opening the windows of heaven and pouring out His blessing on the giver remains valid to this day. The law of the tithe and the ensuing result of those willing to implement it as a lifestyle is unchanging to this day. It still works. We are simply not compelled to do it.

When you believe in Jesus you will not be cursed if you abstain. *"Christ has redeemed us from the curse of the law . . ."* (Galatians 3:13) If you do tithe, however, God's promise remains the same. He will open up the windows of heaven and pour out His blessing. He will rebuke the devourer and provide for you every other benefit that is promised in His word regarding prosperity.

So is the tithe a sacrifice or an investment? If we continue to believe it is a sacrifice, even if you do it you will miss your blessing.

*"So let each one give **as he purposes in his heart**, not grudgingly **or of necessity**, for God loves a cheerful giver. And God is able to*

make all grace abound toward you, that you, always having all sufficiency in all things, may have an abundance for every good work. As it is written, he has dispersed abroad, he has given to the poor, his righteousness endures forever. Now may He who supplies seed to the sower, and bread for food, supply and multiply the seed you have sown and increase the fruits of your righteousness."
—2 Corinthians 9:7-10

True investments are never a requirement. This scripture clearly shows that we have been freed from the *requirement* of giving. However, when you decide to cheerfully make your investment into Yahweh and His kingdom, the words "grace" and "abundance" begin to abound. Grace means God's unearned favor and abundance means more than enough.

In addition, we see the *spiritual* fruit of our investment in the form of righteousness. Isn't that where we *should* be? When you live according to this principle, with total and complete trust in God, it will not be long until your harvest manifests, whatever it is that you are actively believing Him for.

Stop, Thief!

With that in mind it is now time for a little self-examination. Does your life reflect what we have just finished discussing? Are your investments producing righteousness? If all you are doing is sacrificing, you most likely feel that you are being robbed of all of your investment. You are losing your principle and you are wasting your time and your resources. That leads to begrudged giving (if you even continue) out of a compelling sense of obligation and not from the joyful and compassionate heart of the believer in Yahweh.

That was the problem with the Pharisees. They upheld the law, but without the Spirit of God intermingled with the law there can be no love or righteousness. There is only pride and judgment, which results in the devil stealing the love from your life. I can promise you that there is no blessing and there is no joy in that. Unfortunately, most of us have been there at one time or another. Therefore, let us climb to a higher place.

"Let us go up to the mountain of the Lord . . . He will teach us His ways and we will walk in His paths."
—Isaiah 2:3

When your sacrifice to God actually becomes an investment, and you begin to experience God fulfilling His end of the covenant, the joy of watching your investment multiply occurs. So does the number of people who are positively and eternally affected by your life. It is not only your bank account that increases. Maybe it does or maybe it does not. That is God's business and material wealth is the wrong motivation for serving Him. Your relationships, however, both with others, and even more importantly, with God, are guaranteed to prosper. Your compassion will increase. Your sorrow will be turned to joy and life becomes exciting and worth living again. Is that an investment worth making? I dare say it is.

Unmatched Value

God certainly thinks so. In fact, He finds you to be so immensely important and worthwhile that He was willing to make an investment as well. God's investment, however, was so vast that it could only be qualified as a sacrifice. There is no amount of investment return that can surpass or even equal what God has pledged. The capital contribution that purchased your salvation has no price on earth. It cannot be bought or sold. There is nothing of greater value.

God pledged Himself! Yahweh gave His own life. All of humanity combined, now, then, and forever, cannot come close to comparing with the value contained in the life of God Almighty. He is the giver of life and yet the Lord went to the cross and entered the realm of death anyway. He suffered mightily and became a shame and a curse for you—and for what reason?

*"But now Christ has risen from the dead, and has become the first fruits of those who have fallen asleep. For since by man came death, by Man also came the resurrection of the dead. For as in Adam all die, even so in Christ **all shall be made alive.**"*
—1 Corinthians 15:21-22

Do you see that word "all?" It means that your investment in Christ produces the desired return one hundred percent of the time. It also means that Yahweh's investment in Christ produced the desired return as well. *All* are made alive in Christ. Do you want a guaranteed investment? Invest your life in Christ. He will make you alive one hundred percent of the time. When you invest in Him "now," He guarantees "forever." Which is of greater value, a finite now, or an eternal forever?

The endlessness of eternity is a return of immeasurable proportion. It cannot be measured. No value can be placed on it. Eternity continues to compound forever. Who else can provide that?

"He who believes in the Son has everlasting life; and he who does not believe in the Son shall not see life, but the wrath of God abides on him."
—John 3:36

The answer is that no one else can save you. Not Allah, not Mohammed, not Buddha, Rah, Jain, L Ron Hubbard, your government, money, Thor, Odin or whoever and whatever you want to place your trust in.

I Guarantee It

I remember one time a friend of mine gave me a nearly "guaranteed" stock tip. We were to get in on the ground floor of this brand new company. Let me tell you, we thought we were going to be rich! So I dumped nearly all of the money I had saved into this one company. At first it began to increase. As it did I began to get excited. It seemed as if the dream was well on its way to becoming reality.

So I got a nice fat bonus and guess what I did? I sank it all into this one company. I actually believed the information I was getting and since the investment seemed to be growing I believed the information I was getting was true. Hey, other people were doing it too. Have you ever heard that before?

Unfortunately, there was one piece of information that never made it across my desk. A couple of weeks after I sank my second chunk of money into this particular company all of the insiders sold their positions. Within a week the company was liquidated and the next statement I got had a whole bunch of zero's across the bottom. I lost everything.

What I am about to say is very important, so pay close attention. Losing the money was *my* mistake. I disobeyed the instruction of God. There is an investment principal contained in the Word of God that states the following; "*When I saw it, I considered it well; I looked on it and received instruction.* (Proverbs 24:32)

I never took the time to check out the company I was investing in. I did not "consider it well," or, as another translation states, "look well into the matter," nor did I receive instruction from the Lord. I simply took my friend's word for it. The result of placing man's wisdom over God's was a complete financial loss. The stock went to zero. I had done the opposite of Isaac.

Keep this in mind as well. It was not my friend's fault. He was not trying to harm me. In fact, he was trying to help me. He also wound up losing a pile of money. They say the path to hell is paved with good intentions and do you know what? They are right. Whoever "they" are.

So it is with God. Each of us is responsible for our own investment.

> *"Therefore, my beloved, as you have always obeyed, not as in my presence only, but now much more in my absence, **work out your own salvation** with fear and trembling."*
> **—Philippians 2:12**

We all must look well into the matter of who God is and how He relates to us. My advice to you is that you check out the "company" you are investing in. Check out God for yourself and verify whether or not you believe the information contained within this book series is accurate. Look well into His Word. Do not take your friends word for it. Do not even take your parents word for it. I know they love you. I know they have your best interest in mind, but they are merely human and there is a very good chance that they may be wrong.

Do not take my word for it either. I am as fallible as the next guy. Eternity is too important to take lightly. Eternity is forever.

> Therefore, *"work out your own salvation with fear and trembling."* (Philippians 2:12) *"Let it be known to you all . . . that by the name of Jesus Christ of Nazareth, whom you crucified, whom God raised from the dead, by Him this man stands here before you whole . . . **Nor is there salvation in any other**, for there is no other name under heaven given among men by which we must be saved."*
> **—Acts 4:10-12**

I am not really a gambling man but I know a guarantee when I see one. I have read the Q'ran— twice in fact. I have read the Book of

Mormon. I have studied multiple religions and I can only find one claim of a guarantee.

I have studied prophecy in depth, and in all the religious books ever created—of all of the so called seers, such as Nostradamus, or Edgar Cayce, only one book, or one set of writings stands out. In fact, there is only one book that actually has at least one detailed prophecy, which is proven by history, to have come to pass. That book not only has one, but it literally has two thousand. There are just over 3100 specific scriptures, written over a 1500 year period, resulting in two thousand fulfilled prophecies that have been confirmed by historical, archaeological and/or scientific history to be true. I am sure you have guessed by now that the book I am referring to is the Bible. The Bible is the only true source of the Word and wisdom of God almighty. Every other religious book, system or artifact falls short.

The Nuts

If you do not believe that check it out yourself. Look well into the matter. I did, and I continue to do so. Eternal life depends on it. If your religion is Islam, look well into the matter. I certainly respect you, especially your zeal for Allah, but I challenge you to find even one fulfilled prophecy in the Q'ran. I urge you to locate the guarantee of your salvation. Neither exist. It gets dates and times wrong. People are placed in the wrong time periods and amongst the wrong lineages. The Q'ran even describes the earth as being flat where the Book of Isaiah states that *"God sits above the circle of the earth."* (Isaiah 40:22)

Let us not even go down the road of science and the vast amounts of correct information contained in a book written before microscopes, telescopes, and modern forms of technology. There is too much correct information in the Bible to be coincidence or chance.

In poker, *No Limit Texas Hold Em'* in particular, if you believe you have got your opponent beaten you can go "all in." You simply bet everything you have. The only difference is that in poker you can lose because you do not always know what your opponent is holding. That is why it is a gamble. You may have calculated your odds incorrectly, or, just like Lucifer, your opponent may be bluffing.

Bluffing is all Satan can do. He is like the Big Bad Wolf, always huffing and puffing, and threatening to blow your house in, but in reality he has no breath. There is no life in him. Therefore, he tries to bluff you into folding your hand.

In Christ, you have him beat. Jesus Christ possesses the breath of life, and as a result, I know exactly what is in Satan's hand. He knows exactly who is in my heart. Therefore, there is no risk to my investment. Christ is not a gamble at all.

Therefore, if you are an unbeliever consider the fact that you may have miscalculated. Do you want to call my hand and challenge Christ? I am all in. I will place what is in my hand against anyone's, anytime. In Christ, I have what Poker calls, "*The nuts!*" It is a hand that cannot be beaten. Likewise, Christ cannot be beaten.

Are you still willing to bluff? If so, know that I am pushing all my chips to the center of the table. This book is designed to call your bet. Therefore, go ahead and challenge me. Challenge the "forever." You cannot bluff the Almighty, nor can you bluff your way into heaven. Hence, I challenge you to call my hand and read on. You are about to discover the greatest investment known to man. As I flip over my cards in the following pages you will discover exactly what, or better stated, Who, is in my hand—Yahweh revealed.

CHAPTER 9

Blind Faith

The longer I live the more amazed I become by the wisdom and mercy of Yahweh. Recently I was pondering the amazing wisdom of God in the mere fact that He allows us to age. Contrary to popular belief, the golden years are not a curse. They are mercy. Aging is actually the fulfillment of God's love. Most of us believe that the older we get the closer we come to death. Nothing could be further from the truth. As a matter of fact, if we have Christ, the older we get the closer we come to glory.

If heaven is real, can you see the infinite wisdom of God? Think about your life when you were young. You were fearless, daring, and so full of "life." Perhaps that is where you are as you are reading this book. From the standpoint of eternity, however, is it really life that you are, or were, full of? Energy . . . yes. Enthusiasm . . . no doubt—

but if you were, or are, anything like I was, you can add foolishness and sin to the list as well, which no doubt would have meant spiritual death had my eventuality come to pass at that point in my life. I was abounding more in hell than in heaven. How about you? What if God had accounted for your soul today? What if He were to call you into eternity right now?

Through aging we begin to perceive our own frailty which spurns a desire to live. We begin to see more clearly, even if through dimming eyes, that there is so much more to life than ourselves and our own foolish desires. Aging gives us the time and the opportunity to recognize that if death is the end of life, than life is devoid of any and all meaning. We begin to realize that we must *"put on immortality,"* (1 Corinthians 15:53) and that there must be a God who loves us.

We begin to seek and to desire the knowledge of our Father. We yearn to know Him and we learn to recognize the love of God through our own life experiences. We catch a glimpse of His love, for example, through the love of our children. We learn what it truly means to be unconditional, and how we are unable to achieve such when left to our own devices. We gaze into the past and clearly see the multiple times He has saved us from peril.

As we age, we begin to see that there must be something more to life. There must be a purpose and that this place, the universe, is certainly no accident. We begin to see the love of a Creator who is infinitely higher and wiser than ourselves (Isaiah 55:9). We begin to gain knowledge, and to cherish wisdom. We learn how to love and most importantly, through the realization of our own mortality, we begin to seek, and if it is truly our desire, ultimately we discover God. This is not the case for most young people. Of course there are exceptions to nearly every rule, but in truth, *"foolishness is bound up in the heart of a child."* (Proverbs 22:15) The folly of youth is caught up in its own self-will and foolish pleasures. The young man's life and thoughts reside primarily in what they can see, feel, taste, touch, and smell. Thankfully, God is exquisitely patient. He loves us so much that He not only *allows* us to age, He is the cause of it.

As our natural bodies deteriorate, a spiritual longing resurrects to life—a desire for life eternal that for many can never be found in undying youth. As we get closer to death we begin to look for answers. Through aging, Yahweh gives us time to search—to find—and ultimately in death we are reunited with our Maker (Ephesians 1:4). Do not be foolish though. You may not have an entire lifetime to search. Through accident, disease, or natural means, we all have a different life span. Therefore, I would encourage you to *"seek the Lord while He may be found, call upon Him while He is near."* (Isaiah 55:6) Time is not guaranteed. He is calling you right now and as *Meatloaf* so aptly serenaded in his famous pop song *Paradise by the Dashboard Light*, "What's it gonna be boy, yes or no." Being lukewarm will only cause the Lord Jesus to spit you out. (Revelation 3:16) Therefore, *"let your yes, be yes, and let your no, be no. For whatever is more than this is from the evil one."* (Matthew 5:37)

Therefore, in order to help you "enter through the narrow gate," (Matthew 7;13) let us have a look at two men who encountered the living Messiah. Both were faced with the same choice I have just presented to you. Perhaps this ancient drama will help you decide.

A Time to Kill

By the way, the word "decide" is quite interesting as it ends with the letters, "c-i-d-e." Everything ending with these letters is a description of some sort of death. Think about it, suicide is the killing of oneself. Homicide is the murder of another human being. Pesticide is the killing of various pests, such as rats, roaches, demons, Lucifer, etc . . . Genocide is the annihilation of an entire race of people.

So what is the meaning of the word, "decide?" What does it kill? Quite simply, it is the killing of option number two, whatever that may be. When you decide to take your life in one particular direction you have actually killed the other options you were considering. When you decide to follow heaven, you kill hell. When you decide to live your life for God, you kill the power of Lucifer.

Keep in mind, however, that the opposite is also true. When you reject heaven, you empower hell. When you choose to deny God, you empower Lucifer. Think about the choices you have made in life and contemplate whose side you are currently on. Choices have consequences. Where did you think all the chaos came from? With that in mind, let's see the power of decision in action from a biblical perspective. You are about to meet two extraordinary characters.

From an eternal standpoint, one of these two men will live and one will die. Therefore, I would encourage you to pay close attention to what follows. If you have not already, my prayer is that by the end of this chapter you will have seen enough to choose life. (Deuteronomy 30:19)

Who is Good?

Let us begin with a familiar, yet interesting piece of scripture from Mark, chapter 10.

> *"Now as He* (Jesus) *was going out on the road,* **one came running***, knelt before Him, and asked Him, 'Good Teacher, what shall I do that I may inherit eternal life?"*
> **—Mark 10:17**

Just imagine the scene. The disciples are following Jesus down the road when a certain young man of the ruling class chases Him down from behind and desperately falls at His feet. Sweat droplets careen down his reddening visage as rays of sunlight shimmy off the royalty of his gold laced head and torso. His violet tunic melds to a brilliant magenta in evidence of the day's heat. With his chest heaving, and with fragmented words conscripted between frantic breaths, the crowd gazes intently as he poses the above question, *"Good Teacher, what shall I do that I may inherit eternal life?"*

Jesus, never being one accused of conformity replies, *"Why do you call me good? No one is good but One, that is God. You know the commandments, 'Do not commit adultery, do not murder, do not steal, do not bear false witness, do not defraud, honor your father and mother."*

And he answered and said to Him, "Teacher, all these things I have kept from my youth." (Mark 10:18-20)

Although I love Jesus' answer, I must admit that for a very long time I did not understand it. Jesus says, "Good, why do you call me good? No one is good except for God." My reaction was always, "But Jesus, you *are* God. What do you mean you are not good? If you are not good, who is?" Is it just me or did you find yourself pondering the same thought?

Then doubt would begin creeping in. "Did Jesus just say that He is not divine? Didn't He just say that He is not God? The Bible must be flawed. Perhaps God isn't real after all. Was Jesus merely another prophet, or worse yet, was He a *false* prophet?"

The more I get to know Jesus, however, the more I realize that He is the master at drawing forth what is truly in our hearts. This situation was certainly no different. The question was not an admission of mortality. As you will see, Jesus was not focusing on Himself when posing it. As we have previously discussed, Jesus undoubtedly is divine.

In truth, this was a carefully calculated test designed not just for the young man confronting Him, but for every person who will ever read the account of that long lost day's events. Jesus knew this young man's motive before he ever asked the question. When Jesus replied, "Why do you call me good?" He was attempting to reveal something to this young man about Himself. Jesus was trying to open his blind eyes to the deity standing before him. Jesus was actually asking, "Young man, who do you believe I AM? Do you *know* that I AM good? Do you *believe* that I AM God? You say you know the letter of the law, but do you recognize its author standing before you? I AM the eternal life you seek."

Good Teacher

With complete disregard for truth and without even allowing Jesus to finish orating the commandments, (If you read the account carefully you will discover that he cut Jesus off in the middle of His recitation) we are graced with the young man's arrogant, and in my estimation, less than genuine reply. As you will see, his answer reveals both the incredible wisdom of God, as well as, the unrepentant nature of his hardened heart. Like so many of us he had a precise motive for seeking Christ on that fateful day, which unfortunately, was neither love nor submission.

He pompously replies for the benefit of all those within earshot, *"Teacher, all these I have kept from my youth."* (Mark 10:20) There you have it—self-righteousness at its best. If you are anything like me you are undoubtedly thinking, "Seriously dude! You have never broken one?" With that in mind, let's take a closer look at how arrogance manifests itself in the heart of man.

Often times, ego can be difficult to discern, particularly for the victim of its deception. Generosity can be as selfish as greed when the giver is out for personal gain. Ego can masterfully disguise itself as righteousness or holiness. Therefore, in order to unmask this young gentleman's true motivation it is important to note the regard in which he engages Jesus. Consider how the following conversation progresses. His opening reference to Jesus is as, "good teacher." This reference to "teacher" is not worthy of divinity. It is that of a common man. It simply means, "instructor." He could have at least used, "Rabbi" or "Rabboni," and showed *some* respect, but he chose not to.

After Jesus discards the young man's contrivance, He is not even worthy of "good teacher" anymore. He is just "teacher." The Lord asked a precise question in an attempt to get this young man to see that which is of true worth. However, the youth was staring God in the face and completely missed Him. He was so darkened by "*everything in the world—the lust of the eyes, the lust of the flesh, and the pride of life,*" (1 John 2:16) that he was unable to discern the presence of the Messiah staring directly into his sin stained eyes. Thus, his second reference was merely "teacher." He just didn't get it.

Therefore, since the man whom had "never transgressed the law" actually had no spiritual understanding whatsoever, he never even addressed Jesus' original question, "Why do you call me good?" As you will soon find out, it was all a show. I must tell you that this is not all that uncommon, even to this day.

I would imagine that Jesus found this to be a bit comical. He must be thinking, "C'mon man! If you had truly kept all the commandments you would know that God is the only goodness in existence. Therefore son, by calling me good, who are you saying that I AM?" That was the gist of the question—but the blind cannot see.

Treasure in Heaven

If you feel I am being too hard on this young man, remember the opening sequence. He caused a huge scene by chasing Jesus down publicly and falling "desperately" at His feet. With a multitude of eyes fixed upon him he awaits Jesus' confirmation of his own self-righteousness. He longs for the adulation and the exaltation from all those who would acknowledge the triumph of his perceived virtue and greedy self-aggrandizement.

When viewing this scene, do not forget about the Rich Young Ruler's social status. Because of his wealth, adulation is all he knows. Just like today, I would imagine that everyone who knew of his wealth wanted to be his friend. The entire world kisses his "you know what" every day of his life. Therefore, with no real knowledge of God, he believes in his heart that Jesus is no different than all the pretenders in his life. He must be thinking, "Certainly the highly regarded Rabbi, Jesus of Nazareth, will confirm my greatness as well." Is this what he gets? Just like everyone who has a true encounter with the Messiah, he is about to find out that Jesus is very different than anyone he has ever blindly stumbled upon.

> *"Then Jesus looking at him loved him . . ."*
> **—Mark 10:21**

What a profound statement. Unlike anyone the young man had ever met, Jesus had only one thing on His agenda. Jesus had only one reason for engaging him—the saving his soul. Do not let the rich young ruler's claim deceive you. He was a sinner. He may not have known it, but just like you and me, without Christ in his heart he *was* a sinner. If you do not believe that just take a look around you. Watch the evening news. Gaze into your own thoughts. We are all doomed without Christ! "***All have sinned*** *and fall short of the glory of God,*" (Romans 3:23) including this exceptionally wealthy and remarkably egocentric young man.

The law, which he claimed to have utterly fulfilled, could not deliver him from himself. It cannot deliver us either. However, even in his spiritually decrepit condition Jesus loved him. Since "*God is no respecter of persons,*" (Acts 10:34 and Romans 2:11) you can rest assured that He loves us, as well. Not with an earthly, sensual love, but with a truly unconditional "agape" love.

The Greek word "agape" is quite interesting. It describes a love that is so unconditional that the giver does not need reciprocity to remain in love. Of the four ancient Greek words primarily used to describe love, "agape" describes the only love in existence that truly has no strings attached. Agape has no ulterior motive.

Incredibly, Jesus loves this boy with so much "agape" that He is willing to give him the eternal life he seeks. Jesus is ready to die for Him just as He was ready to die for us while we were in the same sin-stained state of being.

"But God demonstrates His own love toward us, in that while we were still sinners Christ died for us."
—Romans 5:80

However, he, just like we, must be willing to acknowledge our own sin, repent, and receive the necessary correction in our lives. Jesus loves him enough to show him that all he is procuring in this present life is a one way ticket to the Lake of Fire. Jesus is calling him to begin making deposits into eternity.

*"Then Jesus looking at him, loved him, and said to him, 'One thing you lack, go your way, sell whatever you have and give to the poor, and you will have treasure in heaven, and come, take up the cross and follow Me.' But he was sad at this word, **and went away sorrowful**, for he had **great possessions.**"*
—Mark 10:21-22

I have heard this scripture not just used, but abused, more times than I can count. Jesus did not tell this young man to sell everything because Christians are supposed to be poor. God receives no glory in your deprivation. This young man's possessions were great but his heart was destitute. His problem was materialism. He had everything a man could want in life, however, he lacked one thing. He was not in possession of Yahweh.

Therefore, he lacked love, compassion, and mercy. He was arrogant and self-righteous. He perceived himself to be full, when in truth he was empty. All he cared about was his stuff and he loved it more than any man, woman or child in his life. He loved it more than God Himself. Therefore, when confronted with his idolatry he chose to walk away from eternal life. I would encourage you to use this example as a mirror into your own soul. Do you see yourself? If so, what choices are you willing to make? Are you willing to make a decision? If so, which power are you willing to kill?

The Shift

Anytime you love anything more than God you are living in idolatry. Jesus' goal was not to make this man poor. It was to give him true wealth from both a spiritual and eternal standpoint. It was to give him *"treasures in heaven, where neither moth nor rust destroys and where thieves do not break in and steal."* Jesus is fully aware that *"where your treasure is, there your heart will be also,"* (Matthew 6:20-21) and that *"the love of money,"* which is *"the root of all kinds of evil"* (1 Timothy 6:10) poisons the soul.

The rich young ruler, just like you and me, had to give up his idolatry, which was *his* way and not God's way (*Go your way*). He needed to deny himself and his corrupt ways (*Take up the cross*) in order to gain the eternal life that may only be found in following Jesus Christ (*Come . . . follow Me*). There is no other road to eternity.

Please understand this great spiritual message. Following God is not about gaining material possessions. Becoming a disciple of Jesus Christ is about loving people regardless of their social status. It is about planting seeds that spring into eternal life. That includes loving the rich, loving the poor, loving the lovable and unlovable, and everyone in between. Agape loves those who are black, white, yellow, brown—gay or straight, ugly or beautiful, and every color of the transgender rainbow. Social status and ethnicity are irrelevant in the kingdom of God. So is religion, by the way. God is not interested in your religion. Yahweh is only interested in your salvation.

*"Bring no more futile sacrifices; incense is an abomination to Me.
The New Moons, the Sabbaths, and the calling of assemblies—I
cannot endure iniquity and the sacred meeting. Your New Moons
and your appointed feasts, My soul hates; They are a trouble to
Me, I am weary of bearing them."*
—Isaiah 1:13-14

Therefore, since agape is God's way it must be ours as well. This was the purpose of Christ's request to "sell" that which the young man truly loved and to "give" to that which God deems to be of true worth—the suffering masses of humanity known as mankind. Love requires a spiritual shift.

Just as we discussed in the previous chapter, God was encouraging the rich young ruler to make an investment into his future. Jesus was offering God culture in exchange for an ancient form of pop culture. He was offering an investment that *"could not grow old, a treasure in the heavens that does not fail, where no thief approaches nor moth destroys."* (Luke 12:33) He was being asked to *"lay up treasures in heaven, where neither moth nor rust destroys and where thieves do not break in and steal."* (Matthew 6:20)

But he was unwilling. So he chose a lifetime of sensual pleasure. He decided to choose everything the dying world has to offer over the love of the eternal God of the universe. In the process he killed his own soul. He committed the most ancient form of suicide. I shudder to contemplate his demise.

Son of David

Let's fast forward a few hours to Mark 10:46. We now find Jesus and His disciples arriving at their destination of Jericho. Apparently rumors have been flying, because a multitude has gathered to welcome Him. We discover an interfusion of societal classes ranging from the affluent, to the impoverished, to the bourgeoisie.

We are then introduced to a blind beggar named Bartimaeus. In society's eyes, Bartimaeus was the lowest of the low. He overhears through the chatter that Jesus of Nazareth is about to enter the city gates. In his desperation he begins to cry out, *"Jesus, Son of David, have mercy on me.' Then many warned him to be quiet; but he cried out all the more, 'Son of David, have mercy on me."* (Mark 10:47-48)

To fully appreciate Bartimaeus, we must understand his place in society. His crying out was a tremendous act of faith. There was no safety net to protect him—no welfare system, no food stamps. There was no such thing as a special needs trust. As a matter of fact, a blind man was not even allowed, according to the Book of Leviticus, to serve in the Temple. Bartimaeus was a broken man. He was damaged goods and he knew it. As a result, Bartimaeus was looked at by society as something less than human. He was even required to wear a special shawl that signified his wretched disability. Bartimaeus was a "nobody!" Therefore, when he began to call out through the crowd, their reaction to him, if I may use modern day vernacular, was, "Shut up Bartimaeus!" As a matter of fact, verse 48 actually says, *"They warned him to be quiet."* The crowd could not even conceive that a man of honor such as Jesus, and yes, at this point in time they still considered Jesus honorable, would even acknowledge a "bum" like Bartimaeus. They actually believed Bartimaeus may get in trouble, and he could have. So there reaction was really to say, "Shut up Bartimaeus, don't you know your place?"

Is it politically correct for me to say that Bartimaeus did know his place? The stench of society would not let him forget it every single day of his rotten, miserable life. As a result, he was desperate. However, inside this desperate soul God had imparted the gift of faith. To be quite honest with you, Bartimaeus was a wealthy man. Obviously not in the physical realm, but there was a spiritual richness implanted within his forlorn heart that would gain him the riches of eternity. Therefore, this humble spirit did not approach the Messiah in search of arrogant self-gratification. He cried out in faith. He cried out in desperation!

> *"Jesus, Son of David, have mercy on me!* **So Jesus stood still** *and commanded him to be called."*
> **—Mark 10:49**

Hold that thought for just a second and let that sink in. *Something* that Bartimaeus said, or did, caused Jesus of Nazareth, the only begotten Son of the only living God, to stop dead in His tracks and seek out *Bartimaeus*! I would encourage you to pay close attention to what follows. You are about to encounter the following biblical principal which also happens to be a part of Yahweh's amazing nature and modus operandi:

> *"All these blessings shall come upon you and* **overtake** *you because you* **obey the voice** *of the Lord your God."*
> **—Deuteronomy 28:2**

What was it that caused the Messiah to stand still and search out a lonely and physically broken blind beggar whom the rest of the world regarded as worthless?

Blind Faith

I want you to first take note of the fact that Bartimaeus did not have to cause a scene by chasing Jesus down and asking a silly theological question like the rich young ruler. There was no need to advertise. Jesus heard his cry and found *him*. Make a mental and spiritual note of this amazing truth. Faith caused Jesus to chase down Bartimaeus. We see this same principle in the story of the Prodigal Son. Do you remember how the father ran to meet his beloved son? Bartimaeus simply did what we all need to do. In faith, and sometimes even in desperation, he cried out to Jesus.

You may be thinking, "What was so much different between the way the rich young ruler approached Jesus and the way Bartimaeus approached Him? Surely Bartimaeus would have chased Jesus down the same way had he not been blind. Bartimaeus also caused a scene for everyone to see."

He may have chased him down if he was able, but their motivations were markedly different. Bartimaeus risked humiliation. The rich young ruler sought self-honor. Bartimaeus *did* chase Jesus down. In fact, he was so aggressive that he stopped Jesus dead in His tracks. In faith you can too! It is funny how God reverses things.

"But God has chosen the foolish things of the world to put to shame the wise, and God has chosen the weak things of the world to put to shame the things which are mighty."
—1 Corinthians 1:27

I must say, however, that I do not know how Bartimaeus would have acted if the shoe were on the other foot. Perhaps it was his desperate situation that caused him to long for deliverance. Do not ever underestimate God's ability to gauge what is right for you. Every situation, trial, and tribulation is an opportunity designed by God just for you. You are unique. Therefore, every circumstance in your life is unique in its nature and its purpose and is designed to reach only the particular target of God's choosing. He will not approach each individual in exactly the same manner. He knows exactly what will work to drive you, and only you, to your knees.

Every problem you encounter is an opportunity waiting to be revealed. Therefore, I would encourage you to nurture and maintain a "forever" mindset. There is no other way to perceive the will and way of the Almighty.

Do you remember how the rich young ruler addressed Jesus merely as "teacher?" Either he had no idea, or perhaps he refused to acknowledge who Jesus claimed to be. Both scenario's are still quite common today. Regardless of how far technology progresses the human condition remains stagnant. Sin leaves no room for progress. Like so many of today's modern men, the rich young ruler was only focused on what he could see in the now—himself. Let that be a lesson to all who seek the presence of Yahweh. You must take your ego out of it. Serving God is never about you. To find God you must look to Him, and incredibly, He always points us in the direction of others.

Therefore, learn from Bartimaeus. He addressed Jesus in a specific manner and later as Rabboni, a title of great honor. This was certainly no accidental or random slip of the tongue either. Everyone within an audible range understood Bartimaeus' claim when he cried out, "Son of David!"

Every Jewish man, woman, and child knew that the coming Messiah must be of the lineage of David, who was descended from the line of Judah. Therefore, when Bartimaeus cried out, "Son of David," he was not crying out for *everyone* to hear. To the Jewish ear his claim was blasphemous and could have landed him in jail, or worse. Bartimaeus was crying out for *Jesus* to hear. He was letting Jesus know that he believed He was the long awaited Messiah. That, by the way, could only thrust him into the kingdom of God.

Unlike the rich young ruler, who I believe felt like **Edward Gibbon**, the eighteenth century English historian and member of Parliament, who proclaimed, "Religion is regarded by the common people as true, by the wise as false, and by the rulers as useful," Bartimaeus had no regard for his safety or his honor among men. He had no honor among men! However, he still could have been put out of the synagogue, or perhaps even stoned, for such an act. Other people were and that was a big deal back then. It humiliated not just you but your entire family. Still he cried out, "Jesus, Son of David, I know who you are, *'have mercy on me, and Jesus stood still.'*"

> *"And throwing aside his garment, he rose and came to Jesus."*
> **—Mark 10:50**

What an amazing act of faith and courage. I believe this is actually the point that Bartimaeus received his healing. Incredibly, all he asked Jesus for was mercy. If only our motivation was that of Bartimaeus. If only we could muster the same unwavering faith as Bartimaeus. He understood that it was not God's will for him to be blind. Bartimaeus understood the mercy of God would make him whole. Remember, blindness was perceived as imperfection and unworthy of God.

Bartimaeus, however, did not see himself this way. He was fully aware of how society perceived him. Bartimaeus saw himself as a son of God. I believe he was convinced before he ever saw a manifestation of his healing that Jesus was able to deliver him. I believe he was fully persuaded before Jesus ever came to Jericho that if he ever had the privilege of meeting Jesus of Nazareth, the long awaited Messiah, he would be healed.

Come to Jesus

We all need to meet this same Jesus. Rather than pursue entertainers, professional athletes and the like, shouldn't we expend our energy in pursuit of the one who makes it all possible? God will make the proper introductions based upon His will for your life. Therefore, shouldn't we cast aside our idols and hunt down the one and only living God? We must *eagerly* pursue His mighty presence. We must come to Jesus. He in turn will heal your most grave disease. He will mend your sin sick spirit and present you alive before Yahweh. Jesus will save your soul.

When Bartimaeus threw aside his garment, he discarded his blindness as well. What are you willing to throw aside for the sake of Him who saved us? What risk are you willing to take? Have you considered whether or not spiritual blindness is hindering you?

When Bartimaeus threw aside his shawl, he threw away his ability to make a living. The shawl identified him as a beggar. At that moment Bartimaeus threw away his wretched past and rejected his disability. In essence, he not only stepped into a brand new future in the now, he also put on immortality. (1 Corinthians 15:53) He gained forever. Remember, Bartimaeus was blind. Unless someone was merciful enough to give back his shawl he had no means of recovering it.

The scripture says he rose *"and came to Jesus."* He came to Jesus with eyes clearer and with greater vision than any man who has ever lived. In total darkness he was able to clearly see and recognize his Lord.

Conversely, the rich young ruler was staring Jesus in the face with 20/20 vision and completely missed the awesome company he was among. He wanted Jesus on his terms and his terms only. Does that sound familiar? C'mon, be honest. We all begin this way.

Jesus then makes another profound statement, *"Go your way, **your faith** has made you well."* (Mark 10:52) Jesus did not claim it was *His* faith that healed Bartimaeus. He said it was *Bartimaeus'* faith. Jesus stands in the gap and escorts you to the throne, but it is the Father who does the works. *Your* faith is the catalyst. Take careful note of each man's end. *"But he* (the youth) *was sad at this word, **and went away** grieved, for he had great possessions."* (Mark 10:22) He died (spiritually speaking) that day, grief stricken and miserable. *"He was sad at His word . . . and grieved."*

This is never the case for the disciple of Jesus Christ. *"And immediately **he** (Bartimaeus) **received** his sight and **followed Jesus** down the road* (Mark 10:52) and into eternity. One went away. One followed. Which are you? Which do you want to be? You are only one choice away. Why wait another moment? It is decision time, my friends. Therefore, I would strongly encourage you to kill the power of the enemy and come to Jesus. Let's enter eternity through the *narrow gate* (Matthew 7:13) who is Jesus Christ alone.

Who Can Be Saved?

As incredible as the last chapter was, we cannot possibly leave this section of scripture without addressing vs. 23-32 of Mark chapter 10. It immediately follows the rich young ruler's rejection of Christ. In it, Jesus sets the tone for His disciples in regard to what is, and is not, true wealth. However, I do not think the disciples quite understood Jesus' message—at least not right away. On the surface, it appears that Jesus is addressing the issue of money. As you will see, Jesus is addressing much more than a simple medium of exchange. Therefore, let us spend some time discussing Jesus', which is ultimately Yahweh's, prerequisites to salvation.

While we are on the subject, let's begin by addressing how God actually feels about the wealthy. As you recall from the last chapter, that is ultimately what has led us into this discussion. For years "the church" has taught that having an abundance of money is evil and all those who acquire riches are doomed to eternal damnation. For centuries, Christianity has erroneously misquoted various passages of scripture to support this misguided view. It is true that money is a substantial part of Jesus' teaching throughout scripture. Money and hell were quite often Jesus' primary topics within the gospel passages and often times the two seemed to be intertwined, as if going hand-in-hand.

When viewed out of context it appears that the wealthy are forever lost, condemned to eternal destruction in the abyss that forever burns with fire and brimstone. Is that the truth about riches? Is money inherently evil, corrupting all those seduced by her lust? After all, the Word of God clearly states that *the love of money is the root of all kinds of evil.*" (1 Timothy 6:10) In verse 23, of Mark chapter ten, Jesus most certainly seems to condemn the wealthy as He states, "*It is easier for a camel to go through the eye of a needle than for a rich man to enter the kingdom of God.*" Is that really what Jesus is teaching? Was He condemning the wealthy? Let's take a closer look.

> *"Then Jesus looked around and said to His disciples, 'How hard is it for those who have riches to enter the kingdom of God?' And the disciples were astonished at His words."*
> **—Mark 10:23-24**

At first glance it appears that Jesus *is* going to condemn the wealthy. Amazingly, His disciples were bewildered. They seem to have received His proclamation the same way. Yet at this point Jesus has simply asked a question, albeit, one sufficiently provocative to garner the attention of the listening masses. As you might imagine, greed is timeless. His disciples, therefore, immediately jumped to an erroneous conclusion based upon the event that just unfolded. Don't we do the same thing all the time—jump to conclusions prior to hearing all of the relevant information? Hold on to that thought for a minute. We will return to this markedly relevant issue shortly. First, however, let's allow Jesus to clarify His teaching.

> *"But Jesus answered again and said to them, 'Children, how hard is it for those **who trust** in riches to enter the kingdom of God! It is easier for a camel to go through the eye of a needle than for a rich man to enter the kingdom of God.' And they were greatly astonished, saying among themselves, 'who then can be saved?'"*
> **—Mark 10:24-26**

That is one heck of a question, isn't it? Isn't that the real issue—*who can be saved?* Isn't that the one question that humanity has been wrestling with from the inception of time? Isn't *who can be saved* at the heart of every religion mankind has ever dreamed up and twisted into his own self-centered, sin darkened image?

Incredibly, as we hear the words of Jesus, it *still* appears that He is condemning the wealthy. However, if you pay close attention you will find that He added the interpretive phrase, "*Those **who trust** in riches,*" to clarify His doctrine. The issue here is not riches. The issue is trust. Where have you placed your trust?

Unlike Bartimaeus, and much like the wealthy of our day, the rich young ruler did not trust Jesus. He trusted his money. Does this ring a bell for you? What is more powerful to you, God or money? Do not be deceived, "*you cannot serve God and money. For either you will love one and hate the other, or you will be loyal to one and despise the other.*" (Matthew 6:24)

Therefore, I would encourage you to take an honest look at yourself in regard to this topic. What do you love more, God or money? Where do your loyalties lie? If you really want to know the answer, look at your lifestyle. What do you spend most of your time doing? Do you make time for God? Notice that I did not ask, "Do *you* have time for God?" In the world we live in it is easy to become ensnared by busyness. Therefore, we must prioritize our time. If you want to claim that God is first in your life, making time for Him requires Him being foremost on your "to do" list.

Furthermore, do you invest in God's kingdom? Do you use the gifts God has given you—your time, talent, and yes, even your money, to better humanity; or are you simply heaping up for your future? Don't get me wrong, I believe in preparing for the future and I believe in saving money. The Bible happens to agree. *"A good man leaves an inheritance to his children's children, but the wealth of the sinner is stored up for the righteous."* (Proverbs 13:22) The question, however, and the point of the matter is; how generous are you?

Do you trust that God will not just replace, but multiply the seed you have sown. Do you believe that *"God is able to make all grace abound toward you, that you, always having all sufficiency in all things, may have an abundance for every good work?"* (2 Corinthians 9:8) Before you answer, keep in mind that the things you truly believe are what you will live out in your life. Therefore, we must take stock of how we are living.

The rich young ruler loved and fully trusted the power of his money. As a result, he had no faith or trust in the power of Christ, or the kingdom of God. Furthermore, and as we have already seen, when Jesus speaks of the "kingdom of God" in this passage, He is not discussing heaven. The Greek word used here for "kingdom" refers to a "realm." Jesus was teaching about entering the realm of God, which is God's way of doing and being right. He was referring to being governed by Yahweh.

When you dwell in a particular kingdom or government, a country in our day, you must adhere to its laws, environment, and culture. Jesus was teaching that it is easier for a camel to go through the eye of a needle then for a rich man to be *governed* by God's way of doing things. Why? Most rich men do not believe they need to rely upon God to have their needs met. They believe their money can do that for them. Do you see the problem within this thought process?

Yahweh is completely disregarded when in truth *"every good and perfect gift is from above."* (James 1:17)

Jesus' main focus was not money. Money was the example before the eyes of the masses, but money was secondary to the real issue. The primary focus was idolatry. Because the rich young ruler was governed by his money he was unwilling to be governed by Yahweh. This misplaced love of money is the definition of materialism, and this, by the way, is what kept him from entering the kingdom of God.

To make matters worse, materialism leads every one of its captors down the road of idolatry. Because it misplaces your trust, it cannot end anywhere else. Anything that is placed ahead of God keeps you away from God. This is the true definition of idolatry. Idolatry is trusting any source other than God to deliver you from the trials of life. Money was the god the Rich Young Ruler's entire life revolved around. The love of money led the rich young ruler down the path of materialism whose ultimate destination always ends in idolatry. Idolatry, by the way, bans you from entering the kingdom of God. That is why it is commandment numero uno, *You shall have no other gods before Him.* (Exodus 20:3) Failure to obey commandment number one nullifies all the others.

What is your idol? Is it work, money, pride, ego, perhaps even your children? Children are a big one, especially for you ladies. It requires immense trust to place the future of your children into the hands of the Almighty.

How about your Pastor, Priest or Rabbi? Have you elevated them to the position of God— relying solely upon *their faith* to meet your spiritual needs? I know that one hits home for many of you. Only *you* can answer the question. Without ever realizing it, you cause Yahweh to burn with jealousy when you demote His position of power to that of the mere figure head of your religious rituals, as much of modern Christianity has become.

"To what purpose is the multitude of your sacrifices to Me?" Says the Lord. "I have had enough of burnt offerings of rams and the fat of fed cattle. I do not delight in the blood of bulls, or of lambs or goats. "When you come to appear before Me, who has required this from your hand, to trample My courts? Bring no more futile sacrifices; incense is an abomination to Me. The New Moons, the Sabbaths, and the calling of assemblies-- I cannot endure iniquity and the sacred meeting, your New Moons and your appointed feasts My soul hates; They are a trouble to Me, I am weary of bearing them."
—Isaiah 1:11-14

What is keeping you from the kingdom of God and living your life according to God culture? Acting upon the answer will change your destiny. With that being said, you may be wondering why Jesus' teaching absolutely astonished His disciples. By their reaction, I believe they misinterpreted Jesus' message as well. That is why He needed to clarify it with the interpretive phrase, *"Those who trust in riches."*

As Christians, we tend to disregard the fact that Jesus and His disciples were Jewish. As a result we have a completely different, and perhaps even, flawed mindset. If you were Jewish in Jesus' day there would have been three historical figures at the forefront of your thinking, Abraham, Moses, and the great King David.

If you are a modern day Christian, I would venture to guess that when pondering the Word of God these are not the characters you conjure up. Most certainly, and rightly so, Jesus and the crucifixion is front and center in your mind. Perhaps as you dig deeper, the teachings of Paul and the Apostles shape your rationale. Therefore, we tend to forget, or perhaps never learned, the progression of covenant within the Old Testament which was built upon, and revolved around prosperity.

"And the Lord said to Abram: Get out of your country, from your family, and from your father's house, to a land that I will show you. I will make you a great nation, I will bless you and make your name great, and you shall be a blessing. I will bless those who bless you, and curse those who curse you, and in you all the families of the earth shall be blessed."
—Genesis 12:1-3

Material blessing was part of the Old Covenant. Consider the following evidence, *"Abram was **very rich** in livestock, in gold, and in silver."* (Genesis 13:2) As a matter of fact, if you recall our discussion from my first book *God Culture*, Abram was so rich that the land could not support both he and his nephew Lot. They had to split up. Therefore, Jesus' disciples must be thinking, "If the blessed such as Abraham cannot be saved, who can be?" Their thoughts would have immediately progressed to Moses and David. King David was extremely wealthy and his son Solomon became the richest man who would *ever* walk the earth. (2 Chronicles 9:13-26) It has been estimated that King Solomon would be worth over *one trillion* of today's U.S. dollars. That is an awful lot of money. Undoubtedly they must be thinking, "Is Jesus teaching that neither of them could be saved?"

How about Moses, was he rich or poor? "Of course Jesus could not have been referring to Moses, could He?" In regard to Moses, I do not believe he was wealthy in the traditional sense, the way David, Solomon, or even Abraham were wealthy. Moses actually had three stages in his life. Stage one was very wealthy. Although born a slave, he was saved from Planned Parenthood, I mean the original slaughter of the innocents ordered by Pharaoh and grew up as the Prince of Egypt, the adopted son of Pharaoh.

By the way, the Pharaoh whom Moses opposed prior to the Exodus was his brother by adoption. Moses and Prince Ramses II (whom many now believe to be Thutmose II) grew up together. The first born of Pharaoh to die was technically Moses' nephew. Let that sink in for a moment. That could not have been easy for Moses and demonstrates his immense faith, trust and obedience to God.

Nevertheless, Moses was very wealthy for the first forty years of his life. Do not forget though, it was all Pharaoh's money. His slaying of the Egyptian guard caused him to flee to Midian. When Moses left Egypt he left broke, having nothing but the clothes on his back. The Midianite's, by the way, were descendants of Abraham through his second wife Keturah. Interestingly enough, Moses did not just randomly run in any direction. He knew exactly where to go at this turning point in his life. Do you?

During the second stage of his life Moses marries Zipporah, the Midianite woman, and daughter of Jethro, who was also not a poor man. He dwells in Midian for the second forty years of his life. Finally, he is called by God to deliver the Israelites from Egypt, which he does, and they spend the remaining third, forty years, of Moses' life in the desert, where he eventually dies.

There's Gold in Them Thar Hills

Perhaps you are thinking, "They certainly must have been poor in the desert." In response to that, allow me to ask a few questions. What was the *golden* calf made of, which Moses not only had ground into powder, he was so ticked off by Israel's rebellious behavior that he forced them to drink it! Most never realize that Moses was an ancient day Bad A#*—no doubt the Original Gangsta and a man after my own heart.

Day after day, the O.G. Moses strutted into the court of the most powerful man in the then known world and bellowed, "Let my people go!" When Pharaoh refused he brought some horrific supernatural plague to display the power of God! And you thought you have it goin' on? You think your gang is rough? Check out the

"*Sons of Israel*," who defied Pharaoh, controlled the weather and ultimately destroyed the Egyptian army.

The next time you think you are "all that," make it rain fire. Split the Red Sea and then drown your enemies in it. Like it or not, "*The Lord is a man of war.*" (Exodus 15:3) Obliterating anarchy amongst men is His trademark. If you do not believe me check out Revelation 19:15.

> "*Now out of His mouth goes a sharp sword, that with it He should strike the nations. And He Himself will rule them with a rod of iron. He Himself treads the winepress of the fierceness and wrath of Almighty God.*"

Yahweh is the pinnacle of power. He is the "baddest" King in existence! Do you realize that even after destroying the Golden Calf the Israelites still possessed enough precious metal to construct the tabernacle? Do not forget about the Ark of the Covenant. It was overlaid with pure gold as well. Have you considered what the utensils and the other items of the tabernacle were made of? Being that oil had not yet been discovered and there were not any refineries I am pretty sure they were not made of plastic. I doubt they used paper plates.

They had gold in addition to other precious metals—and quite a few gem stones as well. You might be thinking that sounds a bit strange. Where could they have possibly found gold in the desert? They were slaves in Egypt. They were not fabricating pyramid bricks for profit.

Although that is true, I must tell you that when God delivers—He delivers! They did not find their gold in the desert. They found it right there in Egypt! Check out the following biblical passage and remember that they were still slaves when this occurred. As Israel is leaving for the wilderness, Moses, under the inspiration of Yahweh, instructs them to make one last request of their slave masters:

*"Now the children of Israel had done according to all the words of Moses, and they had asked **from the Egyptians** articles of silver, articles of gold, and clothing. (Wow! What did I tell you? Moses had brass you know what's!)* ***And the Lord had given the people favor*** *in the sight of the Egyptians, so they granted them what they requested. Thus* ***they plundered the Egyptians.****"*
(Exodus 12:35-36)

Although you may question the plausibility of such an event, I must tell you that I find this to be absolutely fascinating. As you will see, the account is not only credible, it is *incredible*, and completely logical as well.

God, in His infinite power has an amazing ability to simultaneously accomplish numerous tasks and purposes while utilizing only one single event. Did you know that even a single scripture verse can have multiple meanings? It is call the *Law of Double Reference*. Do you recall the various plagues that had been experienced by the Egyptians? There is no doubt that they were acutely aware that all the tragedy they had been experiencing was due to the presence of God's people in their land. Moses would not let them forget it. Day after day he publicly ridiculed Pharaoh as he bellowed, "Let my people go!"

In addition to agonizing illnesses, destruction of property, unexplained natural phenomena, and inconceivable outbreaks of nature, the horror of experiencing the death of every first-born in all of Egypt, both human and animal, was more than the Egyptian people could bear. It was the straw that broke the camel's back and they were collectively in the midst of unprecedented grief. Therefore, when the Israelites obeyed the command of God to plunder the Egyptians, they would have given anything to rid themselves of "those people" *and their God.*

Why is this important? We are *"those people!"* Yahweh is still our God. Think about all the tribulation the Israelites went through.

Four-hundred years of enslavement. They were battle hardened for the journey to come. Why do you think modern history has had so much difficulty defeating Afghanistan? Mighty Russia could not do it. The United States could not do it. Why? War is all they know. They have generations of battle hardened citizens accustomed to hardship, death and chaos. The Afghani's alive today have never experienced peace.

Therefore, consider the plight of ancient Egypt. They were living their plush little pagan lifestyles in the lap of luxury. The hardships bestowed upon them by the judgment of Yahweh broke them physically and emotionally. It was too much, too fast, and I believe they simply crumbled under the pressure. They gave up. They could not handle one more day of adversity. Are you beginning to comprehend the incredible wisdom of Yahweh? I wonder what might happen if our enlightened modern cultures experienced these same hardships. Perhaps we are close to finding out.

Quite honestly, I believe our modern societies would break down the same way under such pressure. Throughout history, we have seen that people will do nearly anything to escape pain and suffering. Heck, my own wife can harass me into giving her nearly anything she wants. Seriously guys, you know it is true.

Can you even imagine enduring what the Egyptian's suffered, basically without any warning and certainly without any preparation? Can you fathom the fear, confusion and grief they would have been experiencing?

The majority of Egypt's citizens were not present in Pharaoh's courts. Their only source of information would have been hearsay and what they were experiencing themelves. Therefore, in their broken-down state of hopelessness they simply handed their wealth over to the newly redeemed of Yahweh. They just wanted the pain to stop.

At some point I believe something similar will happen again. As we just read, the Word of God says, *"The wealth of the sinner is laid up for the just."* (Proverbs 13:22) Hang in there if you are struggling. Your current situation is not permanent. Hold fast to the Lord. A supernatural transfer of wealth may be hard for you to believe, but since the Word says it, I believe it will come to pass.

At some point, and in some manner the wicked of the world will give their wealth over to the righteous. Who knows, perhaps taxation has a higher purpose after all. Why would God do this if wealth is actually evil? The answer is simple. He would not. Therefore, I must conclude that money is not evil, people are.

Money is simply a medium of exchange. I do not know how or when this will occur, or if it already is through social programs, but perhaps we are beginning to experience the birth pangs manifested in all the trouble being experienced by the world's economic systems. Just like the Israelites, we will eventually possess the land. *"Blessed are the meek, for they shall inherit the earth."* (Matthew 5:5) Don't worry, Yahweh is infallible. With Him on our side it is impossible for us to lose.

If you are in a tough situation be encouraged by the plight of Israel. In their wildest dreams the Israeli slaves in Egypt could not have imagined that they would be knocking on Egyptian doors and being handed silver, gold, and very expensive clothing. However, *"God is able to do exceedingly, abundantly, beyond all we can ask or think, according to the power that works in us."* (Ephesians 3:20)

I am not sure we can grasp all that this means. We must, however, obtain, maintain and remain in unity to achieve it. The above scripture proclaims, *"The power that works in us,"* plurally, meaning more than one. If and when we can finally achieve unity, and denominationalism is a tremendous hindrance, we will once again begin to see the wondrous works and miracles contained in both the Book of Acts, as well as, the Old Testament. Unity will lead us to soteria, the salvation of our spirit, soul and bodies. All those in harmony with God culture will be saved. Therefore, let's return to the subject of *who* can be saved? Is it any wonder that the disciples were astonished at Jesus' teaching? In their minds and according to Jewish tradition, financial success was evidence that you were living in the blessing of God. Now Jesus shows up on the scene and obliterates their doctrine.

In truth, Jesus was about to make us all a whole lot richer under the New Covenant. Maybe not in the manner some might expect, however, and certainly not in the way His disciples expected.

> *"But Jesus looked at them and said, 'With men it is impossible, but not with God; for with God all things are possible.'"*
> **—Mark 10:27**

The Narrow Gate

Allow me to reveal a truth to you. Many have interpreted scripture to mean that a wealthy man *cannot* be saved. If you are wealthy I am very pleased to reveal to you that nothing could be further from the truth. Scripture says nothing of the sort. Like various other portions of scripture, we misinterpret Mark's gospel because we have never lived in ancient Israel. Therefore, we are unfamiliar with its landscape. When we see the phrase, "Eye of a needle," we think only of a little pin with a hole at the top. From this flawed perspective there is no way a camel could fit through. It is physically impossible. Armed merely with this erroneous information we make an uninformed judgment and misinterpret the entire message of Yahweh. Unfortunately, the ignorant dissemination of such propaganda has dragged on for centuries causing multitudes to suffer unnecessarily.

Had you lived in ancient Israel you would may recognized the "Eye of the needle" as something quite different, thus bringing clarity to Jesus' reference. Legend has it that the "Eye of the needle" was a nickname for a narrow gate that was one of the entrances to the Holy city of Jerusalem.

A camel *could* fit through it, however, this was accomplished with great difficulty. The camel would sort of have to get down on its belly and do a "slide crawl" through the gate with just inches to spare on either side and on top. It was not pretty, but it was certainly possible. It was extremely difficult and I am sure not very pleasant if you were a camel, but it *could* squeeze through. Nevertheless, this saying astonished the Jewish disciples of Jesus' day. The very thought that Moses, David or Abraham could be unsaved would have been mortifying.

The point is, and as Jesus clarified, nothing is impossible with God. No matter whom you are— rich or poor, young or old, you *can* be saved.

> *"In truth I perceive that God shows no partiality."*
> **—Acts 10:34**

God desires that every one of His beloved children live eternally. However, in order to be saved every single one of us must follow the same process. We must "*seek **first** the kingdom of God* (Seek first to be governed by God) *and His righteousness* (Which is found only in Jesus Christ) *and all these things* (Both material and spiritual blessings) *will be added to you.*" (Mathew 6:33)

Seeking the Lord first and foremost, is how Bartimaeus received his sight, which ultimately led to his salvation. This is always the result of following Christ—your eyes are opened and you clearly see the Lord. Since Christ is the only path to salvation it is also how every man, woman and child receives redemption as well. Do not worry, regardless of where you live or what your religion or culture is, God has "got your back" when you make Jesus your Lord.

Bartimaeus had nothing in the natural, but as he courageously and unashamedly pursued God first, his faith manifested into the restoration of his physical eyesight and ultimately the salvation of his soul. Simply stated, his faith led him down the road to salvation. He became a disciple. The good news is that if you are willing to seek, and to be governed by Yahweh, He can and will manifest the fruit of your salvation as well. Are you willing to put Him ahead of everything else in your life? When you do He will fulfill your heart's desire.

The solution to every aspect of life rests within the Spirit of God. Contrary to what most have been taught, "*it's His good pleasure to give you the kingdom.*" (Luke 12:32) You simply need to recognize His call and obediently follow Him down the path of righteousness. Therefore, I would encourage you to dwell in His Word (the Bible). Take the necessary time to pray and to worship Him. This will connect you to His Spirit and He will save your soul. You will enter His kingdom through the narrow gate of the Lord Jesus Christ of Nazareth.

Incredibly, and without even knowing what happened, you will one day realize that Yahweh has changed your perspective from "now" to "forever." He will have become your number one asset and the only possession that can move you from here to eternity. He *is* the greatest asset any man can possess. Eternal wealth lies through the narrow gate of Jesus Christ. So together, let's squeeze through the "Eye of the needle," and rejoice in the everlasting kingdom of forever. Who can be saved? The answer—*my final answer* is quite simple, "*all those who call upon the name of the Lord.*" (Romans 10:13)

CHAPTER 11

The Kinsman Redeemer

As we continue to reveal the true nature of Yahweh, let's delve into one of the most significant claims made by Jesus regarding His identity. Who does Jesus really claim to be? Why didn't the Rich Young Ruler we read about in the previous chapters recognize Him, while the blind man, Bartimaeus, clearly did? What did Bartimaeus know that most in the crowd seemed to either completely miss or disregard? To answer these questions let us revisit scripture.

In the gospel of John 5:39, Jesus exclaimed, *"You search the Scriptures, for in them you think you have eternal life; and these are they which testify of Me."* That is one bold claim! In modern English Jesus was saying, "You read your Bible, or your Torah, in search of eternal life and the whole book is about Me. If you truly want to know who

Yahweh is look no further. He is standing right in front of you. I am the eternal life you seek"

Can you imagine what would happen if someone made this claim today? Many have tried. Take David Koresh of Waco, Texas, for example, who, like many others before him, returned from his visit to Israel with a Messiah complex. Talk about narcissism! As you no doubt remember from watching the evening news, his apocalyptic message convinced quite a few of his Branch Davidian followers to remain inside their compound as Janet Reno, the former United Stated Attorney General, had it burned to the ground—the smoke and flames apocalyptically engulfing their last precious moments of life.

Perhaps many of the ancient Israelites viewed Jesus the same way. After all, Jesus was saying, "I am the fulfillment of the law. I am the coming of the foretold one. I am the culmination of ancient prophesy," which would have undoubtedly resonated as blasphemy to the ear of the ancient believer in Yahweh. I have no doubt that many viewed the "insane" assertions of Jesus Christ of Nazareth in the same narcissistic manner we viewed the claims of David Koresh of Waco. No wonder they plotted against Him!

Is there a difference between Jesus Christ and David Koresh? How do we know? Was Jesus the Messiah or was He simply some disillusioned lunatic with a charismatic ability to deceive the masses, as many whom dispute His authenticity have asserted? How *is* Yahweh revealed in the person of Jesus Christ?

Without being intimate with the Word of God it is impossible to comprehend who Jesus truly is and the redeeming work He has accomplished. Regardless of your faith, to understand the role Jesus plays in the redemption of humanity we must gain an understanding of Levitical law. While my Jewish friends understand the law, they have failed to discern Jesus as the fulfillment thereof. There is a reason the Shekhinah glory manifest Himself as flesh and blood. He is the end of the law and the beginning of faith. As you will see, Jesus has completely fulfilled the law, thus confirming His true identity.

While we are on the topic, what about Islam and the manifold world religions? Why can't they see the real Jesus? After all, Jesus is a central figure in Islamic doctrine, namely, as one of the preeminent prophets and the judge of mankind in the end of time. How bizarre is that when we see such aggressive opposition to both Jesus Christ and Christianity within the actual practice of Islam? My Muslim friends, however zealous they may be, simply have no concept of the law their religion is rooted upon. In fact, they are *discouraged* from knowing. It may reveal some discrepancies causing them to question their faith. Just like the Pharisees of Jesus' day, the Mullah's are simply unwilling to relinquish their power.

Religion aside, without the foundational concept of the Levitical laws of Moses, the law concerning slavery in particular, Jesus cannot be completely comprehended or positioned in His rightful place as Savior of the entire world. This short study of the Kinsman Redeemer will show you exactly why His claims were not just sane, but divine, and why beyond any shadow of a doubt He is everything He proclaimed to be.

Born This Way

To begin this discussion, we must come to an understanding of what every human being is unwittingly born into—slavery. No matter what country you live in or whatever continent you are on; irrespective of the religion you practice and whatever your ethnicity is, you have been born into slavery. There is just no avoiding it. You are not born free. Due to original sin you are born captive and enslaved by its lusts. Human nature has become nothing more than sin nature.

Many of you will refuse to believe this. Therefore, I will prove it to you with one simple question and one honest answer on your part. Prepare yourself. The word I am about to use has been deemed filthy in our new global culture. In fact, it is considered worse than the most precarious of four letter words. Nevertheless, it is rooted in absolute truth.

The word I am referring to, which has been twisted into the object of pop culture filth, is "sin." Have you ever sinned? If you answer is no, or perhaps, even, "I used to," you have proven my point. You have just demonstrated your captive nature. In your quest for self-preservation you have just told a lie, possibly even to yourself, which simply stated is sin. You have fallen into the same trap of self-righteousness as the rich young ruler. You cannot help it. Anytime enough pressure is imposed and you begin to feel either uncomfortable or endangered you will do it again, regardless of how innocent it may seem. Simply attempting to place a number on the multitude of lies one tells throughout a lifetime proves our captive nature to all of us.

Therefore, consider how Jesus answered both His friends and His enemies when they proclaimed their righteousness was to be garnered by their Abrahamic lineage. Whether you realize it or not, the Messiah is speaking directly to you in the following passage.

"Jesus answered them, 'Most assuredly I say to you, whoever commits sin is a slave of sin.'"
—John 8:34

This is a truth that applies to all of mankind. As a slave you are bound to your master. In times past you may even have been branded or had some sort of mark placed upon you. The brand, or mark, if you will, displayed who owned you. As you will see, some things never change.

When understanding the principle of slavery, the "Mark of the Beast" in the Book of Revelation takes on new meaning as you begin to realize who will place it upon the rebellious and deceived. In truth, the mark of the beast is not merely a future event. As we speak, Satan is continually brandishing mankind with the mark of our sin stained slavery. Without Jesus, mankind is hopelessly lost.

> *"Then I saw another beast coming up out of the earth, and he had two horns like a lamb and spoke like a dragon. And he exercises all the authority of the first beast in his presence, and causes the earth and those who dwell in it to worship the first beast, whose deadly wound was healed.*
>
> *He performs great signs, so that he even makes fire come down from heaven on the earth in the sight of men. And **he deceives those who dwell on the earth** by those signs which he was granted to do in the sight of the beast, telling those who dwell on the earth to make an image to the beast who was wounded by the sword and lived. He was granted power to give breath to the image of the beast, that the image of the beast should both speak and cause as many as would not worship the image of the beast to be killed.*
>
> *He causes all, both small and great, rich and poor, free and slave, **to receive a mark** on their right hand or on their foreheads, and that **no one may buy or sell except one who has the mark,** or the name of the beast, or the number of his name."*
> **—Revelation 13:11-17**

Spiritually speaking, this is not just some way out future event. Its roots have already been sown deep within the spirit of humanity. We have all been branded by sin. It has no doubt left its mark upon your life. Although I realize there will be some sort of physical mark placed upon humanity during the Great Tribulation, you do not need to wait for the revelation of the anti-Christ to receive your mark. If you have not been redeemed by the Lord Jesus, sin is your mark. It is your lord and just like a hardened slave master it drives your every thought, word and deed—all the way from murder to that harmless little white lie. The scene is played out day after day and in every corner of the globe.

There is not a person alive who has been able to speak for more than a couple days who has not sinned. Rebellion comes naturally to man. "No," is one of the first words every child learns. Within hours, and sometimes even minutes, we find the same child using it as an act of insubordination. Because sin is against the law, we have been judged guilty and have been sentenced to death. Therefore, we are held captive until we breathe our last breath on earth. On that day your time has run out. We will be brought to justice and our death sentence will be imposed—unless "Someone" pardons us and sets us free.

Please understand that Jesus is always purposeful with His words. Unlike you and me, He does not, has not, and never will, speak idly. He made the connection between sin and slavery on purpose. He wants you to comprehend His true identity. I would encourage you to gain a clear revelation of the following distinction. He does not want you just to identify *with* Him. He wants you to *identify* Him. Do you understand the difference? He is telling you who He is. The connection He is making identifies Him precisely as the Kinsman Redeemer of Leviticus chapter twenty five. He is the fulfillment of it and in just a few minutes I will show you how and why.

Keep in mind when reading the following passage that God is not the author of slavery—man is. Neither is God condoning slavery. He is mandating how man is to humanely treat such slaves and that there *must* be a means of obtaining freedom. That is, unless the enslaved man *chooses* to remain with His master. This in itself is a picture of redemption.

I would also like to point out that God uses every human situation, past and present, to demonstrate His future plan. It seems to me that humanity is continually play acting the show entitled, *Redemption*. Scene one includes, but is not limited to, man's choice to enslave His brother.

History, which is "His story," is God's way of revealing Himself to you. He has designed every aspect of human life as a compass pointing directly back to Him, but you must learn to recognize where to look. Unlike physical sight, spiritual eyesight is a learned skill. Blind Bartimaeus, whom we learned about in the previous two chapters, is the living illustration of this truth. This is why it is so important to be intimately familiar with the Word of God. He is our true North.

If you choose Jesus, He will gladly set you free and He has the authority to do so. However, if you wish to remain a slave to your current master, you may. It is your choice. So let's check out Leviticus 25. Once you understand what I am about to teach *"you shall know the truth, and the truth shall make you free.* (John 8:32) Therefore, ready or not, here I come.

Justice

> *"And if one of your brethren who dwells by you becomes poor, and sells himself to you, you shall not compel him to serve as a slave. As a hired servant and a sojourner he shall be with you, and shall serve you until the year of Jubilee. And then he shall depart from you-he and his children with him-and shall return to his own family. He shall return to the possession of his fathers."*
> **—Leviticus 25:39-41**

I have previously stated that before understanding why Jesus had to come as a man you must be able to answer the question, why was man created in the image of God? Let's go back and review these foundational questions that so many ask, but so few are equipped to answer. Why Jesus, and why God's image? Additionally, why didn't God just wipe out sin? In order to gain a full understanding I must share the following concepts with you.

First and foremost, is the fact that God always operates according to His own law. How could a holy and just God practice anything different? What humanity is asking God to do, to simply wipe out sin, does not make sense. If God truly gave all authority of the earth to man, which He did, how could He rescind it and remain a just God? The truth is that He will not implement a "do over." If He broke just one promise we could never trust Him with another. Since that is not just an absurd thought, but an actual impossibility, He will not alleviate sin that way. God's integrity will never allow Him to break His own law.

Pardon Me

God's way is to *buy* us out of slavery, not in opposition to, but *according* to His own law. He *is* the wealthy next of kin who has the ability to pay the prescribed price, *"an eye for an eye, a tooth for a tooth, a life for a life . . ."* a man for man. (Leviticus 24:18-20) Consider the following, *"Whoever kills an animal shall restore it; but whoever kills a man shall be put to death."* (Leviticus 24:21) God is a holy God of justice and, by the way, because Satan has murdered humanity, his ultimate end is utter destruction in the Lake of Fire. Justice will be served.

As for mankind, we too have sinned against God. Therefore, our lives have also been required according to the law. As we shall see shortly, the Day of Atonement was insufficient to redeem humanity. The death of an animal was just not costly enough. A life for a life requires equality, a human life for a human life—but not just any human life. The law required a perfect "Life." Because the man Adam, created without sin, became sin, redemption required a life of equal or greater value. With no sinless humans available, (Romans 3:23) Jesus, born of the seed of a woman and apart from sin, became sin, as well. Therefore, Jesus is the only answer. No other life could suffice. Jesus Christ fulfills the archetype that Adam was.

God is perfect. Adam was unmarked by sin when he was created. Even under the law the sacrifice of a defective animal was an unacceptable offering to the King of all kings. As an offering for humanity there is no equity in the life of a man blemished by sin. Yahweh will not accept an animal as a permanent solution to sin. Man is far too majestic to be equated with a bull or a goat. The sacrificial system was a *Band Aid* to plug the whole in humanity until the permanent solution manifest.

Until you make Jesus your Lord you are defective. You are tainted with the mark of sin. It has disfigured you in the eyes of Yahweh. Therefore, you, or anyone else for that matter, can never fulfill the law. As a result, you are prohibited from entering the most holy place in His Temple. You have been expelled from His presence.

No matter how hard you try and no matter how many good deeds you have done, you need help to reenter His gates. The ugly and unwanted tattoo of sin can never be removed nor even covered up by our own undertakings. You need someone to free you from its bondage. You need a Savior. There is no other option. You have nothing of equal value to give. You cannot buy or lie your way out of sin. You need your nearest of Kin to pardon you.

Hence, the law requires the only acceptable redemption price—a perfect man. Due to the problem of sin there could only ever be one. Although man's nature has been altered, I have some good news for you. The *Bin Adam,* (Second Adam) who is Jesus Christ of Nazareth, the perfect and sinless Son of Man did not inherit His nature from Adam. His nature is divine, passed along from His heavenly Father. He was born of a virgin.

Therefore, He did not inherit Adam's sinful nature. Do you see the genius of God? Can you now comprehend both the reason for and the necessity of the virgin birth? The second Adam, Jesus Christ of Nazareth, born of a woman, and having no earthly father did not receive the seed of sin. His nature was not passed down from the descendants of Adam. Yahweh is His Father. It is Yahweh's nature that Christ inherited at birth. Therefore, His nature is perfect. In human form He qualifies as the Kinsmen Redeemer you just read about. He did not just pay the redemption price. Jesus *is* the redemption price!

Image in That

Allow me to refresh your memory from a previous discussion. God had the foresight to know man would sin prior to millisecond number one of creation. Thus, He knows the end from the beginning. With such divine knowledge, He also knew He would need to come in human flesh to redeem us. Without comprehending this you can never fully grasp the concept of why Jesus had to come as a man. You may have peripherally understood it, but then try explaining it. Tongue tied is all I have to say. So why were you created in the image of God? The answer is that God knew the end from the beginning. Allow me to explain.

God knew in an instant that He was coming here as flesh and blood to destroy sin. Do not forget that He also authored and operates by His own law. He knows every jot and tittle of it. He will never violate it. As you read above, it takes one of kinship to redeem a slave. Therefore, not just anyone has the authority to pay the redemption price. It must be your relative. As you also read above, if you have ever committed sin, you became a slave to it. Without a Redeemer you will serve it for the rest of your life, both natural and unnatural.

With the exception of Jesus Christ, all of humanity is imperfect and has been disqualified from serving in the holy presence of almighty God. *"For there is not a just man on earth who does good and does not sin."* (Ecclesiastes 7:20) Therefore, neither Mohammed, Buddha, nor any religious ritual, festivity or observance can save your eternal soul. Only your perfect next of kin, Jesus Christ of Nazareth, the Word of God in human flesh (John 1:1 and 14) has the authority to redeem you.

> *"For He made Him who knew no sin to be sin for us, that we might become the righteousness of God in Him."*
> **—2 Corinthians 5:21**

Jesus Christ is the fulfillment of the sacrificial system. He is the atonement contained within the law. Therefore, in order to accomplish the mission, and contrary to what you may believe, God made it simple. When the time was right, and according to His schedule and not ours, Yahweh became one of our kin. He became one of our brethren—a man of flesh and blood, complete with human blood, DNA and every other characteristic required to be human. Think of the simplicity of His plan from His point of view. He already created you in His image. Being born was a mere formality. It was the accomplishment of the end that was determined from the beginning.

Because of its simplistic nature in relation to His immense power, the better part of humanity fails to recognize the genius of God's plan for salvation. Over one billion Muslims reject it because of its simplicity. "God would never lower Himself to be a man. He would never poop all over Himself as a baby," is how one dear Muslim friend stated it to me. Well, that is exactly what God did, poop and all! That does not limit His greatness. It exemplifies it.

In fact, Yahweh is so inconceivable that He told the entire world exactly when, where and how He would come, and exactly what He was going to do. Search the Old Testament for yourself. You will find Jesus everywhere. It testifies of Him. It is designed for you to understand and has been written down in a place where you can easily recognize, identify and gain access to it. None of the pieces are missing. You simply have to take the time required to put it together.

Once you do, you will even discover that He has also told us when He is coming back and what your ultimate fate will be. Although He has not, and will not, give us an exact date or timeframe, He wrote down all of the events that would occur prior to His feet touching down on the Mount of Olives. (Zechariah 14:4)

I must tell you that He is at the doorstep. It is decision time, my friends. Time is running out. Watch the evening news and note the goings on in the Middle East and throughout the globe. There is no such thing as coincidence—just a predetermined plan to usher in eternity. Therefore, do not wait. Make Jesus your Lord and live. Time is short. *"Seek the Lord while He may be found."* (Isaiah 55:6) His mercy will not be available forever. You have been duly warned.

The simple truth is that you were created in His image because He knew He was coming here to get you. Unbeknownst to many, God is completely logical. How could someone of His preeminent intelligence not be? The most logical method of fulfilling His own law, to redeem you as His kin, was to create you *to be* His kin—then wrap up His glorious image in an earth suit, otherwise known as flesh and blood, and voila, problem solved. "See you in four thousand years or so, when I put on *My* earth suit."

Does that sound strangely impossible? I can assure you that it is not. In fact, here it is straight from the gospel of John. *"In the beginning was the Word, and the Word was with God and the Word was God . . . And the Word became flesh and dwelt among us.* (John 1:14) That is all flesh is, your earth suit. Your spirit is the real you. Just like a space suit, flesh and blood allows you to live and breathe in the atmosphere of the natural realm.

Your mortal body is not who you truly are. *"Beloved, now we are children of God; and **it has not yet been revealed what we shall be**, but we know that when He is revealed, **we shall be like Him**, for we* *shall see Him as He is.*" (1 John 3:2) Your true nature is His image and your true home is heaven. Doesn't that blow your mind? You were created in the image of God because Jesus is *"the Lamb slain from the foundation of the world."* (Revelation 21:8) God not only knew the end from the beginning, He prepared it from thought number one. That is the pinnacle of power. To top it all off, it is perfectly logical and legal according to Yahweh's own law.

Show me Your ID

With that in mind, let us move on to the true identity of Jesus Christ. In the following pages I will show you the law of the Kinsman Redeemer, and how and where, Jesus Christ is the fulfillment within the New Covenant. Without knowing the law we can never truly understand what Jesus meant when He said, *"Do not think that I came to destroy the Law or the Prophets. I did not come to destroy but to fulfill."* (Matthew 5:17) His true identity is that of the Kinsman Redeemer of Leviticus 25. Therefore, you are about to discover His true mission. Do not forget that with God it is always about eternity.

Unlike the fakers, also known as false prophets, when God prophecies He does so in detail. Just as there was no mistaking who Jesus is in regard to the sacrifice of Isaac, there is no mistaking Jesus as the Kinsman Redeemer either. These scriptures are testifying to the true identity of Jesus Christ. They are a witness to all who desire to find Him. So let us break down the law concerning slavery and I will show you exactly where Jesus, and Jesus alone, fits into the picture.

Slave Brothers

Leviticus 25 is so detailed, that in many cases I cannot break this down for you sentence by sentence. I must do it phrase by phrase. In addition, Jesus fulfills a dual role here, that of a slave, in order to be manifested as flesh and blood, and that of redeemer, in order to escort you to heaven. Let's begin with Jesus as the slave.

*"And if one of your **brethren** who **dwells by you** becomes **poor:**"*

There are three identifications here. The first is that Jesus is our brethren. Let's have a look at the law in its fulfillment.

"For whom He foreknew, He also predestined to be conformed to the image of His Son, (I believe that surmises the preceding discussion regarding man's true nature.) *that He* (Capital H, Jesus) *might be **the firstborn among many brethren.**"*
—Romans 8:29

Did you know that when you make Jesus your Lord He becomes your brother? That is of utmost importance in fulfilling the law. It is the purpose of flesh and blood. A slave must be redeemed by one who is their kin. Jesus is God's firstborn, both physically and spiritually. When you accept Him as the Kinsman Redeemer you become one of His many brothers and sisters—a family member worthy of redemption..

The second identification is that he dwells near you.

*"I will set my tabernacle (which means dwelling place) among you, and my soul shall not abhor you. **I will walk among you** and be your God, and you shall be my people." (Leviticus 26:11-12)*

The word used here for "walk" is the Hebrew word "halak." It means to walk in a literal sense and to be conversant. It is the same word used to describe God's relationship to Adam in the Garden of Eden. So here we see the Lord literally walking and talking with His people in a physical, not a spiritual sense. Didn't Jesus, God in flesh (John 1:14), fulfill exactly that. During His time on earth Jesus physically dwelt near us, among us, and literally spoke with and to us. There is no mistaking His identity.

The final identification in this first phrase is that Jesus became poor.

"For you know the grace of our Lord Jesus Christ, that though He was rich, yet for your sakes He became poor, that you through his poverty might become rich."
—2 Corinthians 8:9

We are not talking about poverty in a monetary sense. The scripture is referring to the fact that Jesus Christ, as the third person of the trinity, being an equal part of the essence of Yahweh in all of His glory, gave it all up to become a man.

*"But we see Jesus, **who was made a little lower than the angels**, for the **suffering of death** crowned with glory and honor, that He, by the grace of God, might taste death for everyone."*
—Hebrews 2:9

I do not care how rich you are on this planet. The riches obtained by Bill Gates, Mark Zuckerberg and even the wealth of King Solomon could never compare with the glory of God. As a result, Jesus Christ giving up His glory subjected Him to abject poverty. Let's move on.

The next phrase we see in Leviticus 25:39 concerning the brethren is as follows:

"And sells himself to you, you shall not compel him to serve as a slave." Jesus was neither forced to the earth nor the cross. *"My Father loves Me because I lay down My life that I may take it again. **No one takes it from Me, but I lay it down Myself.**"*
—John 10:17-18

Jesus chose the cross. Amazingly, it appears that He volunteered for the job. As always, Jesus was compelled by love. If you take a close look at the gospels you will find that Jesus was always moved with compassion for the people. That is just who He is. *"God is love."* (1 John 4:8) In other words, Jesus sold himself to mankind for the purpose of becoming sin upon the cross. Let's continue with verse 40:

"As a hired servant and a sojourner he shall be with you, and shall serve you until the year of Jubilee."

Jesus was hired by the Father to perform the task of redemption. What was His pay? You! In truth, Jesus was a sojourner among the people. A sojourner is a traveler. The earth was never Jesus' home, just as the earth is not the true home of the believer in Yahweh.

"For our citizenship is in heaven, from which we also eagerly wait for the Savior, the Lord Jesus Christ."
—Philippians 3:20

Jesus' home is with the Father in heaven. He was simply here visiting until the completion of His God given task. The jubilee was a celebration that occurred every fifty years. If you were a slave on the year of jubilee you were set free. Thus, when you make Jesus Christ your Lord and Savior, you too are set free. Jesus also fulfills the year of jubilee.

I'm Going Home

When Jesus died upon the cross there was a celebration in heaven. It was so great that the veil of the temple was rent, the sun darkened, the earth quaked, and graves were torn open as the dead were raised. A multitude in Jerusalem witnessed the party. Sin and death had been defeated and you, my beloved friend and spiritual sibling, were set free!

> *"And then He shall depart from you—he and his children with him—and return to his own family. He shall return to the possession of his fathers."*
> **—Leviticus 25:41**

Then He was gone . . . having ascended into heaven and returned to His former glory with the *"Father of lights,"* (James 1:17) He was seated at the right hand of God Almighty.

What most people do not realize and what the Lord just revealed to me, is that it was not just we who were redeemed. *Jesus* was redeemed as well. Jesus became sin. Upon His resurrection He was freed from sin. Jesus *"returned to the possession of His Father."* He was restored to His former place of glory at the right hand of Yahweh. That, however, is not the end of the matter. Love is not yet finished. Just as the kinsman redeemer took his family members with him, the Lord Jesus is coming back for you as well.

> *"In My Father's house are many mansions; if it were not so I would have told you. I go to prepare a place for you. And if I go and prepare a place for you, **I will come again and receive you to Myself**; that where I am, there you may be also.*
> **—John 14:2-3**

Therefore, the true question is, are you willing to go with Him? I strongly urge you to start preparing. *"Behold, now is the accepted time; behold, now is the day of salvation."* (1 Corinthians 6:2)

The Case Against You

Let's now turn to Jesus as redeemer. This is equally as descriptive and incredible. However, there is a bit of an interesting twist here. Check out the following:

> *"Now if a sojourner or a stranger close to you becomes rich,* (Jesus the sojourner, upon His ascension to heaven was restored to His rightful place of glory, restoring His unparalleled riches.) *and one of your brethren who dwells by him becomes poor, and sells himself to a stranger or sojourner close to you, or to a member of the strangers family, after he is sold he may be redeemed again."*
> **—Leviticus 25:47-48**

What you have just read is the legal version of what happened in the Garden of Eden. It is the case precedent in Jehovah's courtroom. When Adam sinned he became poor. He lost everything and in the process, so did you. In the late 1920's my Grandfather owned a bakery in my parent's hometown. Business was booming. He had a fleet of trucks delivering baked goods to the surrounding area. Then the Great Depression hit and my grandfather lost his business . . . and I my inheritance. My family and I often joke with one another that we could have been *Wonder Bread!*

What happened to mankind in the Garden of Eden is eerily similar. Although I was not even born, the financial situation of the 1930's and 40's has affected my life—even to the present day. Thus is mankind's plight in regard to original sin.

Adam possessed all the riches of God's Garden of Eden. He enjoyed not just the necessities of life, but every luxury the Garden had to offer. He did not have to work a day in his life. The ground just yielded its fruit. However, when he disobeyed God and sold his soul to Lucifer, *"the stranger"* identified in Leviticus 25 above, his poverty became deplorable. The ground began producing thorns and thistles instead of the precious fruit of life. Not only did work become a necessity, it became drudgery. Does that sound familiar? His greatest loss, however, was his life and the life of his whole family, including you and me. Thank God that He is merciful. God made a way to save us.

> *"After he is sold he may be redeemed again.* **One of his brothers**
> *may redeem him."*
> **—Leviticus 25:48**

Lord Jesus to the rescue—our Kinsman Redeemer! Our wealthy brother has paid the redemption price, His own flesh and blood. You may now be one with God and make heaven your eternal abode. With that in mind, it is time to step into forever. Jesus Christ is Lord! Therefore, shake off the shackles of sin. Accept Jesus Christ and your wealthy next of kin, your spiritual brother Jesus Christ of Nazareth, will redeem you from the bonds of slavery. You too can be set free!

CHAPTER 12

Above the Law

In the previous chapters we have learned *why* Jesus Christ is the only means of salvation. We discovered exactly where He fits into scripture and that the entire biblical text, both Old and New Testaments, testify that He is the Savior of mankind. In the following pages, we are about to find out *how* Jesus saves, and thus, we will lay the chief cornerstone to the foundation of both faith and grace.

How Jesus freed humanity from sin is a question as old as the Bible itself. From a religious standpoint, we have heard the phrase, "Jesus saves" so often that we have become hardened to its truth. Sadly, in the minds of many it has become nothing more than a played out and tired old cliche'—merely the slogan on a bumper sticker that whimsically catches your eye as you peer through your windshield while driving to and from work.

How many people have seen John 3:16 displayed in the end zone of a football game? How many of the same people have ever bothered to look up what it means? Furthermore, how many even know *where* to look? I have actually spoken to supposedly Christian people who do not even know that John 3:16 is a biblical reference. How sad is that? No wonder same sex marriage has become the law of the land in America. Most Americans have no idea they have just spit in the face of God.

In a society that idolizes rock stars, sports figures and pop cultural icons, the majority of its people have no idea what the term "saved" even means, to whom it applies, or how one even becomes saved? The fact that so many are ignorant of the origin of John 3:16 is testament to the deceptive power of the *"prince of the power of the air,"* (Ephesians 2:2) who also happens to be the king of thieves.

How many times have you heard it stated, "Jesus died for your sin?" Most likely more times than you can count. Does the phrase mean anything to you or is it merely a religious idiom? Does it raise additional questions, or have the winds of apathy blown it swiftly past your consciousness while never occupying a second thought?

From a theological perspective, what is it that differentiates the sacrifice of Jesus Christ from the Day of Atonement in the Old Testament? If you are like I was, I just didn't get it. It did not make any sense to me. How can someone's death save us? Furthermore, why did God change religions? No one was able to tell me. I was expected to merely swallow down whatever I was spoon fed while never receiving any genuine answers to my questions. Perhaps you feel the same way.

Although I hate to admit it, spoon feeding does not work well for me. My nature is far too inquisitive. I am just being honest. It is who I am. It also seems to me that it does not work for a host of others within our modern culture either—particularly with the younger generations. That is exactly where the break down occurs, unless the topic is evolution of course. "That's just the way it is," is no longer acceptable to a generation raised on natural science, progressive tolerance and the internet. But Grandpa being a frog or a banana, that's okay. I don't know. I just don't get it. The herd mentality never ceases to amaze me.

Modern man, the younger generation in particular, has begun to question nearly every aspect of daily life—religion being foremost on the list. In our modern day of enlightenment, the internet can provide an answer within seconds. Unfortunately, most never get past the first few items to pop up, which often times are nothing more than erroneously opinionated monologues. Swallowing down whatever information the internet provides, however, seems to be much more palatable to today's modern man than nearly anything coming from the pulpit. Therefore, those who belong to God culture need to provide real answers to real, and sometimes even, difficult questions in regard to the truth of Yahweh.

Simply stated, God has not changed religions. How could He? He is neither religious nor a religion. In Jesus Christ, He has simply fulfilled that which He started however many millenniums ago. That is the true message of the gospel. It is also the sole purpose of the New Covenant—to take back those who were seemingly lost in the Garden of Eden, namely, you and me.

In truth, the more I discover the wonder of who God is, lost seems to be a perception created in the mind of man. God is incapable of losing anything. He knows exactly who you are, where you are, and when and how to reach you. In fact, Yahweh prepared the solution to man's woes before the foundation of the world was laid. (Revelation 13:8) Therefore, the real question is not in regard to *how* God saves the lost. That is easy enough to discern when you take an honest look at the Bible. The life and death question presented by the Lord Jehovah is, will you respond to truth?

In order to provide straightforward answers to an immensely skeptical generation, the gospel message must be communicated intelligently, while remaining without compromise in its authenticity. Time has not yet run out. I realize belief in God is based primarily on faith, but it has been my experience that those who possess the greatest faith are those who have sought the most answers. It is okay to question God's Word. Searching for answers *is* seeking God.

> *"Then the brethren immediately sent Paul and Silas away by night to Berea. When they arrived, they went into the synagogue of the Jews. These were more fair-minded than those in Thessalonica, in that they received the word with all readiness, **and searched the Scriptures daily to find out whether these things were so.** Therefore **many of them believed**, and also not a few of the Greeks, prominent women as well as men."*
> **—Acts 17:10-12**

In truth, our modern day religious systems are failing to accomplish the mission. People need to be informed of the good news in a manner that actually makes sense to our modern culture without demonizing those who have real questions. Just like the Berean's, with all readiness we need to diligently pursue truth, and also like the apostle Paul, we need to learn how to confidently communicate it.

> *"How then shall they call on Him in whom they have not believed? and how shall they believe in Him of whom they have not heard? and how shall they hear without a preacher?"*
> **—Romans 10:14**

Paul made such a solid case for Christ that I have been told the Book of Romans had been used in the past as an example to teach law school students how to build a case. Do not forget that Paul was an expert in Jewish law. Paul was a lawyer. Both he and God purposely used his skill-set to argue the lost right into heaven. Why have we abandoned this principle? Isn't God worth the extra effort? After all, this is how the gospel message was originally disseminated.

The gospel message should not be merely preached. It also must be taught and learned. Even Jesus, in addition to His numerous sermons, taught tirelessly in the temples of Israel, as did Peter, James, John, Paul, George and Ringo. Obviously I am just kidding about George and Ringo.

Revival meetings with attendees numbering in the tens of thousands, (It has even been reported that evangelist's such as Reinhard Bonnke have ministered to numbers in the millions.) are a modern day phenomenon. Unfortunately, with so few discipleship programs to solidify the foundation of understanding, many of those saved at such events are simply left to fall away. This potentially does even more harm than good. In a world filled with unprecedented cultural cynicism, we may only have one shot at the sinner.

Do not misunderstand me. I am not just faulting the preacher. His or her role is absolutely necessary but the pulpit must get back on task as well. Watering down the message to fill the seats will not stand at the foot of the cross. Neither will the supposed body of Christ abandoning their newborn children. The judgment seat of Christ will require an account from all of us. Those of us entrusted with the gospel stand to suffer the greatest scrutiny. (James 3:1)

Therefore, the weakest link, or to use Bible lingo, *"the breach"* which has become the apathetic lack of participation within the body of Christ, must be repaired. (Isaiah 58:12) It is we, the ones filling the church pew's, that are at fault. We are not fulfilling our commanded purpose. The body of Christ has not been designed to simply fill a seat.

"In fact, though by this time you ought to be teachers, you need someone to teach you the elementary truths of God's Word all over

again. You need milk, not solid food!"
—Hebrews 5:12

The gospel cannot survive purely on the emotion of a singular event, or for the purpose of building a congregation filled with spectating theatre groups. Emotions are fleeting at best. The gospel of Jesus Christ is far too critical to be reduced merely to a theatrical worship service, equipped with laser and light shows but devoid of true power.

80/20

I recently spent time ministering in Bitung, Indonesia, which is located on the Northern tip of the Island of Sulawesi. The people of God in Sulawesi cannot afford fancy light shows or most of the luxury's we find in the Western Church. The church is merely a compilation of people, sweat, (Bitung is tropical. I left every service soaked to the bone—and loved every second of it!) their instruments and most importantly, both the Word and the Spirit of God. I must tell you that I was absolutely blown away by the power of the worship when people are in the church for the sole purpose of seeking the Lord Jesus Christ. Never in my life have I experienced such power nor the incredible presence of God in such an intense manner.

The Indonesian church, (At least the one I am a part of) by the way, does not follow the 80/20 rule that we find in America and the West, where 80% of the work is done by 20% of the people. On our final day together we had a service dedicated only to those who volunteer as workers within the congregation. I had the privilege of administering the service and anointing the workers with oil, and not just to symbolize the Holy Spirit in their lives, but to actually impart the Holy Spirit into their lives. It was a wild scene.

In a church of one hundred people or so, you would expect about twenty of them to be at the service. This, however, was not the case. To my great amazement, it was not twenty people, or fifty people, or even seventy-five people who showed up for service. They pretty much all showed up. This is also true of the Indonesian church in America. Nearly all of them minister in some form. I left the island wondering, what has happened to the Western church?

As if that were not enough, we also fed the poor at the conclusion of the first two revival services. Can you imagine? the poor feeding the poor! No wonder God manifested. On the second day not one person left the service without receiving Jesus Christ into their lives. I felt like I was living in the Book of Acts when *"the Lord added to the church daily those who were being saved."* (Acts 2:47)

Trust me when I tell you that it was not me. The majority of the people could not even understand what I was saying. Language, however, is man's limitation. The Holy Spirit spoke exactly what each individual needed to hear. If the body of Christ would stop worshipping politicians, actors, rock stars, and the more recent phenomena of pop culture mega preachers, God will do it in the West as well. Church, I am calling for you to get back in the game! God's power is limitless.

On my final day, I could not help but express my love for this incredible congregation of believers while at the same time letting them know that although I showed up to bring revival to their town, they brought revival to me. The Spirit of God was already well at work in Bitung. God can always be found where the seeker is. I will never forget the experience and cannot wait to return. My life's mission is to bring this same revival home to you.

Go Big or Go Home

As I mentioned, the body of Christ must get back in the game. Discipleship is imperative to the spreading of the gospel. The newly saved cannot be left behind to fall back into the obscurity of an isolated culture. The dry bones must be brought to life. (Ezekiel 37:1-14) If you are reading this God has called you to become a disciple. Therefore, learn the Word of God and find someone else to disciple as well. The eternal fate of the person next to you is depending on you.

How does Jesus save? Fortunately, if you peer closely into the Word of God, the books of Romans and Colossians in particular, it is clear as day. Therefore, let us allow the grace of God to add the chief Cornerstone of Jesus Christ to our foundations.

To begin our discussion, let's have a look at the commandments Jesus Christ implemented in the New Covenant. According to Jesus, adhering simply to three commandments fulfills the entire law. Proselytizing, or as the Bible asserts, becoming a witness for Jesus Christ is the third and final command Jesus implemented just prior to His ascension. Unfortunately, most of today's church goers disregard the commandment "*go therefore and make disciples of all the nations . . . teaching them to observe all the things I have commanded you . . .*" (Matthew 28:19-20) and only practice the first two. The result has devastated to the truth of God.

Therefore, God's message to the church is simply this, "Go big or go home." The gospel is not for the faint of heart. *"For the message of the cross is foolishness to those who are perishing."* (1 Corinthians 1:18) The devil will not go down without a fight and he knows his time is short. Therefore, it is time to lace up the gloves. The coming years are not going to be easy for the disciple of Jesus Christ. The truth of the Bible is being diminished daily in America and the West. It will not be long before the people of God will once again be enduring persecution. Therefore, I have never been more convinced that Jesus is on the verge of return.

"Nevertheless, when the Son of Man comes will He find faith on earth?"
—Luke 18:8

God is Dead!

How do you feel about the following statement? "My religion is personal. It is between me and God." For many of us, this has become the new definition of Christianity. The *Great Commission* has been replaced with the Great *Omission!* Is this how Jesus Christ commanded His disciples to propagate the spreading of the gospel?

To anyone who has ever graced even just a few pages of the New Testament, it becomes blindingly obvious that the new mantra is the antithesis of the gospel message. It is an ingrained excuse to justify our apathy, rebellion, and ignorance of the true purpose of God. With regard to this New Age Christian philosophy, it is important to note that Jesus referred to His instructions as commandments and not suggestions. Biblically speaking, the doctrine of keeping the gospel to one's self is purely anti-Christ. It perverts the nature of the first two principles Jesus taught us to cherish. Self-centered apathy is against everything Jesus ever did or taught.

On the periphery, the first two commandments seem easy to obey. *"You shall love the Lord your God with all your heart, with all your soul, and with all your mind,"* and *"You shall love your neighbor as yourself."* (Matthew 22:37-38) These require one to deal only with themselves. "As long as I go to church on Sundays and do no harm to my neighbor, I'm good," is how New Age Christianity is practiced.

The third commandment, however, making disciples and teaching—that is a real doozy. It requires: 1) That I put forth the effort to educate myself to the ways and purpose of Christ, and

2) That I put myself into some fairly uncomfortable situations by opening my mouth.

To be quite honest, most people do not know how Jesus saves. Therefore, it is just human nature to shy away from a situation that may cause embarrassment. When such theological ignorance prevails, "My religion is personal" is the only possible outcome. You cannot share what you do not have, and, therefore, you simply keep to yourself.

If this does not change, the long-term effect will be the destruction of the gospel. If you think I am being melodramatic just take a trip to Europe. This at one time God fearing region has virtually abandoned Christ. Even the newly crowned Pope Francis has abandoned the truth of God's creation for the world's most recently developed and largest faith based congregation. No, I am not referring to the Vatican or the Roman Catholic religion. The world's largest and most recent faith based congregation is the New Age myth and anti-Christian lie known as *Darwinian Evolution.*

If you believe evolution is scientifically based, think again. The scientific process must be observable, testable and repeatable. No one has ever observed organisms changing from one kingdom, or as the Bible classifies organisms, from one "kind" to another. Nor has it been observed that man has evolved from an ape.

In fact, there is no visible evidence of any kind that unrelated organisms were ever related to one another. Think about it, evolution requires genetic mutations to be shared between organisms of different "kinds," to use the biblical terminology. A man and an ape, for example, are different "kinds" and are not sexually capable of reproducing. The sharing of our genetic material is physically impossible, and therefore, so is our evolving from and into one another. Gene sharing does not occur through osmosis. All that has ever been observed is dogs reproducing dogs, trees reproducing trees, fish reproducing fish, reptiles reproducing reptiles, and people reproducing people. The list goes on and on and the result is the same for every organism known to man.

Therefore, since witnessing what allegedly occurred one hundred million years ago, a single cell evolving into all forms of life, is neither observable, testable, nor repeatable, its occurrence must be taken on faith. Faith is believing what one cannot see. That is all evolution is. However, without evidence, it becomes merely an assumption.

Doesn't that place it on the same level as any other religion? God, however, is not a religion, and undoubtedly you are not the cousin of a banana.

What's the point? If man evolved, God did not create. If man evolved, what need is there for God? If man evolved, God is a myth, the Bible is a myth and God is dead. That is the ultimate agenda of the evolutionary religion. It is no different than any other. Its goal is to proselytize and it was created in the depths of hell. It is designed to steal God from your life and render your immortal spirit and soul to be devoid of salvation. If man evolved, you have no need of Jesus! You are merely an animal living out your primal instincts, and, therefore, sin is non-existent. God is dead!

Shine A Light On It

If you are feeling a bit convicted right now, that is good. That is how attitudes and perceptions change. Conviction is what causes truth to prevail. However, do not allow condemnation to set in. Condemnation and conviction are two different animals. Conviction breeds life. Condemnation can be deadly. Simply move on and put forth some effort into getting to know Yahweh.

Our inability to become a witness for Jesus Christ is simply a matter of not having the proper understanding of the Word of God. This is how anti-Christian doctrines, such as *Darwinian Evolution,* and "My religion is between me and God," pop up and take root. Humanity was designed to have faith. Our genetic disposition to believe causes us to search for answers to our origins, as well as, the mysteries of life. Just like empty faith, however, evolution is an expectation based upon the wrong information. Therefore, like Congress and the President, when the answers allude us we attempt to make the evidence fit by fudging the numbers, so to speak.

Spending less than expected does not create a surplus—just a smaller than anticipated debt. Any debt, however, is still debt.

Ignorance and deception does not have to be a permanent situation. The solution is right at your fingertips. Hosea 4:6 states, *"My people perish for lack of knowledge."* The Lord does not excuse ignorance. He never has and he never will justify deception. Therefore, it has become my mission to love humanity by imparting truth and eternal life into your existence. I am compelled by God to illuminate Jesus' true identity and in so doing to completely obliterate Satan in the process. My prayer is that Christ will become your mission as well and you will in turn learn to shine a light on the truth.

I have also noticed that the majority of those enlightened by our modern day world culture either have a negative reaction to Christ or they are completely apathetic toward Him. Although some folks are appalled, I am neither surprised nor upset by this. It is the truth of those living in opposition to God culture. When viewed from the perspective of God culture it is an opportunity to share the truth of Christ.

John 1:5 warns us that *"the light shines in the darkness, and the darkness did not comprehend it."* The problem is, while the deceived are wallowing in the blackness they often times ask a very simple and sometimes even sarcastic question, "How can Jesus save me?" Unfortunately, that is where it all falls apart. Most *Christians* do not know the answer.

As a result, the precious soul that Jesus suffered for simply walks away as uninformed as when they came and we, the church, justify our own ignorance by telling ourselves we have just planted a seed. Although that may be partially correct, God's lost soul remains prodigal, perhaps even for eternity. Sadly, without ever having been confronted with the gospel there was never a true decision placed before them. Most never hear more than a slogan or two. Therefore, multitudes die with their questions, and therefore, their salvation unanswered. Is it just me or does that sound problematic to you? There is a major difference between dropping a seed on hard, dry ground and cultivating the soil for a crop.

Yet, we know the power to save lies in Jesus Christ and in the Word of God. If this is true, why is there so little response to the incredible good news of the gospel? I have become utterly convinced that the answer is simply that most people do not understand what we are talking about. How could they when we, the supposed body of Christ, do not even understand what we are talking about.

In truth, many *Christians* are not dwelling in the light of the gospel. They are meandering in a simultaneously darkened world and often times in union with the sinner. Sadly, many churches today continue to adopt the world's values over the truth of Yahweh. We have become afraid to confront the lost with their sin. We seem to have a entered a type of "dark age," where even though we have Bibles, it is rare to find someone who actually reads and studies it outside of seminary, and unfortunately, many of the once great seminaries have become nothing more than mortuaries where the hungry go to die of spiritual starvation.

Therefore, we perpetually dance around the issue of how does Jesus save? We do not know and we are afraid to offend. So just throw a slogan or two against the wall and see if it sticks. When it does not, we attempt to tell them to just believe—that some things must be taken on faith. Although that is true, most questions have an answer.

I find it to be mind boggling how biblically illiterate humanity has become with so much information available at the touch of a button, or at the click of a mouse, to be more accurate. The answers are just one click away. Yet biblical illiteracy abounds at epidemic proportions. We do not even need to own a Bible in order to possess one. God and His Word can be front and center on the same device we have our noses stuck in twenty-four hours a day. Yet humanity has become so apathetic toward God that even point and click seems to require too much effort. As a result, belief in God is waning. The definition of darkness is the absence of light. Therefore, it's time to draw the curtains and let some in. In Jesus Christ the veil has been rent.

I was overwhelmed with conviction the other day as my Pastor preached to our congregation. He illustrated how addicted we have become to our not so smart phones by stating that many of us open our eyes first thing in the morning, reach for our phones, and light up the screens before ever getting out of bed. As I realized he was speaking directly to me, (although he did not know that) I concluded that my phone had become the greatest idol in my life.

Psalm 63:1 states, *"Oh God, thou art my God, early will I seek thee."* Psalm 5:3 proclaims, *"My voice You shall hear in the morning, O Lord; in the morning I will direct it to You, and I will look up."*

Nowhere in scripture does it proclaim, "Oh smartphone, thou art my God, early will I seek thee." This, however, is exactly what so many of us do. Therefore, as one who believes in honesty, I refuse to get up on my soap box and declare the end of my smart phone. In fact, I am also honest enough to tell you that my smart phone is still going to be the first thing I grab in the morning. However, I have decided to make one minor change in order to be obedient to the God I so love.

From this day forward, before I go to bed every night, I will open the Bible application on my phone and set it to a particular scripture. I have decided upon the Psalms as my starting point. I will then move on to Proverbs, but the scripture does not matter for the purpose of what I am about to teach. As I wake up in the morning, reach for my iPhone and light up the screen, God's Word will be the first thing to enter my eyes.

*"Oh God, **thou art my God**, early will I seek thee . . . My voice*
You shall hear in the morning, O Lord; in the morning I will
*direct it to You, and **I will look up.**"*

If you are a smart phone addict like myself, I would encourage
you to do the same. "Failure is not an option." **Gene Kranz** I
discovered Psalm five on day two of my endeavor. Good bye idol.

My point is as follows: Have you ever stopped to consider how
you might answer the question, how does Jesus save? Have you ever
considered whether or not you even *know* the answer? Yes, Jesus does
save, and the reason is not as complicated as you might think.
Spending just a little time studying God's Word can bring incredible
revelation into your life.

Therefore, to be obedient to the command of Jesus Christ and
make disciples of all nations, there are two things we must
accomplish. We must gain an understanding of the gospel message
ourselves, and we must learn to communicate it to others. We must
learn how to shine a light in the darkness.

True or False?

The foundation of the gospel is found in the Apostle Paul's
statement, *"Where there is no law there is no transgression."* (Romans
4:15) This is both the reason for and the fruit of the crucifixion. A
friend of mine once stated to me, "I can prove to you the message of
the Bible is false and has been corrupted." Believe it or not, and many
Christian people may find this to be heretical, I have more non-
believing acquaintances than I have Christian friends. That is by
design. I love people. Furthermore, how will the "unsaved" man hear
the message of the gospel if no one ever presents it to them?

Jesus never intended to implement "four-walled Christianity." If
you do not believe me, simply follow the example of His life. Which

congregation did He belong to? The answer is none. The Pharisees rejected Him. The Sadducees rejected Him. He was not a scribe, nor a member of the high council known as the Sanhedrin, and He became an outcast amongst men. Even His own disciples turned tail when pressured. With that said, however, those who are closest to me—those whom I seek advice and counsel from, all know the Lord. I would encourage you to pattern your life in a similar manner.

So I said to my friend, "OK, tell me. If you can prove it, I will change my view." He went on to quote the following Biblical passage:

> "Then Lot went up to Zoar and dwelt in the mountains, and his two daughters were with him; for he was afraid to dwell in Zoar. And he and his two daughters dwelt in a cave."
>
> "Now the firstborn said to the younger, 'Our father is old, and there is no man on earth to come in to us as is the custom of all the earth. Come, let us make our father drink wine, and we will lie with him, that we may preserve the lineage of our father.' So they made their father drink wine that night. And the firstborn went in to lay with her father, and he did not know when she lay down or when she arose. "
>
> "It happened on the next day that the firstborn said to the younger, 'Indeed I lay with my father last night; let us make him drink wine tonight also, and you go in and lie with him, that we may preserve the lineage of our father.'"
>
> "Then they made their father drink wine that night also. And the younger arose and lay with him, and he did not know when she lay down or when he arose. Thus both the daughters of Lot were with child by their father."
>
> **—Genesis 19: 30-36**

When he finished, he said, "There you have it. Lot was not only a drunk but he committed incest with his daughters, yet your "sky fairy" never judged or punished him. How can a God who promotes drunkenness and incest be real, let alone worshipped, especially since he had allegedly just destroyed Sodom and Gomorrah for similar immoral acts? At best, the Bible has been corrupted."

After taking a couple seconds to gather my thoughts, I replied, "I can certainly understand your concern in this matter, as incest in our society is a particularly heinous crime. Therefore, we have laws against it which warrant severe punishment, usually resulting in jail time."

I then asked him the following question, "What is it that defines the punishment of such a crime, or any crime for that matter?"

"What do you mean?" he inquired.

I asked, "What is it that makes incest a crime? What defines any behavior as criminal?"

He said, "It's disgusting!"

"I know it's disgusting, but so is eating liver. That doesn't necessarily make it criminal. What makes it criminal?"

He declared, "It's against the law!"

I said, "That is right, but whose law?"

He replied, "Society's law."

I pressed on, "So why does society frown upon such behavior?"

He exclaimed, "Because it's wrong!"

"What makes it wrong?"

He said, "Behavior that is wrong is either injurious to others or it is morally reprehensible."

"Precisely," I said. "The law is what describes behavior as criminal. So our society has defined that which is injurious to others or morally corrupt as wrong. Therefore, society has created laws outlawing such behavior."

He said, "Yeah, so what's your point?"

I questioned him a bit further. "So if there are no laws against something, is it wrong?"

He said, "It could be."

"How?" I replied.

He said, "It may still be immoral."

I said, "I believe you are correct, but is it punishable?"

"Not if there are no laws against it," he said.

So I replied once more, "So what you are saying is that something can be immoral but not illegal, or in other words, sinful but not illegal?"

He said, "That is correct."

I replied, "Exactly! Not only have you not proven that the Bible has been corrupted, but you have just proven that my "sky fairy," as you so ignorantly call Him, is both a God of mercy and justice. He forgives those who are both immoral and unlawful. In fact, He forgives our sin, which is what occurred between Lot and his daughters, even when the transgression is unbeknownst to us."

"That is exactly the type of God who is to be both loved and worshipped. Just like everyone who has ever walked the blue planet; I am guilty of transgressing God's law and so are you. As for Sodom and Gomorrah, they had been forewarned. The angels that appeared to Abraham warned them of their immoral behavior and impending doom. Additionally, Lot and his family were a living example of righteousness, and as such, warned the people of their sinful ways as well. Yet the people of Sodom and Gomorrah refused to follow his lead. Through Lot, sin had been defined and their lack of repentance brought judgment."

Sin or No Sin?

I ended the conversation by showing him that he had a misunderstanding of the passage which he quoted to me. The situation that resulted in incest, as immoral as it may have been, occurred prior to God giving the law to Moses. Behavior which was both immoral and unlawful, resulting in sin, had not yet been defined to Lot and his daughters. Sin was certainly present. Both

Sodom and Gomorrah and the Garden of Eden proved that, but it had not yet been defined to God's chosen people, of whom Lot and his family were members.

Additionally, the commission of a crime can be further defined by the perpetrators intent to harm their victim. That was certainly not the case between Lot and his daughters. Although intent does not make one innocent it can be a factor. His daughters, the "yuck" factor notwithstanding, were simply attempting to guarantee the lineage of their father. In fact, based upon their statement, *"and there is no man on earth to come in to us as is the custom of all the earth . . ."* (Genesis 19:30) I have to believe they were under the impression that God had destroyed the whole of humanity, or at best, all those their "custom" would allow.

In ancient times, lineage was everything. It still is in many cultures throughout the world. Lineage can be the defining factor in ones legacy. The intent of Lot's two daughter's was to help, not to harm, and quite honestly, at the time they were not breaking any of God's laws on sexuality. Why? Not only was God was yet to orate them, interfamily marriage was a common custom. Even Abraham's wife Sara was his half sister.

As for Sodom and Gomorrah, unbeknownst to most, the Sodomites sin was not the act of homosexuality that they were undoubtedly committing with one another. That was and is sin, but let's be fair, *"where there is no law there is no transgression."* (Romans 4:15) Without the law, God could not have held them accountable any more than He held Lot and his daughters accountable. Sodom's irreversible cause for judgment was not the act of homosexuality, it was their intent to bring harm upon those whom they had violated through the violent act of rape. Rape always steals a piece of the victim. It is grievously injurious and it violates one's soul.

The grave sins of Sodom and Gomorrah, and what caused the outcry to rise to heaven against them is what they were using the act of homosexuality for. They were wielding their sin as a sword to emasculate the souls of everyone gracing their city. This is a warning to the LGBT community. Perhaps you feel victorious today, but beware of how you wield your power. The people of Sodom and Gomorrah intended to injure, degrade and humiliate their angelic visitors through the brutal act of gang rape—and even the spectators were unwilling to intervene. Therefore, they were corporately deemed guilty.

Listen to the words of Paul. Those *"who know the righteous judgment of God, that those who practice such things are deserving of death, not only who do the same **but also approve of those who practice them.***" (Romans 1:32) I am also one hundred percent certain that it was not the first time such a scene occurred in Sodom and Gomorrah. As you will see below, they had apparently crossed over a line from which there is no return.

> *"Look, this was the iniquity of your sister Sodom: She and her daughter had **pride, fullness of food**, and **abundance of idleness**; neither did she strengthen the hand of **the poor and needy**. And they were **haughty** and **committed abomination before Me**; therefore I took them away as I saw fit."*
> **—Ezekiel 16:49-50**

Therefore, I would strongly encourage world leaders and pop cultural icon's to heed Yahweh's words regarding the outcry against Sodom. The only thing holding America together is the prayers of the righteous and our outreach to the needy. Based upon the direction Western societies are headed, we may be next on the judgment list.

> *"And the Lord said, "Because the outcry against Sodom and Gomorrah is great, and **because their sin is very grave**, I will go down now **and see whether they have done altogether according to the outcry against it** that has come to Me; **and if***

not, I will know."
—Genesis 18:20-21

Incredibly, the entire purpose of the angelic visit was to confirm the outcry against Sodom and Gomorrah. It is not as if God did not know. Of course He did. Yahweh is omniscient. The purpose was actually to establish the evidence against them. God was establishing the grounds for judgment. Sodom and Gomorrah were being given one last chance to prove the allegations against them false and repent of their evil ways before being pronounced guilty and sentenced with the capital punishment of death. Just like Nineveh, had they repented God would have relented. Yet still they attempted to steal the souls of their angelic visitors. They demanded that Lot allow them to have their way and violently "sodomize" (Where did you think the term came from?) their angelic guests.

> *"Now before they lay down, the men of the city, **the men of Sodom, both old and young, all the people from every quarter, surrounded the house**. And they called to Lot and said to him, 'Where are the men who came to you tonight? Bring them out to us **that we may know them carnally**.'"*
>
> *"So Lot went out to them through the doorway, shut the door behind him, and said, 'Please, my brethren, **do not do so wickedly**! See now, I have two daughters who have not known a man; please, let me bring them out to you, and you may do to them as you wish; only do nothing to these men, since **this is the reason they have come under the shadow of my roof**.' And they said, 'Stand back!' Then they said, 'This one came in to stay here, and he keeps acting as a judge; **now we will deal worse with you than with them**.'"*
>
> **—Genesis 19:4-9**

As you can now see, the scripture confirms the reason for the visit. Yahweh was giving them one last chance at life—but they were too far gone. The whole city colluded, participated and gathered to participate in the gang rape of the angels sent by Yahweh, Himself. This brings Hebrews 13:12 to whole new level. *"Do not forget to entertain strangers, for by so doing some have unwittingly entertained angels."* Apparently Sodom and Gomorrah were unaware of this concept. Apart from Lot, not one citizen intervened. Their depravity was deplorable. They had passed the point of redemption.

As for the situation between Lot and his daughters, he was simply out of his mind drunk. His propensity for alcohol may not have been the prime example of leadership, but it was certainly not criminal. According to scripture, he woke up the next morning not even knowing what happened. Think about how shocked and surprised he must have been when his daughters turned up pregnant—then to find out that he was the father, O-M-G... Scandaloussss!

Finally, keep in mind that not only were criminal laws undefined, but the laws of morality, to be precise, what is, and is not sin, were undefined as well. The difference between the two, however, was not in the acts of the sexual sin, which were undoubtedly committed in both situations. The judgment upon Sodom and Gomorrah was due to the injurious intent of the crime. Therefore, God, being the most just and holy being in the entire universe did what was right. Just like Jesus Christ would reveal in the future, the intent of the heart is everything. Therefore, according to grace, God followed the spirit of the law and not merely the letter of the law.

Simply stated, when there is no definition of what is criminal or what is immoral, and the intent to injure is not present, there is no resulting crime. *"Where there is no law, there is no transgression."* Therefore, there was no judgment or cause for punishment. Theological rules and regulations had not yet been defined to Abraham and Lot. God had not yet given the law to Israel and, therefore, there could be no transgression against that which was yet to exist.

Therefore, to be clear, if there is no crime there is no punishment. This concept is vitally important to both the giver and the receiver of grace. They say that possession is nine-tenth's of the law. When it comes to grace, intent is the means of possession, and possession of the grace of Jesus Christ is one hundred percent of the law. Therefore, the Apostle Paul communicated it as stated above, *"Where there is no law there is no transgression."*(Romans 4:15) This is perhaps the foremost concept to understanding how Jesus is our salvation. Let us examine where Jesus fits in to this concept.

No Condemnation

> *"There is therefore now no condemnation to those who are in Christ Jesus, who do not walk according to the flesh, but according to the Spirit."*
> **—Romans 8:1**

There are several concepts we must consider within this piece of Scripture. They are: condemnation, being in Christ, walking in the flesh and walking in the Spirit of God. Let's begin with the word "condemnation." According to Noah Webster, the word "condemnation" or "condemn" means: *To express an unfavorable or adverse judgment on, and/or to pronounce to be guilty.* This is precisely where Jesus fits in. If you are in Christ, you have escaped the condemnation of judgment resulting in eternal damnation. Your sin has not just been forgiven, it has been eradicated. Let's examine how.

The next concept involves walking in the Spirit as opposed to walking in the flesh. This is where most folks misunderstand what Paul was communicating. Since most Christians have little or no background knowledge of Jewish law, we more often than not come to an erroneous conclusion. We mistakenly believe that the act of walking in the Spirit is performance based. If we do not fit into a certain manner of lifestyle or behavior, we are walking in the flesh. Speaking in tongues, for example, does not constitute walking in the Spirit, nor does continually performing religious rituals, including going to church on Sunday.

In other words, we desperately try *not* to sin. Once we realize that we cannot stop we become exceedingly frustrated and demoralized. Our discouragement then leads to a low sense of spiritual self-esteem which eventually propels us right back into the vicious circle of our previously sinful behavior and a deepening sense of condemnation.

What is the natural human response? Our fight or flight mechanism kicks in. We react in one of two ways. We either attempt to earn our salvation by working tirelessly in the ministry, church, temple etc . . . sometimes to the point of neglecting our own families, or we leave God behind altogether. In either case, we are avoiding the real issue. We have left God out of our lives and remain ignorant to the true purpose of the Word and will of God.

Modern Christianity has not recognized that Paul is not referring to conduct or behavior when he discusses the flesh versus the Spirit in this particular piece of Scripture. His statement is in reference to hanging your salvation upon Jewish law, as opposed to living in the grace of Jesus Christ Almighty. Paul's reference to walking in the flesh is actually a reference to circumcision.

I'm Jewish?

What is the significance of circumcision? In Paul's day, there was a faction of believers who felt that one must be circumcised in accordance with the traditions of their forefathers to be saved. However, Paul writes in Galatians 5:3, "*I testify again to every man* *who becomes circumcised that he is a debtor to keep the **whole** law."* In other words, if you believe that your justification is according to the law, when you break even one, you are guilty of transgressing them all. In God's eyes the law is one unit. Each component contributes to the whole. Therefore, if one piece is broken the entire unit ceases to function. We refer to this breaking of the law as sin.

Since, *"**all** have sinned (by having broken the law) and fall short of the glory of God,"* (Romans 3:23) the law can only produce judgment leading to condemnation. Why? As stated above, breaking even one component disrupts the functionality of the entire law. It is like having a broken spring in a wristwatch. Until it is repaired, and even though every other component is functional, the entire watch ceases to function. This causes an immediate separation from Yahweh and your justification ceases to exist. Therefore, we have all been pronounced guilty, and God who is always just, will render the punishment deserving of our crime, which is a one way trip to the Lake of Fire. There is no way to sugarcoat the issue.

> However, if you are in Christ, *"You were also circumcised with the circumcision made without hands, by putting off the body of the sins of the flesh, by the circumcision of Christ . . . and you, being dead in your trespasses and the circumcision of your flesh, He has made alive together with Him, having forgiven all your trespasses, **having wiped out the handwriting of requirements that was against us**, which was contrary to us. **And he has taken it out of the way, having nailed it to the cross."***
> **—Colossians 2:11-14**

Let's build upon this a bit further. What is "the circumcision made without hands?" which is the circumcision of Christ. For clarity, let's return to the Book of Romans.

"For he is not a Jew who is one outwardly, nor is circumcision that which is outward in the flesh; but he is a Jew who is one inwardly; and circumcision is that of the heart, in the Spirit, not in the letter (referring to Jewish law) *whose praise is not from men but from God."*
—Romans 2:28-29

The concept of who is a Jew is of foremost significance and has been greatly misunderstood and, perhaps even, ignored by modern Christianity. Boldly speaking, somewhere along the line religious leaders have eliminated Israel from Christianity, thus making it nothing more than another religion. Does anyone remember that Jesus was a Jew and that the entire early church were all Jews?

God has purposely chosen Israel as His holy people and as you are about to see, separating Judaism from Christianity has made it nearly impossible to explain how Jesus is the salvation of mankind. In fact, eliminating Judaism from Christianity quite possibly renders it to be devoid of salvation. Why? According to Jesus' own words, *"Salvation is of the Jews."* (John 4:22) We seem to cruise right past that one. It is as if we have taken a bottle of white out to our Bibles and eliminated the heart of God.

Undoubtedly Jesus could not have misspoken. He most certainly did not lie. Jesus was acutely aware of every word He ever uttered. Jesus Himself exclaimed, *"I can of Myself do nothing. As I hear, I judge; and My judgment is righteous, because I do not seek My own will but the will of the Father who sent Me."* (John 5:30)

Additionally, He said, *"I have not spoken on My own authority; but the Father who sent Me gave Me a command,* **what I should say and what I should speak.** *And I know that His command is everlasting life. Therefore,* **whatever I speak, just as the Father has told Me, so I speak.**" (John 12: 49-50)

Therefore, since Jesus clearly stated, *"Salvation is of the Jews,"* we must conclude that *"Salvation is of the Jews."* If one is not a Jew, they are devoid of salvation. I know that hurts your ears and your first reaction is to reject it, but since Jesus said it, and according to John 12:49-50, Yahweh told Him to say it, I believe it. *"Salvation is of the Jews."*

Does this preclude us gentiles, or non-naturally born Jews? Certainly not! According to Romans above, the true Jew is the man who is *inwardly* Jewish—whose heart has been circumcised by God Himself and not the man who is born of a particular lineage bearing the circumcision of one's flesh. The beauty in this concept is the truth that God is all inclusive. It is your choice. Race, ethnicity, social standing, etc . . . is completely irrelevant to God's plan for salvation. You get to choose your spiritual ethnicity and whether or not you qualify for salvation. It is all a matter of entering into *God Culture.* Consider the following in regard to the Jews rejection of Jesus Christ:

> *"Have they stumbled that they should fall? Certainly not! But through their fall, to provoke them to jealously, salvation has come to the gentiles . . . if some of the branches were broken off, and you, being a wild olive tree, were **grafted in among them**, and **with them** became a partaker of the root and the fatness of the olive tree, do not boast against the branches."*
> **—Romans 11: 11 and 17-18**

The scripture could not be clearer that the gentile believer in Jesus Christ has been grafted into Israel in order to become partakers of the gift of salvation. Israel has not been nullified. We, the gentile believers, have expanded Israel. As believers in Jesus Christ we have been invited to become a part of God's chosen nation. In essence, we are grafted into the lineage of Abraham.

God through His Spirit, and by your acceptance of His way, which is Jesus Christ crucified, has grafted you into the vine of Israel and converted you to Judaism in your heart. The fulfillment of this prerequisite qualifies you for salvation. How? As a believer in Jesus

Christ you have become one who has been grafted in, or stated another way, a spiritual Jew. Remember, *"Salvation is of the Jews."* You must be part of the family to be saved.

We have become so ignorant of this truth that Christian people continually persecute their Jewish brothers and sisters, even to the point of genocide. Consider this truth the next time you may find yourself persecuting a Jew. You are oppressing your own flesh and blood.

It is Finished

This now leads us right back to the concept of Jewish law. Now that you realize you are a partaker of the vine of Israel by having been grafted into the lineage of Abraham, does that place you back under the law of Moses and reproduce condemnation, *"because the law brings about wrath?"* (Romans 4:15) Let us reexamine Colossians 2.

> *"And you, being dead in your trespasses and the uncircumcision of your flesh, He has made alive together with Him, having forgiven you all your trespasses,* **having wiped out the handwriting of requirements that was against us** *which was contrary to us.* **And He has taken it out of the way, having nailed it to the cross.***
> **—Colossians 2:13-14**

In ancient times, when you were convicted of a crime and imprisoned, the authorities would keep a handwritten list of your crimes on file. For each crime, you would have a list of required punishments that needed to be fulfilled in order to complete your sentence. You may have been sentenced to hard labor, time in the dungeon, etc. As you fulfilled each requirement the authorities would physically cross that particular crime and punishment off the list, thus, *"wiping out the handwriting of requirements that was against you."*

Once finished, they would nail the list to a wooden post outside of your prison cell, thus letting everyone know that you had fulfilled the punishment for your crime and that you had been set free. Just as Paul stated above, the handwriting of requirements against you was wiped out. It was nailed to the prison cell. You had fulfilled the sentence required by law.

Do you see the resemblance and grace of Christ Jesus having been nailed to the cross? This one incredibly unselfish act of both unimaginable horror and love has taken the law, the handwriting that was against all of us, out of the way. In Christ, your punishment has been fulfilled. He took upon Himself all of your guilt and thus the hand of Yahweh nailed Him to the cross, just as the ancient prison guard would nail his prisoners fulfilled sentence to the prison cell wall. In His grace, the law has been fulfilled—it has been nullified. You are still guilty, but your sentence has been suspended for time served—not your time served, His. Therefore, *"when you make His soul an offering for sin"* (Isaiah 53) you are set free.

But wait! There is one more piece to the puzzle. What about your next transgression? Let's be real. I doubt you will live the rest of your life having never committed another sin. Therefore, let's refer back to our previous example of having fulfilled our punishment.

As human beings, we are all under God's law which defines sin. Unfortunately, and as referred to above, we all continually break God's law. Let's be honest: we lie, cheat and steal continually, and that constitutes merely three of a multitude of sins a man or woman may commit on a daily basis. Therefore, without grace we are continually pronounced guilty when we are living our lives according to the flesh, that is, according to the law. Thank God for Jesus Christ.

"As far as the east is from the west, so far has He removed our transgressions from us." (Psalm 103:12) The beauty in this concept is that the East never meets the West. The two directions move infinitely away from one another. Therefore, there is no longer any law that remains against us. Jesus Christ has fulfilled the law. Thus,

the good news, or gospel, is that Jesus Christ has removed the law. We are no longer subject to it. It no longer exists when we abide in the grace of Jesus Christ. Your sin has been removed for eternity and just like Lot and his daughter's you are not held spiritually accountable for breaking a law that no longer applies.

That brings us full circle. We began with the concept, *"Where there is no law there is no transgression"* (Romans 4:15) and, therefore, where there is no transgression there is no sin. When one is in Christ sin is no longer judged. Its effects no longer remain. God's grace has conquered death. Jesus, having served our punishment has taken the law out of the way and pronounced us innocent. Therefore, we are free to live. Grace has triumphed. We are now right back in the same position as Lot and his daughters—guiltless.

This is why *"anyone who has been born of God does not sin, for His seed remains in him; and he cannot sin, because he has been born of God."* (1 John 3:9) It is not that the redeemed will never again transgress the law of God. It is my opinion that unless God translated you to heaven like Enoch or Elijah, never again lapsing into transgression is, if not an impossibility, it is . . . yeah, it's impossible. Why else would we need a Savior?

Redemption lies in the truth that when we are in Christ we cannot sin because sin is no longer judged according the law. In Christ, there is no law to break, and, therefore, there is no transgression to punish.

"For by grace you have been saved through faith." (Ephesians 2:8)
Therefore, *"sin shall not have dominion over you, for you are not under law but under grace."*
—Romans 6:14

Perhaps you are thinking, "Does this give us a license to sin?" Absolutely not! *"For if we sin willfully after we have received the knowledge of the truth, there no longer remains a sacrifice for sins, but a certain fearful expectation of judgment, and fiery indignation which will devour the adversaries."* (Hebrews 10:26-27) Remember, intent equals possession. Therefore, allow Hebrews 10:26-27 to enlighten you, not frighten you. It is no longer our nature. Our old desire for sin has passed away. Along with your sin, your old nature was nailed to the cross as well.

"Therefore, if anyone is in Christ they are a new creation, old things (the law) *have passed away; behold all things become new,"* (2 Corinthians 5:17) including your inner most desire to walk with God and do what is right. Jesus Christ in heaven, who is seated at the right hand of God the Father, *"who has been given a name above all names,"* (Philippians 2:9) has renewed you. He has set you free. His grace is **above the Law.**

CHAPTER 13

Forever One

The nature of Yahweh is perhaps the most misunderstood concept in all of scripture. It may be the most ill-conceived concept in all of theology. Therefore, I would like to spend some time discussing two immensely misunderstood aspects of both the plan and nature of God—the bride of Jesus Christ and the trinity. As you will see, they are intimately related. In God's forever plan they go hand in hand.

Let's begin this discussion at the end of time as we know it. At this midway point in our journey, it is time for us to visit with John the Apostle, whom is also known as, "John the Revelator." In addition to the gospel of John and the epistles of John, he is the author of the Book of Revelation. While exiled on the Island of Patmos for preaching the gospel, John had an astonishing visit from the one and only Jesus Christ, who opened a window into eternity and showed Him the eventual and unchangeable plan of Yahweh. As we did with the Genesis account in my previous book, *God Culture,* and as the great Sports-Caster Warner Wolf declared in times past, "Let's go to the videotape . . ."

Come, I Will Show You the Bride!

*"Then one of the seven angels . . . talked with me saying, 'Come, **I will show you the bride, the Lambs wife.'** And he carried me away in the Spirit to a great and high mountain, **and showed me the great city, the holy Jerusalem,** descending out of heaven from God, having the glory of God."*
—Revelation 21:9-11

Let's peer into a couple of amazing truths that will bring clarity to the two aforementioned and immensely misunderstood subjects; the identity of the bride of Christ and the trinity. Allow me to first comment on the bride of Christ as shown to John the Revelator.

As Christians, we have always been taught that we, "the church," also known as the body of Christ, is the *bride* of Christ. This concept does not seem to line up with scripture. Interestingly enough, I have seen evidence in the Word of God where *Israel* is described as being betrothed to, and even married to Yahweh. (Jeremiah 3:14, et al) Additionally, God was perpetually accusing them of playing the harlot by chasing foreign gods. Therefore, Israel, as a nation, is undoubtedly married to Yahweh, but keep in mind that the nation of Israel is not the church. Therefore, we must make a distinction between the different administrative functions, for lack of a better term, of Yahweh and Yeshua (Jesus). In our present condition, Yeshua is approachable by man. Yahweh is not.

Comprehending the roles of Father, Son and Holy Spirit is vital to understanding God's plan for salvation, as well as, the totality of Yahweh's ultimate plan for all of eternity. Israel (Jacob) is the lineage that God chose to bring the Messiah through in order to save both the Jews and the gentiles. Therefore, in order to preserve, protect and provide for them, He betrothed Himself to Israel. God is married to Israel. Why do you think they have not only been able to survive, but have prospered for thousands of years while being completely surrounded by an enemy whose chief aim is to destroy them. *"For your Maker is your husband, the Lord of hosts is His name"* (Isaiah 54:5) was spoken to Israel. Applying this concept to the body of Christ is a major faux pa.

The church consists of gentile believers who have been grafted into the vine of Israel by faith in Jesus Christ. I suppose you could argue that a Messianic Jew is part of the church, but the naturally born Israelite, whether they are Messianic or not, is part of Jacob's natural lineage. This is not true of the gentile. The problem is that nowhere in scripture does it state that *the church* has been, or will be, wedded to Jesus Christ. In fact, when John was carried away in the Spirit and shown *"The Lambs wife,"* which is the bride of Christ, he was not shown Israel, or the church. He was specifically shown God's holy city, the New Jerusalem.

Many have argued that the New Jerusalem consists of God's people and that makes the church the bride of Christ. As I will show you shortly this is just not the case. In order for that to work we have to "make it fit" by liberally, and I might add, inaccurately interpreting scripture. As you will see, God is clearly referring to the physical nature and beauty of the city when He shows John "the bride." In other words, God was talking about the city! That was intentional. If God wanted John to see the church as the bride, that is what God would have shown him. The church certainly has its function in the eternal plan of Yahweh, but it is not that of being wed to Jesus Christ.

The only bride of Christ ever named in the Word of God is the New Jerusalem. Therefore, I must conclude that the church is not His bride, the New Jerusalem is. According to scripture, the church is His body.

> *"Now you are the body of Christ, and members individually."*
> **—1 Corinthians 12:27**

That is what scripture plainly states. These are two very important distinctions in understanding our true role within the eternal plan of God. Think logically for just a moment. *"God is not the author of confusion but of peace, as in all the churches of the saints."* (1 Corinthians 14:33)

We cannot be Jesus' body *and* His bride simultaneously. That makes no sense whatsoever and we, the church, are never named to be His bride. According to 1 Corinthians 12:27, we are specifically identified as being the *"body of Christ."*

Revelation 21:9 clearly and undeniably names the New Jerusalem to be the Lamb's bride with her wedding gown, or "adornment," according to Revelation 19:7-8, *not* being the saints themselves, but the righteous *acts* of the saints.

> *"And His wife has made herself ready. And to her it was granted to be arrayed in fine linen, clean and bright, for the fine linen is the righteous acts of the saints."*
> **—Revelation 19:7-8**

The saints are defined in God's Word as all who believe in and serve Yahweh. We have been misled to believe that the "Saints" are those who performed supernatural feats and miracles and have been given a special place of worship within the Roman Catholic Church. That is not scripturally accurate. If you believe in Jesus Christ you are a saint of Yahweh.

Therefore, it is important to keep in mind that it is not the saints of God that formulate the bride of Jesus Christ. It is our righteous acts that merely adorn and add to the city's majestic beauty and elegant nature. Righteousness is the nature and the culture of the heavenly city.

We, the redeemed of God, are Christ's body. Think logically once more, the bridegroom never marries the dress, earrings or any other ornament arraying the bride; nor does he marry his own body. The adornments certainly make the bride more attractive, but it is she whom is wearing the jewels that marries the groom. In these versus of scripture, and nowhere is it ever stated differently, the bride of Christ is identified as being the New Jerusalem.

As you will see shortly, the importance of this scriptural concept is for gaining a clear understanding of *God's* oneness with all of creation. Its implications are in regard to the trinity, not our becoming one with Him. That was accomplished at the cross and *"it is finished."* (John 19:30) The remission of our sin has reunited us to God. Creation, however, is still in the process of redemption.

> *"For the creation was subjected to futility, not willingly, but because of Him who subjected it in hope; because the creation itself also **will be delivered from the bondage of corruption** into the glorious liberty of the children of God."*
> **—Romans 8:20-21**

The unveiling of the New Jerusalem in conjunction with the New Heaven and the New Earth is imperative to our recognition of God's redemption of the entire creation, not just mankind. As human beings we tend to be self-centered. We seem to think everything is about us. As a result, nearly every biblical theologian has inserted themselves into an arrangement that has never been agreed upon by the Lord, namely, exchanging wedding vows with Jesus

Christ. There is no biblical basis for the concept and yet I hear it coming from every Christian pulpit day after day.

If we have to *make* a concept fit, chances are it is misinterpreted. God never leaves us guessing. He tells us very plainly and openly. *"Approach Me! Listen to this! From the very first I have not spoken in secret."* (Isaiah 48:16) To me, the unveiling of the bride seems to be clear as day. She is distinctly identified in very clear and simple language to be the New Jerusalem. I do not believe the New Jerusalem is an allegory.

According to Matthew 22:2-13, we; the body of Christ, have been invited to attend the Marriage Supper of the Lamb *as guests*. We have not been proposed to as participants in the marriage vows as the bride. Furthermore, and with that important detail in mind, a wedding is always about the bride and groom, and not the guest list. Have you ever been to a wedding where the guests were the honorees, let alone being married to the bridegroom? Perhaps if you were an old time Mormon that might work. I have seen *Sister Wives*. In truth, however, the guests are there simply to participate in the celebration and to support the union. It is after the wedding that the friends and family members of the new union become an active part of their new lives together as husband and wife.

Therefore, why would this marriage be any different? It is God who ordained marriage. He is the creator of it. Of course He knows the rules. The Marriage Supper of the Lamb is between Jesus Christ and the Holy City for the redemption of creation. Do not forget that *"all things were made through Him, and without Him nothing was made that was made."* (John 1:3) In essence, just like the believer in Jesus Christ, when God creates a *"New Heaven and a New Earth"* creation will also get "born again."

*"Now I saw **a New Heaven and a New Earth**, for **the first heaven and the first earth had passed away**. Also there was no more sea. Then I, John, saw the holy city, New Jerusalem, coming*

down out of heaven from God."
—Revelation 21:1-2

At the celebration of the union, we the church, are neither the bride nor the groom. Man was redeemed at the cross, but creation was not. The Marriage Supper is not about us, it is about God. It is about His love for the whole of creation. In the following paragraphs you will discover just how important this concept is.

So what is the point? Why make the differentiation? It is a matter of accuracy. It is a matter of understanding our relationship with the Lord and how and where we fit in to the Lord's eternal plan. Ultimately, it is a matter of discovering our roles which allows us to understand *His* will and *our* purpose. Wisdom and understanding is what breeds Godly vision and a supernatural purpose in your life.

Therefore, take careful note of what follows. When we accept the Lord Jesus Christ we are cleaned up and made a righteous part of the Lamb's body—spotless and without blemish. Thus, as inhabitants of the Holy City our spiritual righteousness adorns the bride who is to be joined in unity to the Lamb. In the end, all of creation will become one with God.

Since Christ is one with the Father, (John 10:30) all joined to Him become one with the Father as well, including we, the members of His body, as well as, the New Jerusalem. This connection of singularity joins all of creation in oneness with God and completes Yahweh's ultimate plan for eternity, which is the eternal bliss of the oneness of heaven on earth. Heaven and earth will become one.

Since becoming one is what any marriage is about, oneness with the Father, Yahweh, is what the Marriage Supper of the Lamb is all about as well. (Revelation 19:9) Oneness is the purpose of redemption and God is in the process of redeeming *all of creation,* not just mankind.

The Trinity

This is also perfectly consistent with God's method of blueprinting. Just as a husband and wife are joined together in holy matrimony to become one flesh (Genesis 2:24), God the Father, Son and Holy Spirit, together with the whole of God's creation will be wedded as one, in, and for all of eternity, and dwell with mankind forever. In essence, Eden will be recreated, but on an even greater spiritual and physical level.

Thus we will see the scripture fulfilled, *"Hear O Israel, the Lord our God, the Lord is one!"* (Deuteronomy 6:4) In fact, Zechariah 14:9, which peers into the future giving us a glimpse at the Day of the Lord, clearly declares the following: *"And the Lord shall be King over all the earth. In that day **it shall be** the **Lord is one, and His name one.**"*

It is my opinion that the trinity as we experience Him, is a temporary decoupling of the Father, Son and Holy Spirit for the purpose of providing redemption. In eternity, there will be no more need for redemption, nor the infilling of the Holy Spirit. The work will already have been completed. Therefore, there will no longer be a need to penetrate either the realm of sin, or the heart of man. Both the coming of Christ and the Holy Spirit to planet earth is, and was, for the sole purpose of breeching the natural realm in order to provide the redemptive work of Christ. The trinity will remain alive, well and active. The essence of God will never change, but in that day all will be reunified in Yahweh. Thus, as Zechariah 14:9 declares, *"In that day **it shall be** the **Lord is one, and His name one.**"*

Take careful note that this verse of scripture is describing a future event. *"In that day it shall be . . ."* At some future point, which in my opinion most likely occurs at the Marriage Supper of the Lamb, the Lord will reunite Himself in complete and total inseparable oneness. However, in this present dispensation, where the death of Christ became necessary for the remission of sin, the Lord *became* separate in order to *become* sin for the sole purpose of experiencing death.

Had there been no separation of Christ from the Father, the death of Almighty God, if it were even possible, would have ended the universe. The dispensation of the trinity, if we can call it that, potentially answers not only the question of why God became a man, but also how God could become sin and die without the catastrophic end of the universe, and, in fact, the entire space-time dimension in which we reside.

Almighty God becoming sin in His totality would be beyond cataclysmic. If we view the trinity as inseparable, the death of one equals the death of all. That would simply put an end not just to mankind, but to the entire universe and everything under God's authority. Since God, *"who being the brightness of His glory and the express image of His person, **and upholding all things** by the word of His power"* (Hebrews 1:3) is the unseen force that holds creation together, all life and all matter would instantly cease to exist. That is simply incomprehensible and not an option in God's eyes. Thus, God has dispensed Himself in the form of the trinity.

*"And **the Word became flesh** and dwelt among us,"* (John 1:14) and *"behold, I send the Promise of My Father upon you; but tarry in the city of Jerusalem until you are endued **with power from on high**."*
—Luke 24:49

*"And suddenly there came a sound from heaven, as of a rushing mighty wind, and it filled the whole house (Just as the Shekhinah glory would fill the temple.) where they were sitting. Then there appeared to them divided tongues, as of fire, and one sat upon each of them. **And they were all filled with the Holy Spirit** and began to speak with other tongues, as the Spirit gave them*

utterance."
—Acts 2:2-4

Are you beginning to understand what an immense problem sin had become? Thank God that Yahweh *is* Almighty because only He possesses the foresight, wisdom and ability to overcome sin. Neither Satan nor any other god could ever accomplish such an immense task. They simply do not possess the power, the glory (the Shekhinah), nor the wisdom and foresight to do so. The trinity is a stroke of genius from the most incredible and powerful being in the universe.

I realize this may be a new concept, but it is perfectly consistent with the purpose of God and in my opinion reveals not just the existence, but the *necessity* of the trinity, and why salvation is non-existent in any other than Christ.

*"For there is no other name under heaven given among men by which we **must** be saved."*
—Acts 4:12

Redemption requires death. This is why no amount of works, or the law, can ever bring you the point of total forgiveness of sin. The death of Jesus Christ is God's only path to salvation.

Do not forget that God is efficient and logical. A power so brilliant and immense could only be. It is in the essence of God's purpose that we discover the mystery of His will and begin to understand His marvelous ways.

Mankind has been desperately attempting to explain and understand the concept of the trinity without ever giving consideration to God's purpose for it. When purpose is separated from concept, the trinity appears to be nonsensical and perhaps even idolatrous. It breaks commandment number one. Try explaining how three is one. I have heard it described not as 1+1+1, which = 3, but

1x1x1, which = 1. Who decided upon the math? People who believe it do not get it. Try convincing an unbeliever. They walk away shaking their heads.

Now that you understand purpose and foresight, however, the trinity makes perfect sense and Zechariah 14:9 illustrates it at fruition. *"In that day* **it shall be** *the* **Lord is one, and His name one.** *And the Lord shall be King over all the earth."* I purposely reversed the sentence order for clarity. Isn't it comforting to know that all of the sin, corruption, violence and evil will be completely annihilated, and we will live in a recreated universe in oneness with the most powerful and loving being in all of creation—for all of eternity?

We catch a glimpse of God's eternal oneness in the gospel of John which describes a point in history that lies even beyond the creation event of Genesis chapter one and prior to the dispensation of the trinity.

> *"In the beginning was the Word, and the Word was with God and the Word was God. He was in the beginning with God."*
> **—John 1:1-2**

Here we see the nature of God as time as we know it begins, and perhaps even prior to that, unified in complete and total oneness. There is no separation. The Word is identified as existing, but is with God in complete and total unity. God is one. Verses three through thirteen of the gospel of John go on to describe the problem of mankind's rejection of God, and in verse fourteen we see the manifestation of the trinity come to fruition.

> *"And the Word became flesh and dwelt among us, and we beheld His glory."*

Many believe that Jesus gave up the glory of God to be made manifest. This is simply untrue. The scripture states, *"We beheld His glory."* How would that be possible if Jesus gave up the glory. The more accurate statement is that Jesus Christ masked the glory of God. He made it palatable, for lack of a better term, by covering it in human flesh.

As we discussed earlier, Jesus Christ is a manifestation of the Shekhinah glory of God. Just like the cloud in the tabernacle that masked the glory of God and made it palatable for human interaction, Jesus Christ is God with His preeminence masked by human flesh. Through Him, sinful man is able to enter God's presence and live. Without the Shekhinah, no one can see God and live. (Exodus 33:20) In fact, without the Shekhinah no one can gaze upon God at all. This is why the scripture states, *"No one has seen God at any time."* (1 John 4:12) We haven't. We have seen His Shekhinah glory manifested in various ways, but until sin is eradicated from the heart of man and redemption reaches its completion we will not see His face. (Revelation 22:4)

Additionally, it is not until after the resurrection and ascension of Jesus Christ that He sends the Holy Spirit, who is the third aspect of the trinity, and serves as a helper to mankind in the bodily absence of the Savior. He, the Holy Spirit, fills our spirit and leads us to the truth of who God is and how to obtain salvation through faith in Christ. In other words, Yahweh is revealed by the Spirit.

However, with sin out of the way in eternity, and mankind being eternally united to Yahweh by the Spirit of God, there will be no need for the dispensation which allows for the infilling of the Spirit to lead and to guide us into the truth. Sin will have been overcome. The essence of our existence will be in the truth of our eternal oneness with God. We will be complete and inseparably united to Yahweh. That is the definition of redemption.

The trinity, quite simply is God's dispensation for obliterating the problem of sin. It is His means of redemption through the gift of death, knowing that even *He* would need to participate. It appears to be the only way that God, in whom is life, (John 5:26) could ever die. In essence, by physically separating from His immortality and in small part, separately entering into and becoming an element of His own earthly creation. It is complete and total genius from the mind of the highest power in existence. In truth, only death can separate mankind from his sin.

FaceBook

To better understand the concept of the trinity, consider the following. I recently had a rather interesting conversation with a gentleman on FaceBook. To protect the innocent, let's just say his name was Paul. Paul is an atheist, and he confronted me over an advertisement I had placed for my first book, *God Culture.*

Paul contacted me to express his displeasure at my "propaganda," and to assure me that there is no God. "He is merely a figment of man's imagination, and has been invented by evil human beings to control the masses." Obviously, my first task was to explain the difference between God and religion, but nevertheless, we took the conversation in the direction of the truth of God's existence.

After several days of bantering back and forth, I asked the following question, "Paul, do you believe in anything non-physical?"

Fully expecting to see the word, "no" appear, my eyes lit up as my computer screen replied, "Yes, love." So I asked my new friend to define love. He answered, "Love has many characteristics, but basically it is a physical reaction leading to an emotion."

Most people in this instance would have asked, "Are emotions physical or non-physical?" thinking they had sealed the argument, but God is too smart for that. Besides, this was not about winning or losing. It was about salvation. It was about heaven or hell. Who cares about "winning" when the stakes are that high.

So I replied, "Is love physical or non-physical?" In all honesty, love is a combination of both.

After a short pause he agreed, "both," he replied.

So I stated, "Then you agree that something can have both physical and non-physical properties?" I was doing my best to keep this in the scientific language in which he communicates.

He said, "I hadn't thought about it that way . . . but, yeah, I guess so."

I asked, "Is love eternal?"

He said, "No. It dies when we die."

So I replied, "How can something that is not physically alive die?"

He countered, "It cannot."

So I reiterated, "If that is true, and you believe love is both physical and non physical, and you agree that anything that is non physical cannot die, you must agree that love cannot die. Therefore, love is eternal."

"I guess it is," he shot back.

So I asked, "Can love inspire you to speak, and to do? Can you experience the non-physical phenomenon we call love?"

The computer screen immediately lit up, "Of course."

I replied, "Well, congratulations are in order. You quite accurately just described the nature of God."

"What," he replied. "You are insane!"

"Perhaps," I replied, "But you just described the nature of God. God the Father is the non-physical eternal entity you just described. 'God is love.' (1 John 4:8) Until now, you simply have not recognized Him. God ever lives and He cannot die. But He is so much more than what you classify as an emotion. 'God is Spirit.' (John 4:24) Love is the supreme power in all of creation."

"In our physical realm where sin reigns, man became separate from God, and, therefore, to reconnect us to God death became necessary. (Hebrews 9:16) To rectify the problem, God poured out a finite piece of Himself as a sacrifice for our sin. In other words, Love stepped into the physical realm where man resides. A small aspect of God, human flesh and blood, became temporary. He was still love.

He was simply the physical aspect of love that you just acknowledged to exist. His purpose was to connect the physical to the non-physical—to reunite man with God. We know God in this manner as Jesus Christ of Nazareth, whose death on the cross alleviates the power of the law and reunites us to the eternal power of love, who is the Father."

"To make sure we all know about Him, Love in the person of the Holy Spirit, bridges the gap from the spiritual to the natural by infilling, inspiring, and empowering humanity to speak, to do, and to declare the good news of the gospel for the salvation of all of mankind. The Spirit becomes one with both man and God, just as love becomes part of two human beings in love.

It is not only a physical connection. Two people in love do not all of a sudden become Siamese twins. God, by the Holy Spirit bridges the gap between the physical and natural realms, just as to people in love have both a physical and a spiritual connection. Like two people in love, God joins Himself together with us, thus giving humanity access to the power and wisdom of Yahweh, as well as, the eternal life that only exists in that non-physical entity known as Love. Through the Holy Spirit, the power of God speaks and leads humanity into all truth. You see, Paul, you *do* believe!"

Unfortunately, that was the last I heard from my new friend. Perhaps that was his last day as an atheist. My prayer is that he and I will continue our conversation in eternity.

Stick um

With that in mind, let's continue our conversation regarding sin. Sin is an especially sticky substance. This is why it is so difficult, if not impossible, to live a life without sinning—even *after* you have accepted Jesus as your Lord and Savior. Sin is like "stick um," the adhesive substance similar to pine tar, that football players used to wear to give them a better grip on the football. If you have ever used it, you realize how difficult it is to wash off. It would take hours for some of the old timers to wash it off. In fact, sin is so persistent that only death can separate you from its grip. While still breathing, you are only half way there. Physical death is required to complete the process of redemption.

Christ's death and subsequent resurrection is the perfect pattern of the process of redemption. We too will rise again to a glorified body. In the meantime, even the Apostle Paul struggled with sin and no one can argue that he was unredeemed by Jesus Christ. Therefore, take note of how he expressed his never ending daily battle with sin.

> *"For what I am doing I do not understand. For what I will to do, that I do not practice; but what I hate, that I do . . . but now,* ***it is no longer I who do it, but sin that dwells in me.*** *For I know that in me (that is, in my flesh) nothing good dwells; for to will is present with me, but how to perform what is good I do not find. For the good that I will to do, I do not do, but the evil that I will not to do, that I practice."*
>
> *"Now if I do what I will not to do,* ***it is no longer I who do it, but sin that dwells in me.*** *I find then a law, that evil is present with me, the one who wills to do good . . . O wretched man that I am!* ***Who will deliver me from this body of death?*** *I thank God* ***through Jesus Christ our Lord . . ."***
> **—Romans 7: 15, 17-21, 24-25**

If you are honest with yourself, I know that there are times when you feel just like Paul did in the above scriptural reference. Especially, *"that evil is present with me"* part. That explains a whole lot doesn't it? Our propensity for evil is part of being human. It may be the greatest illustration of why every man, woman and child needs a Savior, regardless of race, religion or sex. However, just like Paul, if you have made Jesus your Lord, you will not have this problem in eternity.

You will have been separated from your sin by faith in Jesus Christ and the death of your mortal body. Jesus Christ and death are the two mandatory components to obtaining eternal life.

Forever One

In my opinion, both are cause for celebration! If you have been redeemed by the Lord Jesus Christ you have no need to fear death. Just like a seed that falls to the ground appearing to be dead, you will instantaneously sprout into eternal life.

> *"We are confident, yes, well pleased rather to be absent from the body and to be present with the Lord."*
> **—2 Corinthians 5:8**

Most people do not realize that man was created as an extension of God's love. Although human beings are not, and never will be divine, the Lord created us to be joined together as one with Him. Separation from God was a consequence of sin. With sin out of the way, the dispensation of God's plurality will no longer be necessary and God, man, the Holy City, along with an entire newly created universe will become one in Spirit for all of eternity. The resulting paradise will be known as heaven. The trinity will still exist, however, He will have been reunified.

I bet you had no idea how important a piece of God's puzzle you actually are. Even more amazing is the fact that you had no idea up until you read those last several pages what it truly means to be a part of the body of Christ and where you fit into eternity. Eternal life will be spent in oneness with God *and* creation. Do not forget that God created the entire universe just for you. The natural realm was created to be the dwelling place of humanity and God loves it.

*"Then God saw **everything that He had made**, and indeed it was very good."*
—Genesis 1:31

Notice that God saw *everything* that He had made, not just man, *"and indeed it was very good."* I believe the "world" gets a bad rap from many Christians. God adores everything He created, the things of the world included. The problem arises when we make the "world" our object of worship and leave God out of our lives. In God's eyes, creation was *very good* because it was perfect. It was perfect because all of creation was functioning exactly as God designed it. Creation was in harmony with its Creator. What most never come to realize, and where the problem arose, is that when humanity fell, creation fell along with it.

"Then to Adam He said, 'Because you have heeded the voice of your wife, and have eaten from the tree of which I commanded you, saying, 'You shall not eat of it': 'Cursed is the ground for your sake; In toil you shall eat of it. All the days of your life. Both thorns and thistles it shall bring forth for you.'"
—Genesis 3: 17-18

Along with the redeemed, creation will ultimately be reborn, as well. This is what redemption is all about. Oneness is the end game and God's ultimate eternal goal.

I do not think we have ever realized what an amazing role we will play in eternity. With Jesus as the head, and His believers as the body, we bring to fruition the eternal plan and glory of God's oneness. We see the precursor to this event in the Book of Genesis when the two, Adam and Eve, become one flesh through the spiritual unification of holy matrimony. Marriage is not consummated by the ceremony. It is consummated by sexual intercourse which reunites the man and woman as one flesh, with God in the middle of it by covenant.

Torn Asunder

This connection between you, your spouse and God is why adultery is prohibited by scripture. It is a heinous perversion of God's will. It separates that which man should not tear asunder and introduces an unintended third party into the middle of a private relationship between man, woman and God. Why do you think God cried out to Adam in the Garden of Eden, *"Where are you?"* (Genesis 3:9) It is not that God could not find them. God was standing right in front of Adam and Eve. Why do you think they tried to hide? The sin of Lucifer simply got in the way. The unintended third party, known as the devil, procured his place in the heart of man.

In essence, Adam and Eve entered into an adulterous relationship with Lucifer For the first time God and man had been separated. As a result, God felt the pain of what was never intended to be. Just like a child leaving the womb, sin had cut the umbilical cord, which was the lifeline between man and God. Although it was not visible, death was instantaneous. Man had been torn asunder from God.

Redeemed

As we have seen, the body of Christ has been joined together with both the Father and Israel at the cross. At the Marriage Supper of the Lamb, we will once again be reunified with a new creation, (The new heaven, the new earth and the new Jerusalem) thus completing the Lord's eternal plan. Remember the holy city, the New Jerusalem, proceeds from the Father. It is part of His glory. Thus, when Christ is joined together with the Holy City which is adorned as a bride and proceeds from the Father, all of creation together with mankind will be united with Yahweh. Thus the scripture, *"Your Husband is your Maker, the Lord of Hosts is His name,"* (Isaiah 54:5) is fulfilled once and for all.

Since the work has been done and the Father has redeemed His bride, the marriage supper of the Lamb will complete the everlasting reunification of the Father, Son and Holy Spirit for all of eternity. There will be no more need for redemption and there will be no more need for Yahweh's separation. *"The Lord He is One,"* (Deuteronomy 6:4) and as the redeemed of the Lord we are alive in Him.

At the cross, we have become part of His unity. (John 17:21) That is deserving of a hallelujah. As you can now clearly see, we serve an incredible God who will stop at nothing to save what has become the most glorious and wretched of all He created—an arrogant and apathetic humanity who has utterly rejected His Lordship.

Three in One

But wait, there is even more! Once again let us apply simple logic for just a moment. According to the Book of Genesis 2:26 man was created in the image of God. Not that we physically look like God, only God knows the answer to that. Mankind was created as a triune being just as the Lord is a triune being. A man is a spirit, has a soul and has a body. 1 Thessalonians 5:23, states in regard to mankind, *"Now may the God of peace sanctify you completely; and may your **whole spirit, soul, and body** be preserved blameless at the coming of our Lord Jesus Christ."* In this gem of scripture we see undeniably that a man is a triune being. What most do not realize, however, is that the Lord who is a Spirit also has a Body and a Soul. We are truly His image.

Note the following scriptural evidence of this truth: *"**God is Spirit**, and those who worship Him must worship in spirit and in* *truth."* (John 4:24) We see here that God is a Spirit. Now check out Isaiah 53:10. *"Yet it pleased the Lord to bruise Him; He has put Him to grief, when you make **His soul** an offering for sin."* Yes, as amazing as it may seem God has a soul which was personified in the miracle of Jesus Christ. To bring the final piece of this small portion of God's puzzle to fruition, we read in John 1:14 that, *"The Word became flesh and dwelt among us,"* a physical body.

There it is; the image of God and how you *are* His resemblance. Implanted within the oneness of the Father, Son and Holy Spirit, is a Spirit, a Soul and a Body just like you and me. We have been created in the image of God and because we are His image we have a spirit, a soul, and a body—just like He does.

However, here is the importance of this little known truth. When I look at you I do not see a fragmented human being. I only see you. Your spirit, your soul, and your body exist as one in harmony with one another. Only death can separate them.

Cloud Cover

The same is true with God and that is exactly what we see in the death of Jesus Christ. In His infinite power and because of His majestic love, the Lord extended Himself for the purpose of redemption. He became the manifestation of sinful flesh thus masking His true glory, *"which no man can see and live."* (Exodus 33:20)

By manifesting in the flesh, the Lord Jesus covered Himself as Yahweh did with the pillar of cloud in the desert as He spoke with Moses and the Israelites. The evidence of this truth exists in Jesus' transfiguration on the mountain in Matthew 17:2.

"And He was transfigured before them. His face shone like the sun, and His clothes became as white as the light . . . while he (Peter)

was still speaking a bright cloud overshadowed them and suddenly
a voice came out of the cloud saying, 'This is My beloved Son in
whom I am well pleased. Hear Him!'"
—Matthew 17: 2 and 5

For a brief moment Jesus uncovered His divinity which brought about the cloud to mask the presence of Yahweh. Had the cloud (Shekhinah) not not manifested the glory of the Lord would have brought Peter, James and John to instantaneous judgment and annihilated them. Sin cannot exist in the manifested presence and glory of the Lord.

If you carefully search scripture you will find that whenever the glory of the Lord encounters mankind the cloud (Shekhinah) shows up to mask His presence. This "covering" is what allows man to encounter Yahweh. The covering of flesh is what allowed the Lord Jesus to walk among us sinful human beings without annihilating us, as well. The preeminence of divinity was masked momentarily by the likeness of sinful flesh. Thus we could see Him face to face and live. Yes, the scriptures do testify of Him.

Isn't that amazing? Even the pillar of cloud in the desert was a revelation of Jesus Christ and a pattern for His future interaction with mankind. I cannot speak enough about His absolute brilliance and foresight.

Volunteer

In truth, the Lord Jesus was only spiritually separate from the Father for the twinkling of an eye when the sin of the world was laid upon Him. Thus, Jesus cried out in fulfillment of Psalm 22, *"Eli, Eli, lama sabachthani? That is, My God, My God, why have you forsaken Me?"* (Matthew 27:46) While the crucifixion of Jesus Christ mortified His physical body, it was the separation from God that actually caused the death of Jesus and the obliteration of sin. Just like any viruss sin cannot survive without its host.

> *"For I was once alive without the law. But when the commandment came, sin revived, and I died."*
> **—Romans 7:9**

Death is always the consequence of sin. It is not that Jesus sinned. He most certainly did not. He voluntarily *became* sin and the beauty of Jesus Christ is that it was not forced upon Him by the Father. In love He offered Himself.

> *"Nevertheless, not as I will, but as you will."* (Matthew 26:39)
> *"For He made Him who knew no sin **to be sin** for us, that we might become the righteousness of God in Him."*
> **—2 Corinthians 5:21**

Because of this one incredible act of love and selflessness, all of humanity has the opportunity to exist in unity with God in the New Jerusalem. We are His body, and *"in that day it shall be the Lord is one."* In that day we will be eternally one with Him. In the forever, all will be one.

CHAPTER 14

All Things Made New

S everal years ago I had the honor and the privilege of conducting a man's funeral. Although that may sound ordinary enough, keep in mind that, 1) I am not an ordained minister, and 2) I had never met the gentleman in person until the day I gazed upon his lifeless body in the casket. You will often times find yourself in strange but exciting situations when you chase after Yahweh. As you will see shortly, this incident happened to be both—strange and exciting.

Allow me to explain. I was involved with a church plant in Canada and was spending a couple weekends per month in the Toronto area, Mississauga to be exact. During the course of my mission several extraordinary families had "adopted" me and I was spending significant amounts of time with them.

Several months after my assignment had ended one of our members brother-in-law was diagnosed with terminal cancer. In fear, and with nowhere else to turn, his family turned to me. The only problem was this beloved child of God had never met his Savior.

One evening I received a phone call from his sister-in-law who desperately introduced me to the man via telephone. I felt impressed to pray for his soul and for physical healing. So upon calling him and hearing the fear and desperation in his voice, I began to minister and pray with him. He knew he was dying, but he had no idea where he was going or how much time he had. The uncertainty of his eternal fate, and even more specifically, the soon to be realized reality of hell was more than he could bear. It terrified his desperate soul. It is funny how things change when a man is faced with forever.

Over the course of the next couple months we communicated several times per week. Often times, I would receive a phone call in the middle of the night. Andre would be in tremendous pain and quite literally scared nearly to death. As we would pray, his fear and his pain would begin to gradually subside. As time passed, and the end drew visibly closer, a sense of peace began to fall over Andre and his family. Andre had accepted Christ!

Late one afternoon I received a phone call from his wife. The inevitable had come. Andre had passed from death to life and to my great surprise his wife asked me to preside over his funeral. Did I mention that I am not an ordained minister? I did not go to seminary. I am one of you—just a simple guy who loves Jesus, but in all of Andre's life he had never known a Priest or Pastor.

As a preacher of the gospel and having been ministering to Andre over the previous several months, I suppose I was the closest thing he had. Therefore, in honor and celebration of Andre's newly found eternal home they felt it should be me to comfort the family. As far as I was concerned, this was to be a celebration of a man's life, in particular his eternal life, and not a despondently hopeless forever farewell.

So I gladly agreed, hung up the phone, experienced feelings of inadequacy and called my Pastor for advice. Not in regard to whether or not I should do the funeral, I did not doubt *that* until the *day* of the funeral. My question was, how do I even *do* a funeral? I had no idea. I will never forget how the funeral director's had to guide me through the church. I did not even know which aisle to walk down! Have I mentioned yet that God has an incredible sense of humor? I can only imagine how silly I must have looked to God during this entire affair and how tickled He must have been while gazing upon my idiocy.

Incredibly, and always keep this in mind, only God and I were aware of my inadequacy. The funeral directors barely noticed and the people at the funeral thought it was routine for me. To them, I appeared to be an old pro. The funeral director seemed to think I was simply unfamiliar with the layout of the church. Since Andre's wife was OK with my inexperience, who was I to get in the way of God's plan? Therefore, I squelched my fear and pressed on.

Meeting Andre's extended family will be forever etched into my memory. I remember it like it was yesterday. The machismo of my youth was completely incapable of preparing me for this moment. I will never forget how incredibly inadequate I felt and how intimidated I was by the whole scene. I grew up fearing no man and yet I do not ever recall having to overcome such unprecedented terror. At the same time, mere words could never communicate how incredibly honored and joyful I felt.

As I walked through the door of the funeral parlor, I could not have anticipated the reception I was greeted with. The family's love, grace, and humility immediately calmed every fear and feeling of inadequacy I had been experiencing. That alone made the trip worthwhile.

On the day of the funeral the church was packed full of family and friends. Even more importantly, however, the Spirit of Yahweh had preceded me. I was overwhelmed with peace knowing the presence of God had met me in Canada. What transpired that day in the land of our northern neighbor's has boggled my mind, even to this day. The following is an account of the miraculous events that occurred through the Spirit of God on what most would consider a day of tragedy.

Look Ahead, Live Today

I realized in the days prior that if Andre had not known the Lord Jesus Christ, or even a minister of the Lord for that matter, there was a good chance that his family and friends did not either. As a result, the Lord had laid upon my heart a message of hope and peace for his family. I pray that by telling you this story the same message of hope will be delivered to both you and your family as well, regardless of whether or not you have experienced tragedy. Even greater than hope, however, what follows is a glimpse at eternity.

As human beings, we should be excited about the future. Not in a sense that we are forever living in the clouds. We must, as previously recorded, learn to live in the "now," but at the same time we must also keep our eyes fixed on our eternal home, "the forever." Otherwise we simply live, die, and cry, with no understanding of what transpired over the course of a human life. Perhaps even more importantly, what transpires after that life is extinguished.

Here is the message that the Lord laid on my heart on that cold Canadian winter day. I hope in the "now" you will enjoy this momentary glimpse of perpetuity while discovering your eternal habitation in Yahweh's "forever!"

Relocating

After a brief introduction I began the message with the following glimpse into the future of mankind. *"Now I saw a new heaven and a new earth, for the first heaven and the first earth had passed away. Also there was no more sea. Then I, John, saw the holy city, the New Jerusalem, coming down out of heaven from God, prepared as a bride adorned for her husband.*" (Revelation 21:1-2)

"May I begin by emphasizing to you that heaven is real? It is as real as if you were to hop on an airplane and land in some other city. It is not located somewhere off in the billow, with a bunch of pudgy winged cherub's fluttering from cloud to cloud. It is a real place that has both spiritual and physical properties. It is presently located in a realm somewhere outside of our dimension, but one day it will be home to all those who have been redeemed."

"What is even more fascinating is the truth that ultimately, heaven, the holy city of the New Jerusalem, the Lord God Almighty and His redeeming Lamb who takes away the sin of the world, along with all those who have trusted in Christ, will be located on the planet which you are now standing. The evidence points to its location as remaining in the same physical dimension in which we currently reside. God will translate His Super to our natural and what we now know as the third rock from the sun will someday be known as heaven, God's everlasting abode."

"Eternity will not possess the imperfect state, form or condition of our presently known earth. It will be recreated by fire and fabricated into an existence more in the resemblance of Eden than our present fallen abode. It will be even greater and more majestic than Eden, the garden of God ever was. The New Jerusalem is God's holy and eternal city.

The new heaven and the new earth will no longer be known as the third planet from the sun. It will become the *first* planet *with* the *Son!* Even the sun and moon will have been blotted out. The city will have *"no need of the sun or of the moon to shine in it, for the glory of God illuminates it. The Lamb is its light."* (Revelation 21:22-23) The Shekhinah glory of God will no longer manifest as a cloud to cover the the preeminent power of Yahweh. The all consuming fire of God will light world with the glory of eternity through our Lord and Savior Jesus Christ. The Lord will dwell amongst His people for time everlasting."

"If you have trusted Christ as your Lord and Savior this is your destiny. I know my friend Andre will be there. I heard it from his own lips that he trusted in Christ. Therefore, *we do not grieve as others who have no hope.*" (1 Thessalonians 4:13) Will we miss him? Yes. Have we lost him? No. In fact and truth, we have found him. Andre is now "forever."

"Yes, we will be temporarily separated from his physical presence, but we will be forever reunited with, and in, the presence of Him who created us, the Lord God Almighty, the heavenly Lamb who is the Lion of the tribe of Judah. When we trust Jesus Christ, He perfects us. In Christ, we will spend an eternity in paradise. So let's take a look at and for a brief moment begin to experience what, and who, my dear friend Andre is "now" and "forever" experiencing—the Lord God and His holy city, the New Jerusalem."

The City of Peace

At this point, rather than reproduce the whole sermon, please allow me to expand on its principles. I am sure it will be of greater benefit to you in this format. It will also allow me to add the necessary details where required.

The New Jerusalem contains important insight into understanding our glimpse into eternity. Let's, therefore, gaze into the Holy City in which we will not only live, but spiritually become a part of—the heavenly "Jeru-Shalom", which means, "the City of Peace."

What I find interesting is that the angel that shows John the Holy City, first and foremost, describes the spiritual nature of the New Jerusalem before any physical characteristic is ever revealed.

"He showed me the great city, the holy Jerusalem, descending out of heaven from God, having the glory of God."
—Revelation 21:2

Here we discover three spiritual characteristics of this marvelous city. First and foremost, it is holy. It is from God, connoting that it proceeds from within and as a part of the essence of Yahweh it contains His glory. This makes perfect sense when you realize that anything that proceeds from Yahweh is adorned with His Shekhinah glory. As a result, anything sinful is prohibited from existing there. Sin cannot abide in the presence of the King. The holy city is separated from sin for God's glory. The word used here as "glory" comes from the Greek word "doxa" and it means "glory, as being very apparent." In other words, there will be no mistaking who the ruler, designer and governor of this city is. It belongs to Elohim.

In addition, when describing the physical characteristics of the "bride," which is the New Jerusalem, the angel makes no mention of its people. The angelic vision is of the incredibly pure and unsurpassed elegance of our future home. Take note of what follows. All your life you have desired to live in the nicest place you could possibly afford. Many of you have gone way over your heads into debt in order to obtain it.

This home—your eternal home, has already been purchased with the blood of the Lamb. He has been preparing it from time everlasting so you can bank on the fact that it will be spectacular. Keep in mind, however, that you will never have enough money to buy property in the New Jerusalem. The blood of Christ is priceless. In the New Jerusalem the Hope Diamond is just another rock. No mere mortal can buy their way in, no matter how wealthy, or how good the world may perceive them to be. There is only one way to enter its gates. You must take possession of it by faith in Christ. Without Him, you will never be granted the Certificate of Occupancy.

So let's take a spiritual walkthrough of our heavenly abode. The following is a description of the most beautiful city in all of existence. If you play your cards right you will take up residence there. If not—well—that is between you and God.

> *"Her . . ."* Please take note of the gender specific language used to describe the Lamb's beautiful bride. *"Her light was like a most precious stone, a jasper stone, clear as crystal. Also, she had a great and high wall with twelve gates, and twelve angels at the gates, and names written on them, which are the twelve tribes of the children of Israel."*
> **—Revelation 21:11-12**

> *"Now the wall of the city had twelve foundations, and on them were the names of the twelve apostles of the Lamb."*
> **—Revelation 21:14**

By the way, I believe we should stop being so hard on Judas. I do not know if we will find him in heaven, but whether you like it or not, his name is on the foundation of the holy city. Never forget that he was an integral part of the Lord's ultimate plan. Even the Apostle Peter recognized this amazing truth.

> *"Men and brethren, **this scripture had to be fulfilled**, which the Holy Spirit spoke by the mouth of David concerning Judas, who became a guide to those who arrested Jesus, for he was numbered with us **and obtained a part of this ministry**."*
> **—Acts 2:16-17**

Judas was cast as a "now" player on the "forever" stage of God's literary tragedy. Therefore, do not be surprised if you find him accompanying Saint Peter at the pearly gates. Now back to the city:

*"The construction of the wall was of jasper; and the city was pure
gold, like clear glass. The foundations of the walls were adorned
with all kinds of precious stones . . . The twelve gates were twelve
pearls: each individual gate was of one pearl. And the street of the
city was pure gold, like transparent glass."*
—Revelation 21:11-21

Note here that it is after a brief description of the physical
characteristics of our eventual home that we get a peek at its
inhabitants, as well as, those who will never grace the golden streets of
the New City of Peace.

"But I saw no temple in it (there will be no need of a
"religious" system) *for the Lord God and the Lamb are its temple.
The city had no need of the sun or of the moon to shine in it, for
the glory of God illuminated it.* (Note that there is no longer a
need for the cloud to cover the Shekhinah glory. It now
illuminates the city.) *The Lamb* (The Shekhinah of God
manifest on earth who, *Shone like the sun* [Matthew 17:2] on
the Mount of Transfiguration) *is its light."*
*"**And the nations of those who are saved** shall walk in its
light, and **the kings of the earth** shall bring their glory and honor
into it. Its gates shall not be shut at all by day (there shall be no
night there). And **they** (those who are saved) shall bring the glory
and honor of the nations into it. But there shall by no means enter
anything into it that defiles, or causes an abomination or a lie, but
only those who are written in the Lambs Book of Life."*
—Revelation 21:22-27

We now return to the physical characteristics of this fantastic
city:

*"And he showed me a pure river of water of life, clear as crystal,
proceeding from the throne of God and of the Lamb. In the middle*

*of its street, and on either side of the river, was the tree of life,
which bore twelve fruits, each tree yielding its fruit every month.
The leaves of the tree were for the healing of the nations. And there
shall be no more curse, but the throne of God and of the Lamb
shall be in it, and His servants shall serve Him. **They shall see
His face,** and His name shall be on their foreheads. There shall be
no night there: they need no lamp nor light of the sun, for the Lord
God gives them light. And **they shall reign forever and ever.**"*
—Revelation 22:1-5

Going Home

As I looked up from my Bible all eyes were fixed upon me. Many were sobbing with tears flowing down their faces. I was not sure what to say at this point, so I looked back down at the Word of God. As I lifted my eyes once more I began to state, "My friends, as surely as I am looking into your eyes right now, Andre is peering into the eyes of the Almighty. Andre sees His Lord face to face and he is alive! He will live for eternity. His pain and suffering is over. Perhaps right now, Andre is strolling down a street of pure gold, as clear as glass, and basking in the everlasting light of the Almighty God in, and for all of eternity. There is no more curse, no more pain, no more fear and no more suffering." In Revelation 21:3-5 the Lord makes the following declaration:"

*"Behold the tabernacle of God is with men, and He will dwell
with them, and they shall be His people. God Himself will be with
them and be their God. And God will wipe away every tear from
their eyes, there shall be no more death, nor sorrow, nor crying.
There shall be no more pain, for the former things have passed
away. Then He who sat on the throne said, 'Behold, **I make all
things new.**'"*

I looked up once more and stated, "My friends, do not grieve for Andre. He is with God. Grieve for yourself. I know you will miss him and I know his young boy will have to grow up without a father, but Andre has not been lost. He has been found!"

I turned to his wife and declared, "According to Isaiah chapter 54, God will be a Father to your young child and he will be a husband to you, His beloved son's widow. He will be a provider for your needs and a teacher to your child. He will never leave you nor forsake you all the days of your life."

"As for Andre, you have no need to fear. If you continue in the Lord you will be reunited with Andre in eternity. As for the rest of you here today, God loves and desires to be with you. His will is for you to dwell in the same eternity in which He has welcomed our beloved brother. He wants to bring you home. Will you say yes to Him?"

At this point there was not a dry eye in the place. I continued on, "But the Lord does require one thing from you. If you fulfill that one thing all that belongs to Andre belongs to you as well. You must be born again. *'For God so loved the world that He gave His only begotten Son, that whoever believes in Him shall not perish but have everlasting life.'* (John 3:16) *'Therefore, if anyone is in Christ he is a new creation; old things have passed away, behold, all things become new.'"* (2 Corinthians 5:17)

Once again I peered into the eyes of the audience. "Brothers and sisters, you do not have to wait for this newness of life. You do not have to wait to pass into eternity to experience the Lord Almighty and His goodness. God wants to renew you right now. He wants to give you that second chance that the world will never be willing to give you. He wants to forgive your sin and permanently engrave your name in the Lambs Book of Life. *'Behold, I make all things new,'* is a call to you, His beloved children."

"'So let not your heart be troubled, you believe in God, believe also in Christ. In His Father's house are many mansions, if it were not so He

would have told you. He went to prepare a place for you. And because He went and prepared a place for you He will come again and receive you to Himself; that where He is, you will be also.' (John 14:1-3 Adapted to the second person) You will dwell in eternity with your husband, your son, your brother, your father, and your friend."

"But there is only one way to get there, my friends. *Jesus is the way, the truth and the life. No one comes to the Father except through Him'* (John 14:6) Your parents cannot take you there. Your friends cannot escort you there. Neither religion, nor Mary, the mother of Jesus, can buy your ticket. Your ticket has been bought and paid for with the only price worthy of redemption, the blood of Christ. It is the blood shed at Calvary that purchases your everlasting abode. Only in His blood is there forgiveness of sin and you can only receive it by faith—by believing in the one and only Jesus Christ of Nazareth who takes away the sin of the world. Will you receive Him today?"

"I cannot leave this funeral celebration without extending an invitation to you. I would like to invite you into my Father's house. If you repent of your sin and receive Him today your name will be engraved into the same Book of Life that Andre's name now indelibly resides in for all of eternity. You must make Jesus your Lord and Savior."

"Andre did not meet the Lord until his last days were upon him. Do not make that same mistake. We will never know how much time we have. Nevertheless, God has used Andre to bring you to this very point. In death, as in life, Andre has glorified his Lord."

"Therefore, I would like to ask you a question and I do not want you to be shy. Today is not a day of condemnation it is a day of glorification. If you would like to make Jesus Christ your Lord and Savior, if you would like to have all of your sin forgiven and your guilt and shame taken away forever, just raise your hand into the air . . ."

To my amazement nearly half the hands in the church burst forth. The tragedy of death had been transformed into the miracle of eternal life. The sin of Satan had been eternally cast into the Lake of Fire and rejoicing broke out in the heavenly realm. Another name(s) had been added to the Lamb's Book of Life.

Last Call

My friends, I call you friend now that you have come to the end of this second journey. I trust that this is not the end for you but a beginning. It is the beginning of a brand new adventure in the Lord Almighty and I must admit that I am excited for you. You cannot even comprehend the joy and excitement that is ahead of you if you will just allow Jesus to be Lord, and if you would allow yourself to know Him. Will it be easy? Certainly not! Is this the end of your trouble? To the contrary, it is just the beginning and there are a whole new set of tests and challenges that lie ahead.

Therefore, stay in faith, read the Word of God, pray and worship daily and listen for His still small voice to lead and to guide you. Of utmost importance, find a faith filled church and surround yourself with like-minded believers. Become a true disciple. I promise that you will never regret it.

My prayer is that you will come to know the Lord in a more intimate way. My ultimate prayer and reason for penning this discourse is that you will have been saved and renewed, and that you have become that new creation, transformed into the image of Christ, and that you will pay it forward and become a witness to the one and only Son of God.

If you have not already done so, I would like to extend one final invitation. It is last call if you will. I will ask the same question that I asked Andre's family and friends so many years ago on that cold but glorious winter day in Canada. Your answer may determine the difference between life and death, and, therefore, this is no time to be shy.

Talk of the end times has no doubt been declared so many times that you have become numb to it, but I must ask you to begin to feel again. The end *is* drawing near. Terrorism, tsunami's, earthquakes, plagues, famines, hurricanes, tornadoes, floods, wars and the domineering effects of sin and evil is proof that the birth pangs are becoming inevitably more frequent. Time is running out. Jesus' return is imminent. All of creation is on the verge of being birthed into eternity.

I have never been more convinced of this than I am right now. If Jesus tarries one more day, His return is only that much closer. Although you and I may never meet in this life, what a joy it will be to visit with one another in the beauty and fellowship of the New Jerusalem.

With that said, I must ask you one more time. If you would like to have your sin forgiven and enter into eternity—if you would like to give me the honor and the privilege of escorting you into the heavenly realm, and most importantly, if you would like to make Jesus Christ your Lord and Savior and become a new creation— sinless and eternal, and one with God, just raise your hand. It does not matter where you are or what you are doing. It does not matter who is watching. Just smile, lift up your hand and say, "Yes Lord, I accept your call." May the Lord bless you and keep you "now" and "forever." See you in the Holy City . . . Amen!

Conclusion

I would like to take a moment and thank you for taking the time to read *Yahweh Revealed*. If you made it this far, (assuming you already read *God Culture*) you are two thirds of the way there—that's two down and one to go and thus, I hope you have enjoyed getting to know our Lord in a more intimate way.

By this time, I am sure that you have learned some things about our God that you were previously unaware of. Therefore, I would like to encourage you to continue in your pursuit of the Almighty. Although God does not require perfection from us, and we are not saved by works, but by the grace found in Jesus Christ of Nazareth, (Ephesians 2:8) Yahweh certainly requires that we be diligent in regard to getting to know who He truly is and how He operates in our individual lives. Anything less devalues His majesty.

Having come this far, you are now aware of His culture, His personality and His love for humanity as a whole. Now it is time for you to get personal with the God who not only loves you, but created you to be the unique personality that you are. You may not realize it, but you are the only you who will ever exist. In God's eyes you are perfect when saved by grace. Therefore, the Lord God Almighty desires not only to know you, but to become one with you.

Thus, I have prepared *Secrets of the Father* for those desiring more of God. Most of us have never realized that God yearns for you to know Him on a personal level, and, therefore, He has set aside secrets that are designed just for you. Keep in mind, He is not hiding His secrets *from* you, He has prepared them *for* you from the foundation of the world. (Ephesians 1:4)

My prayer is that you will continue your journey and progress from merely having the knowledge of God *(Yahweh Revealed)* to having a personal relationship with God (by knowing the *Secrets of the Father)*. If and when you are willing to do so, God will draw you from the land of common place and compromise, and thrust you into the Land of Promise where miracles make their home.

May God bless you!